Jewelry Craft for Beginners

BY GLORIA R. MOSESSON AND
VIRGINIE FOWLER ELBERT

Photographs by VIRGINIE FOWLER ELBERT
Drawings by LORETTA TREZZO

BOBBS-MERRILL INDIANAPOLIS NEW YORK

Published by The Bobbs-Merrill Company, Inc.
Indianapolis, New York
ISBN 0-672-51902-X
Library of Congress Catalog Card Number: 73-22680
Manufactured in the United States of America
First printing

DESIGNED BY JACK JAGET

Contents

Jewelry Craft for Beginners

1. Jewelry Is for Everyone

TO ADORN oneself with jewelry seems to be a universal human desire. It is found in all cultures, whether primitive or highly developed, and in all eras of human history. Cave dwellers used their crude tools to turn shells and animal bones and teeth into pendants, bracelets, and hair ornaments. The Bible is rich in descriptions of the jewelry that was part of religious ritual. And for rulers and noblemen, jewelry reflected their rank and office. Thus, jewelry has always been important to mankind, not only as personal adornment, but also as a symbol of function and position.

In many parts of the world, the jewelry crafts practiced today are identical with those in use hundreds and even thousands of years ago. In other areas, the ancient techniques have been combined with new ones to create modern forms of jewelry or to use new materials to execute old designs.

In other countries, particularly those of the Western world, technological changes throughout the centuries have altered and refined jewelry crafts so that ancient basic techniques are used in modified forms. Mass production of jewelry is one of the results of this development.

But many of us seek individuality in adornment, just as

our ancestors did when they created their own personal decoration. It may be just a matter of wanting an ornament of a particular color or size for a certain outfit, or of *not* wanting to wear what everyone else is wearing. Or perhaps you wish to have a piece of jewelry that you could otherwise not afford or obtain—a copy, say, of a very expensive or a one-of-a-kind piece. Or it may simply be the urge to create something for oneself.

Whichever it is, it is now possible to have a self-made, unique collection of jewelry of any type, even if you have never done anything similar in the past. This book starts with simple tools like needle and thread and proceeds to more complex designs and techniques. The materials can be simple and inexpensive, easily obtained anywhere.

As your skills develop, you can go on to use expensive metals and stones, all handled with the same simple tool requirements. Throughout, we emphasize simple directions and equipment—and the importance of imagination and taste in opening up the possibilities for new creations.

The final chapter of the book is a discussion, with examples, of designing and creating jewelry from found objects. We hope it will encourage you to look at all kinds of small objects with imagination, and to create new jewelry from old pieces or from materials no one else would have dreamed of using in exactly the same way. There is also a list of sources of supplies and tools.

Just remember that every new skill or craft takes learning. Don't be discouraged or give up easily. If you've never worked with your hands before, start with the simplest jewelry at the beginning of the book. The satisfaction of finishing and wearing your first piece will be all the incentive you need to keep turning the pages to new accomplishments!

2.

CREATING jewelry of beauty, usefulness, and appropriateness does not necessarily require costly and complex equipment and materials. As these first projects illustrate, you can achieve wonderful results with common, everyday tools and with inexpensive, easily obtainable decorative materials.

TOOLS

To do your threading, you will need an assortment of needles. The thickness and length of the needles will depend on the thread to be used and the size of the holes to be threaded. Needles may also be made from fine-gauge wire cut to a desired size and bent into a loop at one end. The loop is then flattened down over the thread after it has been inserted. This is a particularly useful trick when you are stringing beads that are very long and heavy and it is difficult to find a long enough needle. If the beads have a very small hole, you may find that extra-fine wire, such as that used for some electrical work, serves your needs best.

You don't have to worry about rethreading wire needles once the loop has been closed tightly over the thread. Just discard the used needle and make a new one for each new use.

The rest of the tools you'll need are of the simplest sort—ordinary *cosmetic tweezers;* small *embroidery scissors;* and a *wire cutter* and *chain-nose pliers,* obtainable at any hardware store.

MATERIALS

All kinds of materials can be used to create the jewelry projects in this chapter, so before you start collecting supplies you'll want to decide on a project and figure out just what you need to carry it out. Here we want to run through some of the basics—as well as a few of the variations—to give you a rough idea of the kinds of materials you will be working with.

For threading necklaces and bracelets, a number of materials are available to you. One of the simplest to obtain and easiest to use is *thread,* which comes in many types and weights. You can use *mercerized cotton thread* of appropriate color to fit a jewelry design. Make sure, though, that it has a thickness of at least 40 gauge. You'll need a heavier thread for heavier beads. *Carpet thread* is the strongest of all. Nylon thread is especially useful for beads with small holes, because it is finer than mercerized cotton and very strong. *Waxed craft thread* is excellent for heavy beads, and it has extra endurance.

There are lots of other threading materials—*shoelaces,* all sizes and colors from 26 inches up, in cotton or leather; *leather thongs* of varying widths and colors; *stiff package string* or *cord* in various colors; and *elastic* in all colors and types—elastic thread, round elastic, and dressmakers' soft elastic ribbon, which comes in widths from 3/8 to 2 inches. You should also have on hand a ball of ordinary soft-quality package string or cord—it's indispensable for making preliminary estimates of lengths for chains, necklaces, bracelets, and so on.

A few projects in this chapter suggest *wire* as an alternative threading material. We'll talk more about wire—types and weights, and how to work with it—later on, in the metalworking chapters. But right now you should know that you can buy copper, brass, and steel wire for these projects in hardware stores and hobby shops. Wire comes in different thicknesses, and the thickness of a wire (as with thread) is its *gauge*. The projects here call for 14-gauge wire. Remember, the higher the gauge number, the finer the wire.

A few projects also make use of *dressmaker's flat cording*. It comes in widths from 1/8 inch up, in all kinds of colors.

You won't just be stringing beads, of course. You'll need all the other elements that make up jewelry as well—the parts known as *findings*. In these and all the projects in this book, you'll be making use of *pin backs, cuff-link backs, earring backs* (you can get screw-back, clip-on, and pierced-ear types), as well as *ring shanks* (with holding receptacle), *jewelry hooks* and *clasps* for single and multistrand pieces, *jump rings*, and *spring rings*.

Don't worry about all the names now—as you work your way through the projects and develop your skills, they will become very familiar to you. For a start, take a look at

SCREW-BACK WITH RING FOR HANGING

SCREW-BACK

CLIP-ON

PIERCED-EAR

PIERCED-EAR DROP RING

SPRING RING WITH RECEPTACLE

JEWELRY HOOK

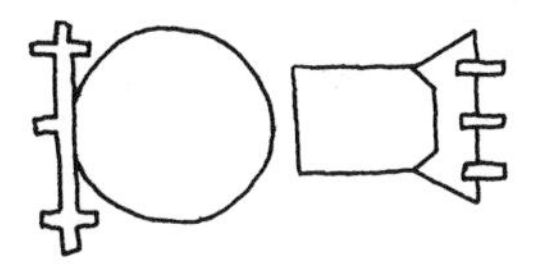

MULTISTRAND CLASP

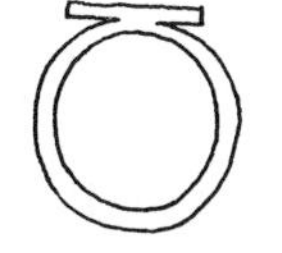

RING SHANK WITH RECEPTACLE

PLAIN RING-SHANK

what's available in a good notions department or five-and-ten-cent store.

Now for the decorative materials that will be the main element of your first jewelry-making projects. We'll be using *beads* of all sizes, styles, shapes and colors, *buttons* (preferably lightweight) in all their endless variety, *sequins* —anything, in fact, that suits your design and the techniques described. You'll be able to find what you want by visiting milliner's and dressmaker's trimming supply departments, craft shops, hobby shops, notions departments, jewelry supply stores. It just depends on what you have access to and what strikes your fancy. (And, of course, you can also order supplies by mail.)

A couple of projects call for the use of *felt scraps*—again, in any color you like—and ordinary *dressmaker's snaps* and *hooks and eyes.*

Last, get yourself a tube of *clear contact cement.* You'll use it to assemble jewelry pieces and secure knots.

DESIGNING JEWELRY

Before starting a design, you must make some basic decisions. You'll probably start with a color or colors in mind, as well as some idea of the types of materials you want to use. You should also have a sense of the size of the piece—whether it is to be heavy or light in feeling, whether you want a long or a short necklace, and so on. How complicated do you want it to be? And how much work are you prepared to put into it? Also ask yourself how many matching pieces you want to make—bracelet, necklace, earrings, ring, pendant, belt, and so on.

Next, draw a picture of the design you have in mind and of the various pieces you want to make. For instance, suppose you want a heavy, four-strand, simple beaded necklace, with beads of different sizes but all in shades of blue. You'd sketch it to look like the one shown here.

You probably wouldn't want the bracelet to be as wide and heavy, so you'd design it with fewer strands, or smaller beads.

And you certainly couldn't get all the different sizes and

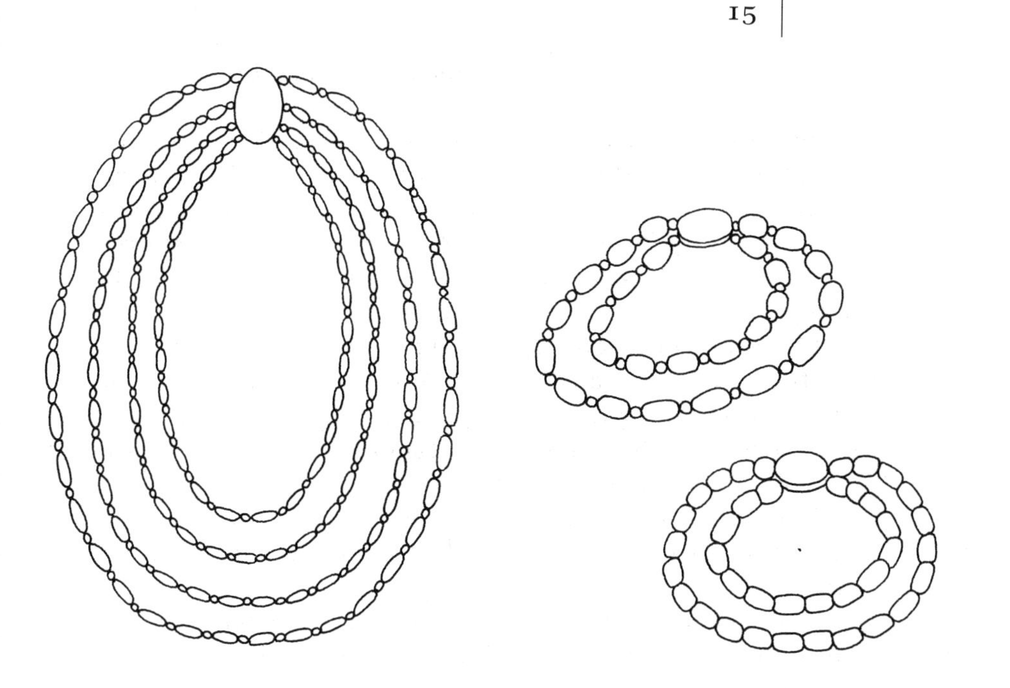

shades of blue beads into one pair of earrings and still expect them to be graceful looking, so you'd select one or possibly two tones or sizes of blue beads to be used in the earrings.

In more complicated designs, you will probably find that the matching pieces cannot accommodate all the basic design elements of the main piece. You must then select the part of the main piece that you want to pick up for the smaller pieces, and sketch its variations for each use. For instance, if you have a design like the one shown here, the pattern is simply too much to repeat in a pair of earrings. But you certainly can use part of it for earrings. Here are a couple of possibilities.

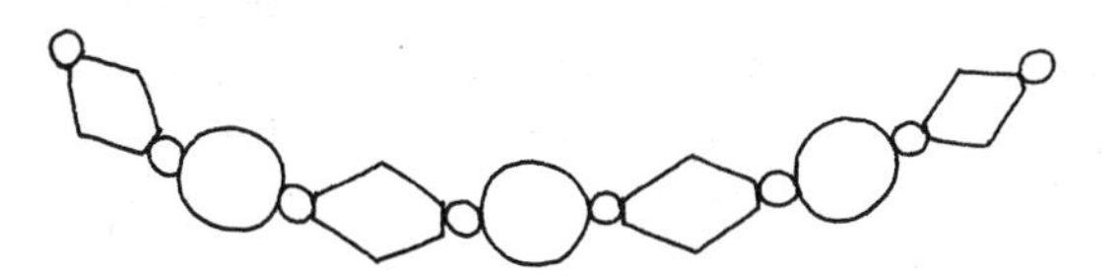

Unless you already have your materials or know exactly where to buy them, be prepared to alter your design depending on what the marketplace offers. Frankly, we get many of our ideas by looking at what the stores have and basing our designs on what we know is available. Remember, too, that styles change and that what is available today may not have been on the market a few years ago and may disappear in another few years. Certain things like sequins can always be found, of course. So enjoy shopping and browsing and have an open mind about designs. It may lead to startling variations from your original sketch, and many fresh plans for the future.

There is one more step before you actually purchase your materials. You will need to measure the lengths and widths of the pieces you are planning to make so that you know what quantities to buy. You cannot figure out in advance how many beads you need for an 18-inch necklace, because you won't know until you've selected them exactly how large the beads will be. But you know you need 18 inches' worth, and that you'll need twice as many ½-inch beads as 1-inch beads to complete your design. So be prepared to do some arithmetic to figure out how many will fit into the size you've measured. And if your design calls for a mix of colors and shapes and sizes, make sure you estimate in advance—again, by measuring—what proportion of each you need, so you won't run out of a particular element midway in your work. Some stores are very nice about letting customers who are not sure about quantities have return privileges on extra materials, and if you can find a supplier like this, it will take some of the measurement problem out of your work. It is always wise, too, to buy a few extra of whatever you are using—beads, sequins, buttons—just for emergency.

This measurement principle is important also for the cording, elastic, wire, and other materials you need for your work. So again, sketch and measure in advance so that you buy wisely and economically.

Most of the projects in this chapter will show beads or other materials of ordinary shape with not too much variation in sizes. This is because it is easiest to draw and explain the work in this way. But keep in mind that these designs can be used as the basis for wildly imaginative jewelry in a wide range of materials, shapes, colors, and sizes. Really exciting supplies from all over the world are available almost everywhere. So feel free, please, to take any of the patterns sketched or photographed and do your own thing with them.

A SINGLE-STRAND BEAD NECKLACE

Let's start with that most basic form of jewelry making—threading beads—and with the easiest type—large beads with big holes that can be threaded without the use of any tool.

Steps

1. Choose an easy design of large-holed beads that you can use as the base of other designs as your skills increase. The design shown here uses three sizes of wooden beads in contrasting colors (blue and green or orange and brown) or several tones of the same color. With a simple style like this, the bracelet can be identical in design.

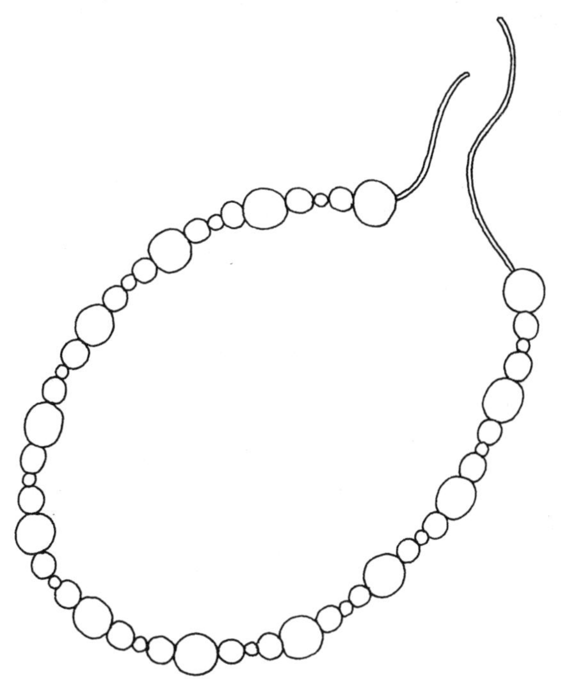

2. Take a piece of the soft package string and use it to determine how long you want your beaded necklace to be. Put it around your neck and try it on for size, then measure the length it should be. Allow an additional 10 inches for tying it behind your neck, and another 1¼ inches for knotting the end beads into place at each side.
3. The necklace can be strung on a shoelace of a color that blends with the beads, on ⅛ inch dressmaker's cording, or on appropriately colored, firm (nonstretching) package twine. A leather thong may also be used, but it is more difficult to work with and to tie. If you use a shoelace, the tip will act as a firm needle for threading. If you use the cording or twine, you may want to moisten the threading tip to make a "point" to go through the bead. Or you can pull the end of the cord across an ordinary household candle to wax it, and then shape it into a point. Thread all the beads in the desired design.
4. When all the beads are on, hold up the strand so that the ends meet, as shown, and the beads are perfectly centered on the string. Mark the spot where the beads end on one side; shift the beads slightly so that you can make a knot in the string at this spot. The knot should be larger than the bead hole so that it becomes an anchor for the end bead.
5. Slide all the beads to the knotted end by holding up the entire strand. This will enable you to make a tight end knot at the other side (X on the drawing). Your beads will be held firmly in place and centered. To wear them, simply tie them around your neck with a small bow. And to make sure the end of the cord or string doesn't ravel, make a small knot in each ending, just as you would at the end of a piece of thread in ordinary sewing.

If the necklace is long enough to slip over your head, measure the exact length you want it to be and allow 3 inches extra. Skip steps 4 and 5 and make just one knot to join both ends. Make sure the knot is firm by making it a double one, trim the ends closely, and wear with the knot at the back of the neck.

If you do this, and your design is a repeated one with dif-

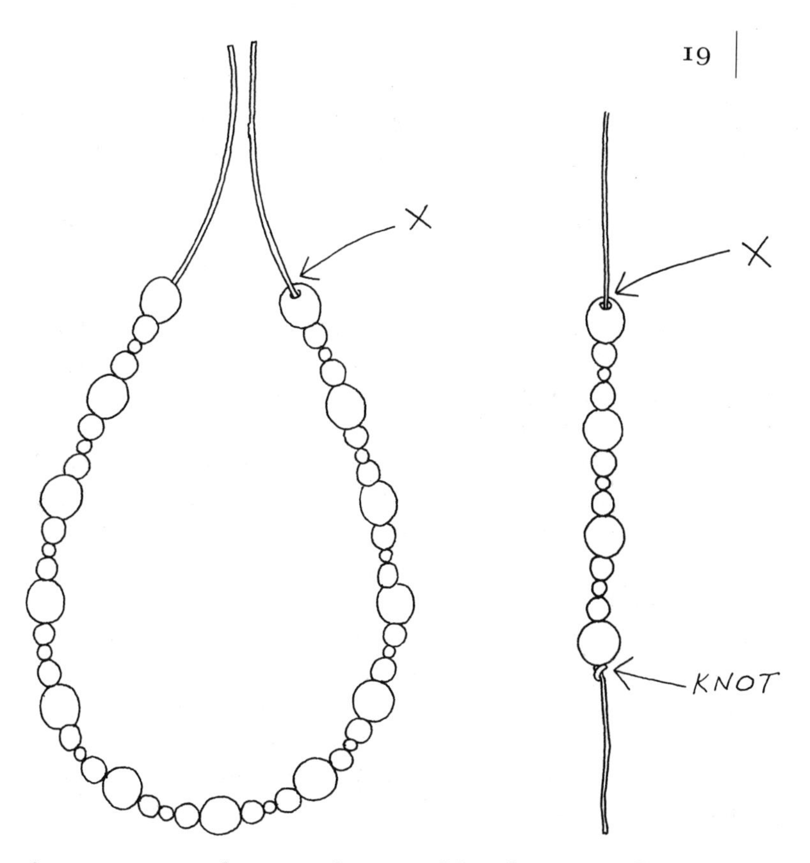

ferent sizes, colors, or shapes of beads, you will not want both ends to be the same, because when they are joined you will have an off-pattern repeat of the same bead sequence. For instance, if your design sequence is

You will not want the joined part to look like this.

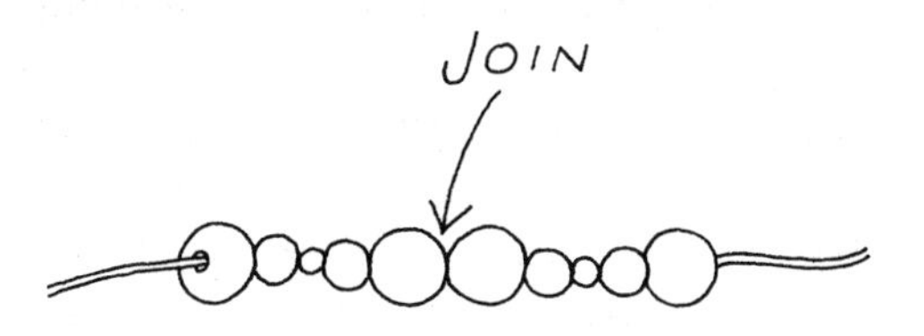

You will want to make sure that it runs in an unbroken pattern, with the knot as small and neat as possible.

A necklace of varied sizes and shapes of beads is strung on a shoelace. It encircles a bracelet strung on elastic thread (see page 18).

A long necklace that slips over the head needs no clasp. The thread ends are joined and the knot is hidden in a bead. It surrounds a choker made of snail shells that have been pierced for stringing. The choker closes with a spring ring and a jump ring.

A long necklace made from beads created from rocks cut into various shapes and polished encircles another long necklace made from carved wooden beads. The wooden beads are in two sizes, which are alternated in the necklace. Both necklaces are strung on nylon thread, which is simply knotted for the closing, as they are long enough to slip on over the head. Wire or heavy-duty sewing thread could also have been used.

SINGLE-STRAND BEAD BRACELET

Steps

1. Use a length of round elastic or heavy elastic thread exactly equal to the size of your wrist, plus 6 inches for handling. At one end of the thread, make a knot that is larger than the bead hole so that the beads cannot fall off.
2. Thread the beads onto the elastic in the same pattern as that used for the necklace, remembering that you want an unbroken pattern where the ends meet.
3. When you have added enough beads to cover your wrist exactly, shift them all on the thread by holding up the two ends of the elastic, as you did for step 3 of the necklace.
4. Knot the elastic ends together exactly where the beads meet, so that the elastic is not stretched and the beads cover it completely and it cannot be seen. Again, make sure that the knot is small and firm; this time try to have it smaller than the bead hole so that you can slide the beads over the knot to hide it. The bracelet is now a continuous design. Put it on by sliding it over the hand onto the arm.

BEAD EARRINGS

Steps

1. Purchase the appropriate earring backs for your ears (screw-back, clip-on, pierced-ear type). All are available with concave bases for stones or other decorative inserts.
2. Using contact cement as directed on the package, glue onto the earring bases one large bead from your basic design and let dry. Make sure you select a bead that is large enough to cover the earring base.

MULTISTRAND NECKLACE

The basic idea of the set of jewelry pieces we've just described prevails in all beading work. Only the materials

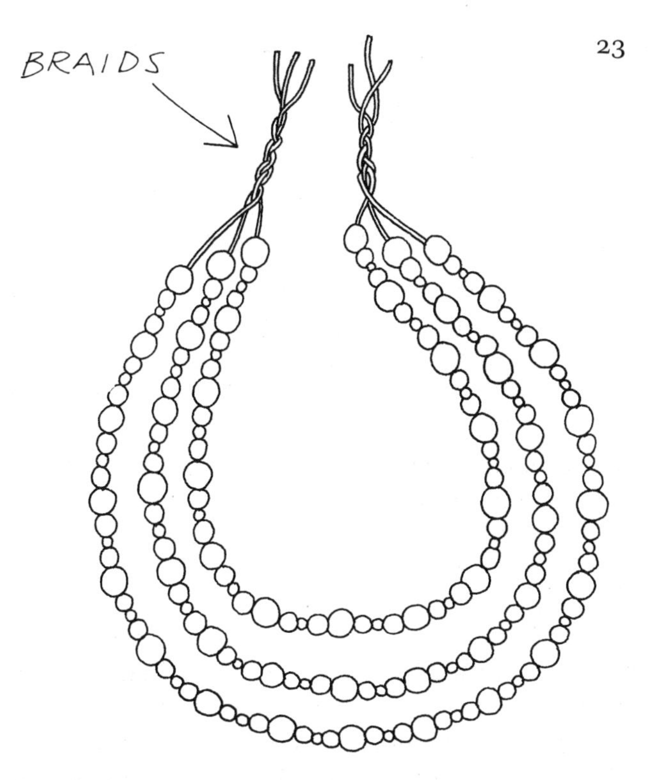

and the designs change, and you can use this simple method to make more elaborate jewelry with no more complicated tools. For instance, here's how to modify it into a multistrand necklace and matching pieces.

Steps

1. Decide how long you want your strands of beads to be, then string them following the directions for the single-strand bead necklace. Knot each strand at the ends as described in steps 3 and 4. You will need to allow 5 or 6 inches of extra lace or cord beyond what you used for the single-strand necklace for tying.
2. Usually the strands in a multistrand necklace are different length, with the shortest strand closest to the neck so that the necklace falls correctly on the body. In this case, however, all the strands have the same number of beads and the adjustment is made in the length of the strings or laces at the ends of the strands. It would be very difficult to tie separately several strings to the proper length around the neck, and they might become

tangled. Therefore braid the ends together to keep them neat.

To get a proper fit, put all the strands down on a table and lay them out as you would have them look on you. Start the braid on each side flush with the end of the last bead on the inside strand, leaving as much "blank" string on the outer strands as the size of the beads and your preference for fit demand. A bow is too bulky for so many strands, so it is best to join the ends with a simple knot, which is easily opened by hand.

MULTISTRAND BRACELET

Steps

1. Make your individual strands in the same way as you made the single-strand bracelet, with elastic thread. Do not close up the strands, but knot them loosely at each end to keep them neat and on the thread.
2. Lay your bracelet strands out side by side, exactly as you want them to look on your arm. Cut four lengths (6 to 8 inches, depending on how much extra thread you like to work with) of the fine elastic thread. Tie the strands together in four places with the elastic threads, spacing them equally along the length of the beads. Tie between the beads so that the elastic threads will not show. Do not tie them tightly, as this would make the strands bunch up and overlap each other, but tie them with just enough pressure to hold the beads in line. Make small, firm knots, and trim the ends.
3. Now join each strand at its ends with a small knot, as you did for the single-strand bracelet.

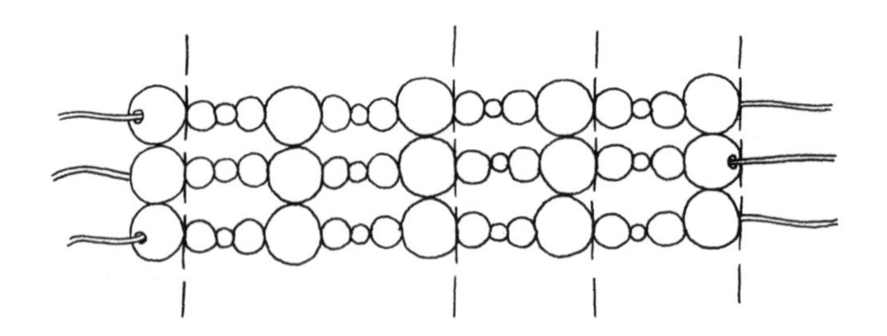

SINGLE-STRAND BELT

Make this belt exactly as you did the single-strand necklace, allowing enough extra string or lace for tying in the front. You might want to decorate the ends of the ties with beads. Just add a bead or beads at the very ends of the string, then tie a simple knot and trim it at the end.

MULTISTRAND BELT

Proceed exactly as for a multistrand necklace, braiding the extra string or lace to make it neat and easy to tie or untie. Again, you might want to end with a decorative bead or beads. In this case, make a knot at the end of the braid 2 or 3 inches before the ends of the strands. Put the decorative tassel beads on the loose ends, holding them in place with a trimmed knot.

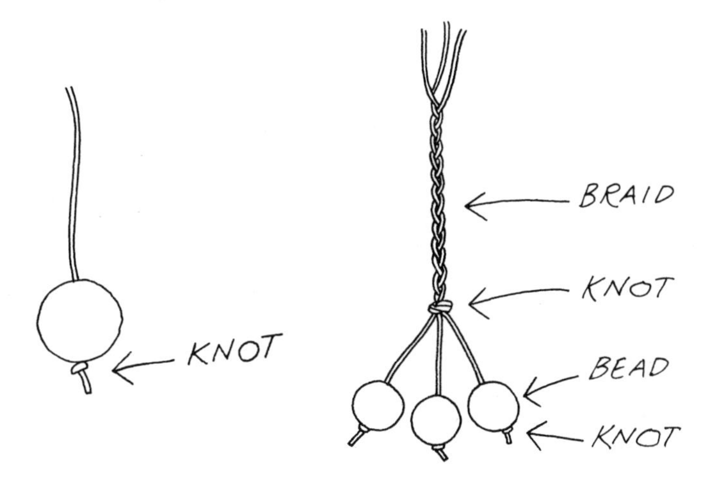

SINGLE-STRAND THREADED NECKLACE

Needle and thread make possible much greater variety in design and materials than does the basic beading method just described. The range of potential bead sizes and designs is so enormous that we will describe only basic working techniques and then give a selection of some designs that can be created by using them. After that, your imagination is your guide.

This single strand (for which directions are given opposite) is also part of the multistrand necklace shown on page 31.

Steps

1. Design all the pieces of the set you wish to make—for example, a single-strand necklace of several types of beads, with matching bracelet and earrings.
2. Measure the length you want for the necklace. (By this time you should know your wrist dimension and not have to measure it again.) Using these measurements, determine how many pieces of each different kind of bead you will need. Make a scale drawing of the pieces to be sure that your final piece will be symmetrical. You may even want to take your beads and lay them out in the design pattern on a table, checking to make sure they look right and that your measurements are correct. This will also help you to string them in the right order.
3. Take the jump ring end of a spring-ring closing set and knot your thread firmly around it several times, using a buttonhole stitch to make it firm. Your thread should be as long as your intended necklace, plus at least 10 inches as a safety margin. It may look like a lot when you start, but by the time all the beads are on most of it will be gone, and you still need some for finishing off, etc.
4. Start to string your beads according to the pattern—in this case, following the drawing, five small gold beads, two black jet beads, two gold disc beads, a round crystal bead, another jet bead, and so on. After you pass the center of the necklace, the pattern goes on in reverse, so your design will be symmetrical.
5. Hold up the entire strand of beads and push them down against the end with the ring attached.
6. Make a small, firm knot at the loose end of the beads. Try not to let them loosen up while you are making the knot—holding them up in the air is the best way to accomplish this. If you have trouble holding the knot firmly against the end of the beads, start by making a loop in the thread as close to the beads as possible. Do not tighten it by hand; instead, using a pair of small cosmetic tweezers, ease the knot down toward the beads until it is right against them, and then tighten it. Another way to do this is to attach the ring end of the beads to a fixed ob-

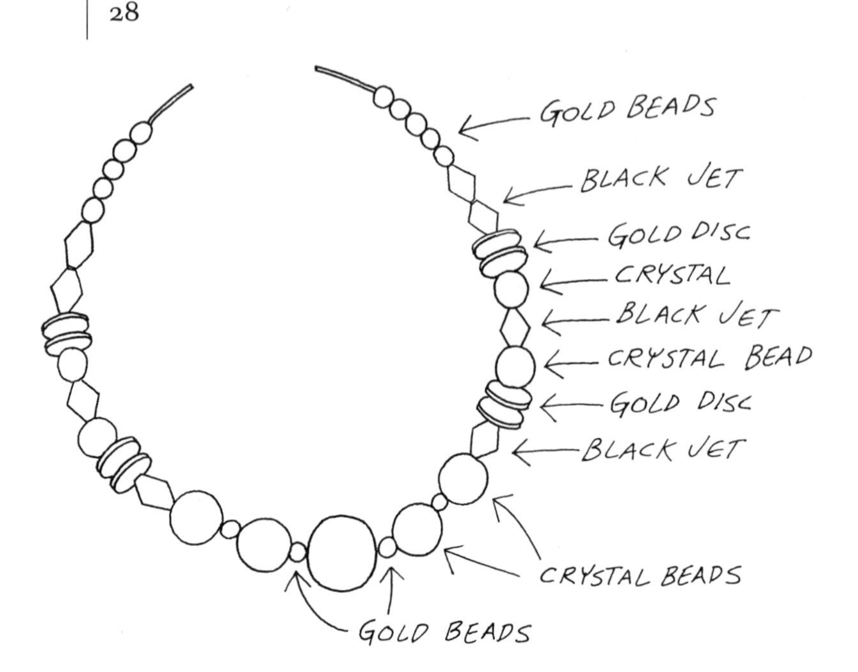

ject (you can loop it over a nail fixed into a board). Then, holding the strand horizontally, you can ease the knot up against the end in the same way.

7. Attach the spring-ring part of the closing, using several knotting stitches or buttonhole stitches.

MULTISTRAND THREADED BRACELET

Steps

1. Since the necklace design uses so many different kinds of beads of differing sizes, you will not want to repeat every part of the necklace in your bracelet. Rather, you will want to select that part of the pattern that will look best on the arm. High and low elements together do not look as well in a bracelet as they do in a necklace, so you probably will not want to use the larger beads. On the other hand, one strand of the smaller beads alone may look too tiny and insignificant on the arm. So you may want to go to a two- or three-strand matching bracelet. One possible variation on our necklace pattern is shown here.

2. If your bead holes are large enough, you can use fine elastic thread and make the bracelet exactly as you did the multistrand bracelet already described. If your holes are not large enough, or if you prefer a bracelet with a clasp, obtain a jewelry clasp that provides for the number of strands you are making. Working with the smaller end

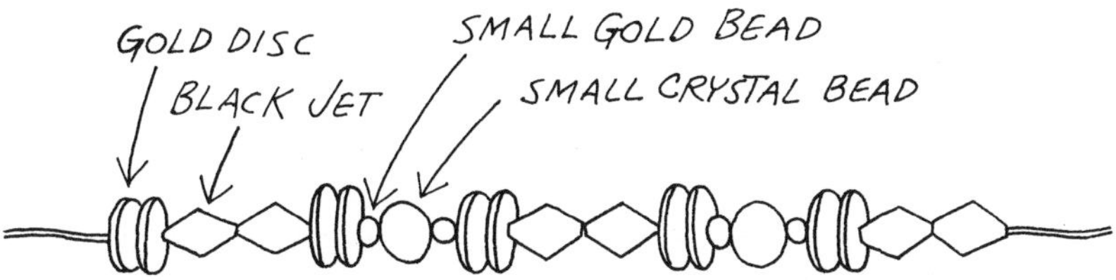

of the clasp, knot one of the threads for the strands onto the clasp. Thread the beads in the design you selected, and attach the thread to the larger end of the clasp, using the techniques already described to secure it neatly and firmly.
3. Repeat with the other strands of the bracelet.
4. If your bracelet has more than two strands and you do not want them to separate on your wrist, tie them together with elastic thread as you did for the multistrand bracelet, step 2.

THREADED EARRINGS

Steps

1. Design your earrings, bearing in mind that with needle-and-thread beading it is possible to attach hanging beads on any type of earring base.
2. Join your beads to each other and to the earring with thread or wire. If you use thread, make a small, firm knot and add the beads, starting with the bottom one. Your thread should match the bead and be flattened against it so that it is not seen when the bead hangs straight down.
3. At this point you can complete your design in one of two ways. In the first version a larger bead is glued to the earring base. Simply thread the beads together, tie and knot

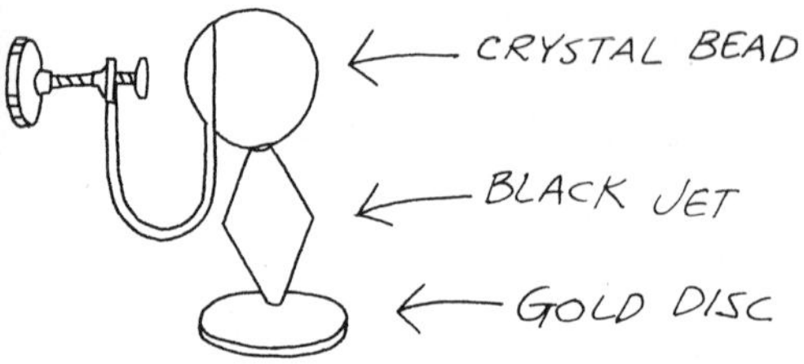

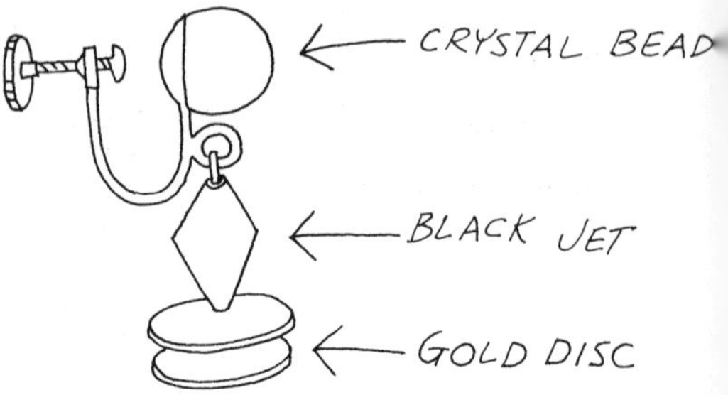

them off in the usual manner, and glue on your main bead.

In the second version the beads are attached to a ring on the earring, and you must loop your thread around the ring before tying and knotting it off. It is really easier, in this case, to use fine wire and avoid the chance that your thread will show or ravel. To do this, take a piece of wire about 4 inches long. With your tweezers or pliers, make a loop at one end of it. String your beads on it and make a loop at the end of the beads. Then simply attach this loop to the ring on the earring and you are set.

MULTISTRAND THREADED NECKLACE

If you want to adapt this design for a multistrand necklace, you have to make certain changes in your work after you sketch the design.

Steps

1. Measure the length of each strand using the limp package string; also lay out your beads on a table to make sure that they fall properly into the layout you want. Each strand should be shorter than the one below it so that you have a graduated effect.
2. Choose the type of multistrand closing you want to use. There are two basic styles generally available, a hook type and a clasp type.

If you use a clasp type, as you did for the multistrand threaded bracelet, follow the same directions for attaching it to the ends of the beaded strands.

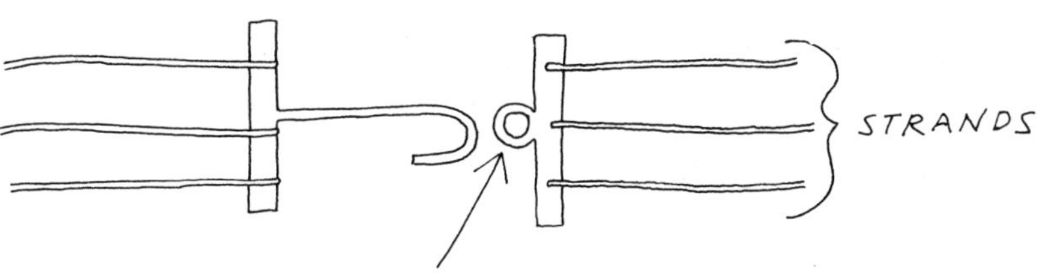

If you use a jewelry-hook closing, attach one end of each strand to the jewelry hook, the other end to the bar that accompanies it. You must then provide a piece of chain onto which the hook can be caught. You can either purchase a small length of chain from a notions or craft shop, or make one yourself from the wire you have already used on the earrings. This can also be more decorative, as you can string beads on the wire. The hook from the other side can be looped over any part you wish to adjust the length of the necklace.

The multistrand necklace, shown with a hook closing.

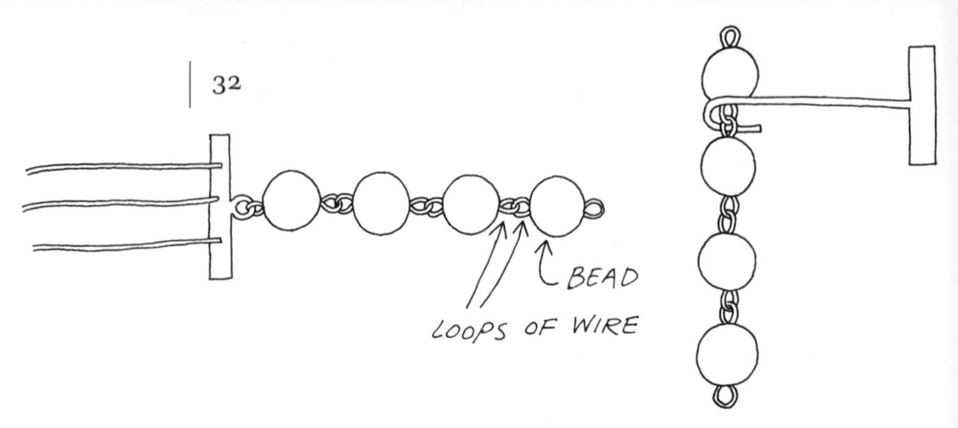

TWISTED SEED-BEAD NECKLACE

Seed beads are very small, approximately 1/16 of an inch in diameter (their threading holes may or may not be small). The beads are never used in single strands, because no matter how pretty they are, they are too small to show up well in single units. In the nineteenth century, Oriental seed pearls were used for baby jewelry, but this has long since gone out of fashion. Seed beads are often used as accents with larger beads or as "spacers" and parts of larger pieces.

This and the following projects show some ways you can use seed beads (or artificial seed pearls) alone to great effect. Design the pieces you want, and select the colors, deciding whether or not you want each strand the same, each strand a different color, mixed colors on each strand, and so on.

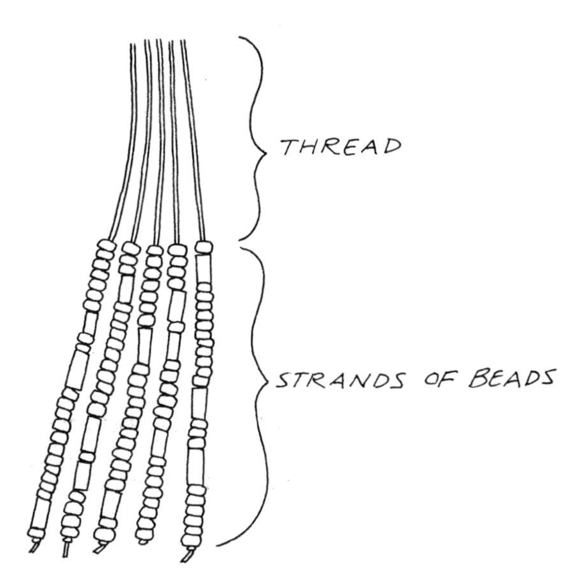

Steps

1. Measure the lengths of the strands you will need, allowing for the twist, which will take up some of the length. To eliminate guesswork, use the soft package string to measure and actually twist the lengths of string as you are planning to twist the beads. You will find that you "lose" some of your length, so make sure that you allow for this in planning the final length of each strand. In addition to this, allow at least 8 to 10 inches of extra thread for working material.
2. Unless they have a large hole, seed beads require a fine needle and thread, preferably nylon. Knot the thread about 3 inches from one end so that the beads cannot fall off, and thread each strand individually, setting it aside unfinished when it is the proper length.
3. When you have completed all the strands you are planning to use, pick them up by the loose ends and hold them in the air. About 3 inches from the end of the threads, knot the strands together firmly.
4. Turn the strands upside down and hold them by their opposite ends, so that the beads now rest against the knot made in step 3. Twist the strands in any fashion you choose to make the design you originally selected. You

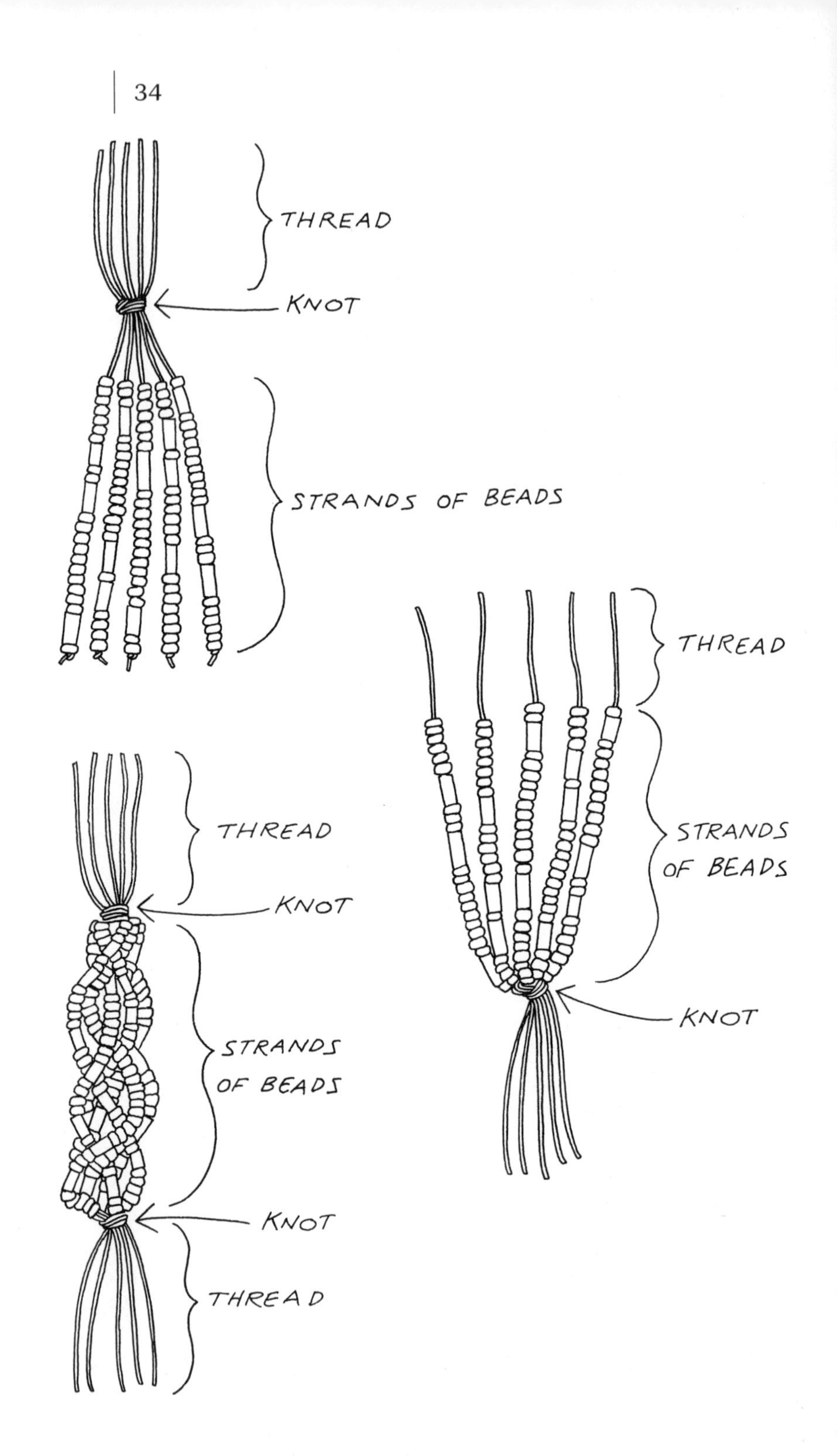
THREAD
KNOT
STRANDS OF BEADS
THREAD
STRANDS
OF BEADS
KNOT
THREAD
KNOT
STRANDS
OF BEADS
KNOT
THREAD

may crisscross, braid, or roll the strands. Make sure that all the strands are as tight as possible after you have "arranged" them.

5. Using a pair of tweezers to bring the knot as close to the beads as possible, knot all the strands together. Both ends of the necklace are now secured.
6. This is an optional step. If you want to be absolutely certain that your beads are secure and that the thread will not give way at the ends, apply a drop of contact cement to each knot in such a way that it flows over the end bead of each strand.
7. Attach a 3/8-inch or 1/4-inch spring ring to one end of the threads, knotting it as firmly and as closely to the beads as possible. Use buttonhole stitches to do this, and trim the excess thread closely for a neat effect. Attach a jump ring to the other end in the same manner.

Twisted multistrand seed-bead necklace, made as described.

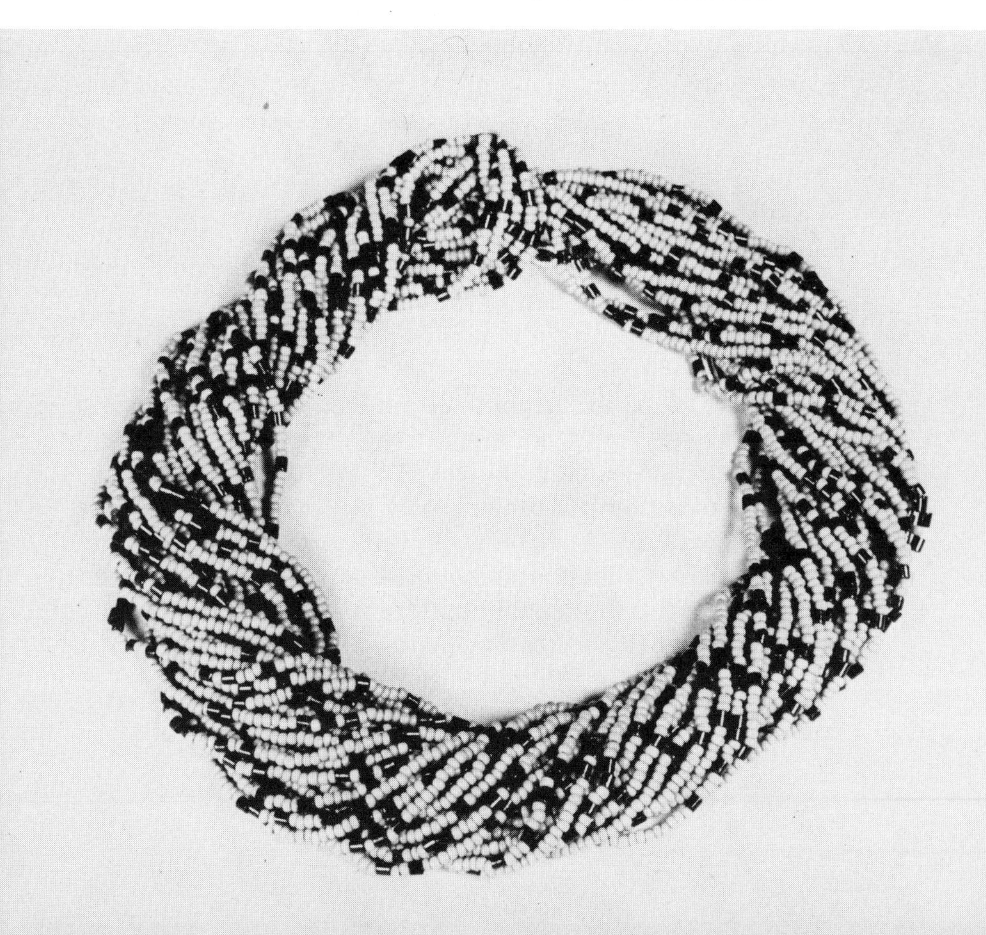

SEED-BEAD BRACELET

This is made in precisely the same manner as the necklace, the only difference being the size. Allow an extra 1/2 inch beyond the normal wrist measurement to allow for easy sliding and for closing with the spring ring and jump ring set. If it is too tight (that is, if it fits exactly), there will not be enough "give" to secure the lock. And be sure to allow for the size of the rings in measuring.

Alternatively, if you do not want to use a ring set, you can thread the beads on fine elastic. Follow the same procedure as for the seed-bead necklace through step 4. After you have twisted the strands, simply tie the two ends together with a firm knot and cut off the excess thread.

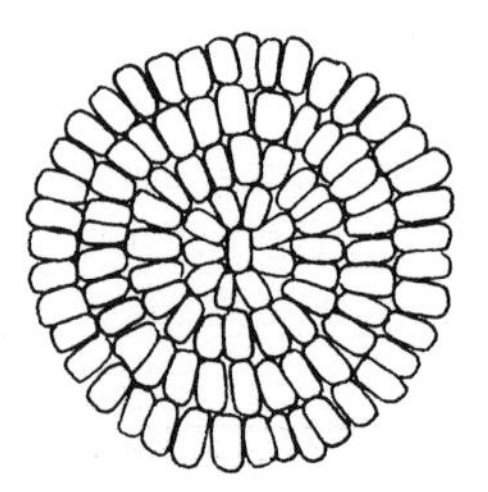

SEED-BEAD EARRINGS

There are at least three types of earrings that can be made with seed beads to match the rest of your set.

Steps (Type 1)

1. This is a plain button-style earring. Since most earring backs are not large enough by themselves to make a good-sized earring, however, you will have to use a mounting for the beads before putting them on the earring back. Find two buttons of the size you want your earring to be. Pick a suitable color and make sure the buttons have a flush back. Using contact cement according to the package directions, spread a layer of beads on the buttons and let them dry thoroughly.
2. Repeat the cementing process, spreading a second layer

in the same manner. Add a third layer if you wish a deeper effect, but remember that you do not want the earrings to be too heavy. Two layers will probably be enough.

To create a domed effect on your earring, layer the beads in a convex fashion after you apply the second flat layer.

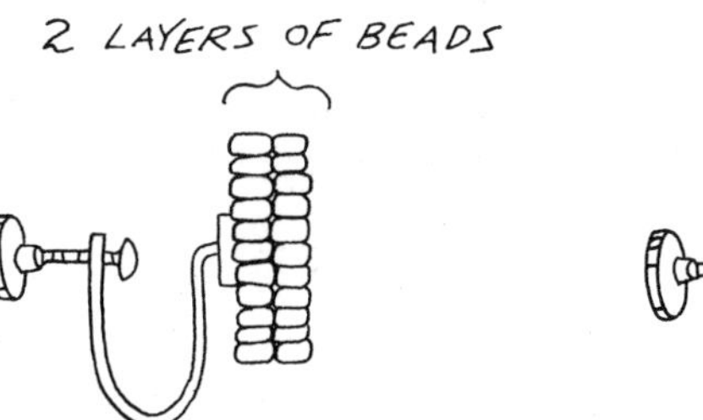

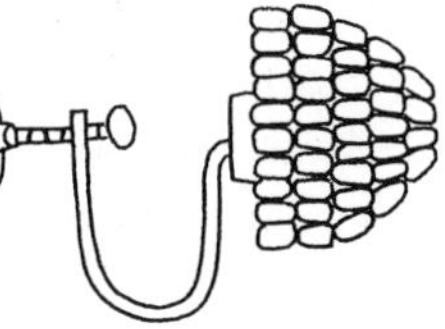

Steps (Type 2)

1. This is also a button-style earring, but the beads are twisted or arranged before they are glued onto the earring back. Begin by making two 8-inch strands of beads. Use whatever colors or combinations you want on the strands. Secure them in the usual manner with a knot at each end.
2. Twist or knot each strand around on itself until it is a ball-shaped piece about ½ inch in diameter.
3. Pour a small amount of clear contact cement over each ball to keep it firm, and let dry.
4. Attach to earring back with cement, as with other earrings.

Steps (Type 3)

1. This is a tassel-type earring; it can be made with a matching top, or on an earring base that has a decorative metal top. Following the instructions on page 38, make tassels the length you prefer for your earring. At this point, you should be familiar enough with your beads to know how many tassels you want and how full you wish the earrings to be. Just remember that the earrings cannot have as many tassel strands as the necklace or bracelet has strands. And the shorter the tassel, the fewer the strands you should use.

2. Attach the excess thread end of the tassels to a small jump ring, knotting as closely and neatly as possible. Contact cement at the tip of the knot will help prevent it from unraveling and enable you to use one small inconspicuous knot instead of several bulky ones.
3. Attach the jump ring to the earring loop, and close with your tweezers or pliers.

Variations

1. Using a bought ring shank, you can make a matching ring following the instructions for type 1 or type 2 earrings.
2. Using a purchased button form with a shank back, you can make buttons with the instructions for the type 1 or type 2 earrings.

SEED-BEAD TASSELS

Seed beads lend themselves well to tassel use because they fall gracefully in bunches. Use them as a finishing touch on accessories.

Steps

1. Decide how full you want your tassel to be—that is, how many strands you want on it. Also decide on colors, color sequence, and so on.
2. For each strand, make a small, secure knot at the end of the thread so that the end bead is held firmly. A drop of contact cement over the knot will help, too.

3. Thread each strand to the length of the tassel desired.
4. Hold all the strands vertically and knot them tightly.
5. Use the extra thread to attach the tassel to a jump ring, which can then be attached to another piece of jewelry or accessory.

SEED-BEAD CHOKER

Seed beads lend themselves well to use in chokers. You can use slightly larger beads, too.

Steps

1. Design your choker and matching pieces. Too wide a choker may be uncomfortable, so do not plan to make it more than 1 inch wide, unless you are looking for a special effect, such as on an African neckpiece. If you use seed beads, you will need seven or eight strands to form a choker 1 inch wide. Larger beads will need fewer strands.

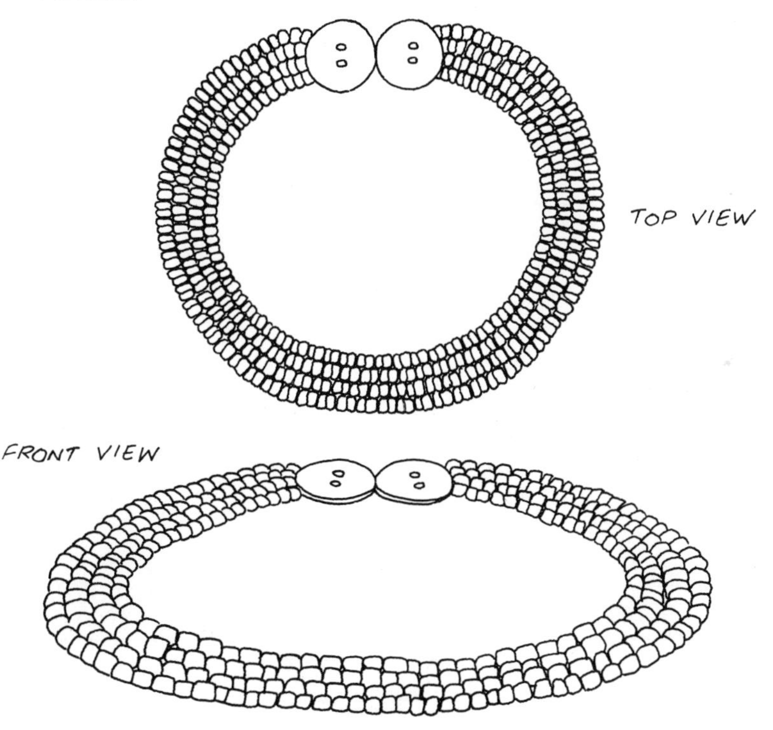

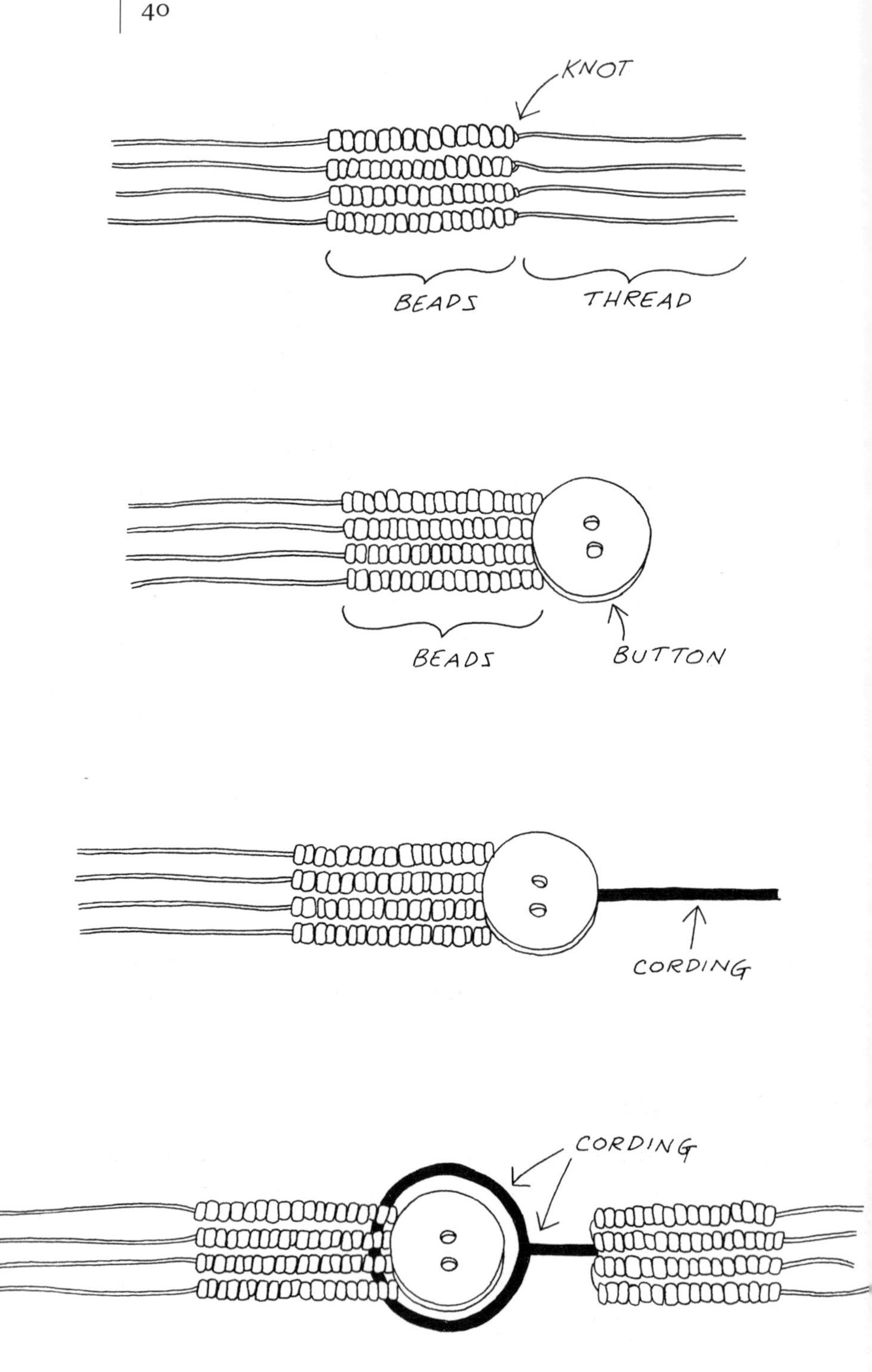
KNOT
BEADS
THREAD
BEADS
BUTTON
CORDING
CORDING

2. Measure the length you will need for your strands, remembering to allow for the clasp.
3. Make a knot about 8 inches from the end of the thread. Then string each strand to measure. Make a knot at the end of the strand, again leaving about 8 inches of free thread. You now have 8 inches of excess thread at each end of each strand.
4. Use the excess threads from all your strands to attach a two-hole button to each end of the choker. This joins the strands together and also secures them. Knot the threads under the button where the knot cannot be seen.
5. Cut about 6 inches of dressmaker's 1/8-inch cording in a color matching the beads. Sew it to the undersides of the buttons, knotting it at the end to prevent raveling. Repeat for the other side. The choker will close with a small knot or bow made with this cording.

Variations

1. Attach a button to only one side of the choker. To the other side, attach dressmaker's cording that has been sewn into a loop large enough to fit around the button and secure the choker around your neck.
2. Use a jewelry-hook set for the ends of the choker. If you have used large beads, make the chain as described on page 31. Seed beads, however, are not large enough to hold the hook in place, so in this case use a gold- or silver-plated chain from a hobby shop or notions department.
3. Make a bracelet to match the choker, using the button and loop for the closing. Alternatively, use elastic thread and hold the strands together and finish them off as you did for the multistrand bracelet.

AN AFRICAN NECKLACE

This design will give you some idea of the techniques you can use to add design elements to a main piece. The basic necklace can be varied by using more or fewer strands, and beads of different sizes, colors, types, and shapes. We show beads of uniform size and shape here so that the steps in the assembly process will be clear.

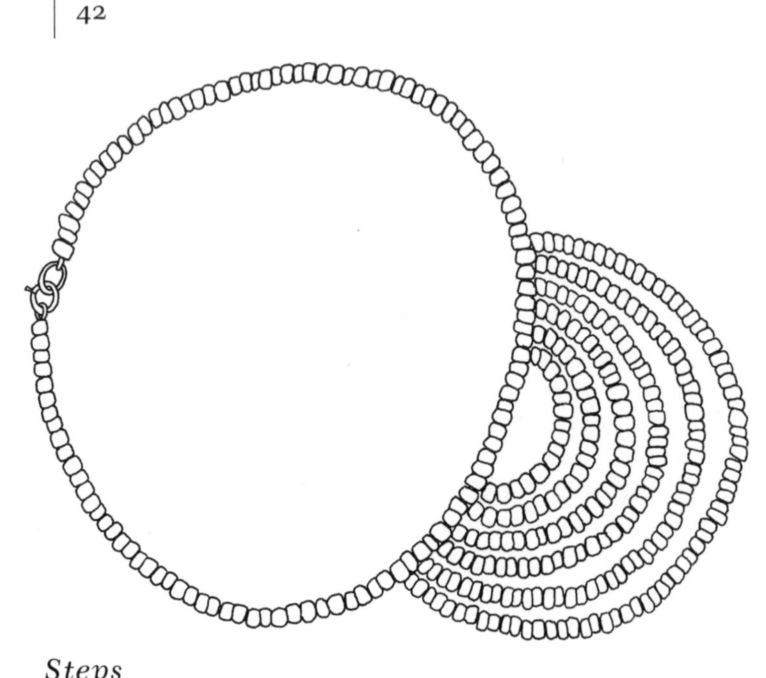

Steps

1. Measure the length of your neckpiece. This design should come up around the collarbone and not droop low. Next measure the lengths of the individual hanging strands. Again, the limp package string is useful in measuring; so is actually laying out your beads in the arrangement and sizes you want.
2. After making a knot 10 inches from the end of each thread, thread each strand to the desired length. Finish with a knot as for the other necklaces you have made, again leaving 10 inches of excess thread at the end of each strand.
3. Thread onto the neckpiece the center beads that fit between the ends of the first strand on the necklace.

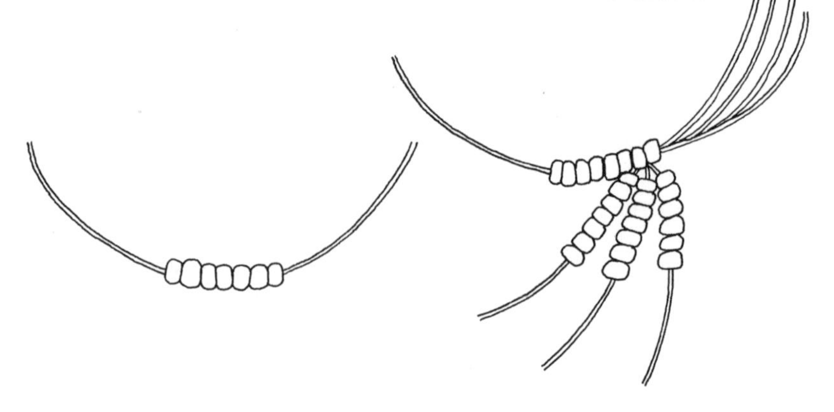

4. If your beads have a large hole, attach the strands to one side of the neckpiece by pulling the neckpiece thread through the end bead of each strand with a needle. Use a needle with a large eye, for each time you add a new strand you also add the thread of the strand to the needle. At the end you will have several threads in the needle, all of which pass through the end bead of the final strand. Next add the rest of the beads to that side of the neckpiece, and finish off with a spring ring.

If the bead holes are not large enough for the larger needle and the multiple strands, you will need to proceed differently. After stringing the center beads of the neckpiece (step 3), loop and tie the free ends of the smallest hanging strand to each side of the center beads. After tying firmly, twist back the extra thread into the first bead of the strand and, with your embroidery scissors, cut the thread very close to the bead. Repeat in proper order for each of the hanging strands. After the last strand has been attached, add the rest of the beads to that side of the neckpiece and finish off with a spring ring.

5. Add the other ends of the hanging strands to the other side of the neckpiece center beads, following the same procedure as in step 4. Finish with the rest of the beads for the neckpiece and a jump ring on which to catch the spring ring.

Variations

1. Matching bracelets and earrings can be made similar to those described for other types of beads.

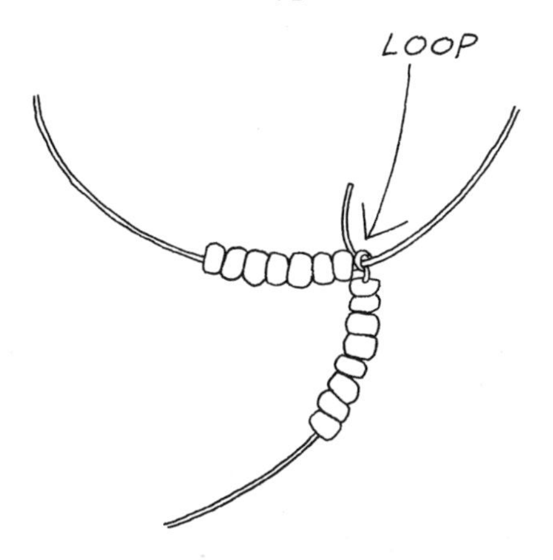

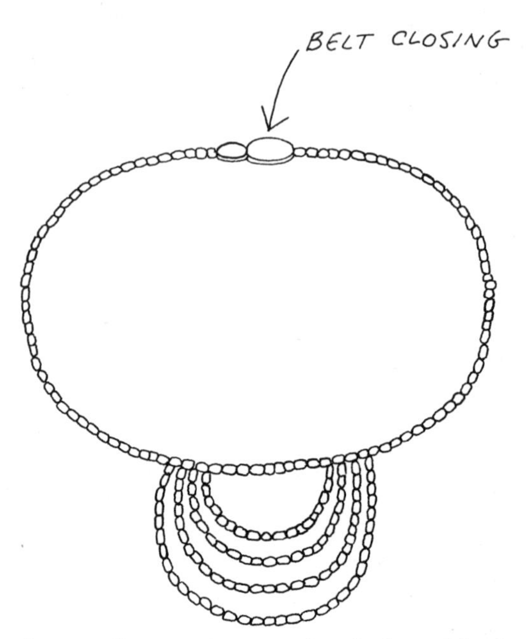

2. This design makes an interesting belt, with the loops at the front and the closing at the back. The belt part should be threaded on elastic thread. You can make it a double strand of beads if desired. An alternative pattern with multiple loops, based on the same African design, is good for either belt or necklace.
3. If you prefer, you can make this necklace by using wire thread for the hanging strands. This makes it somewhat easier to add them to the main neckpiece.

Black-and-white African necklace, made on wire.

In this version, thread all your strands individually on fine wire. End each with a small ring or loop, made by twisting the wire around with a pair of tweezers or pliers. These should be as small as possible.

Thread the center beads of the neckpiece, then thread the wire loops onto the neck thread, tightening them with your tweezers or pliers so that they are firm on the thread, as close as possible to those center beads. Follow the pattern of the necklace, and repeat for each loop. You may prefer to do one side at a time, or to complete each in order, in which case the neckpiece must be threaded through a needle at each end. Finish off as for the first version.

A BUTTON NECKLACE

Ordinary buttons can make some of the most interesting and individualized jewelry imaginable, at little cost and with a relatively small amount of work. Here's a necklace to start you off.

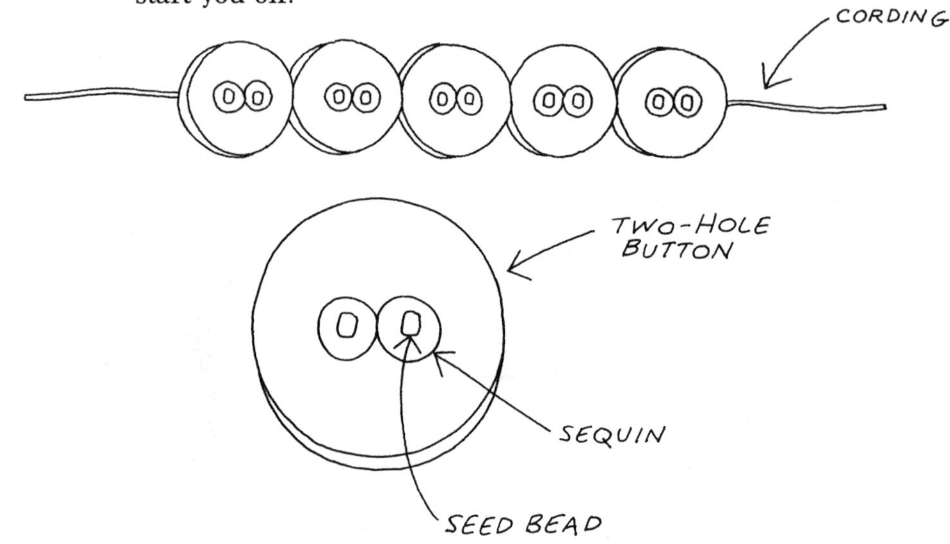

Steps

1. Design the piece you want to make, deciding on color, length, style, and so on. The design followed here tops each two-hole button with two sequins and two seed beads.
2. Measure the length you want for your necklace, planning it so that the length of the necklace is equal to the length of the buttons when they are placed end to end.
3. Take a piece of 1/8-inch dressmaker's cording in a color that matches the buttons you are using. Add 3 inches to the length of your necklace and cut. Fold over 1 1/2 inches at each end of the cord, making a small "hem" so that there is no rough edge showing, and stitch it down.

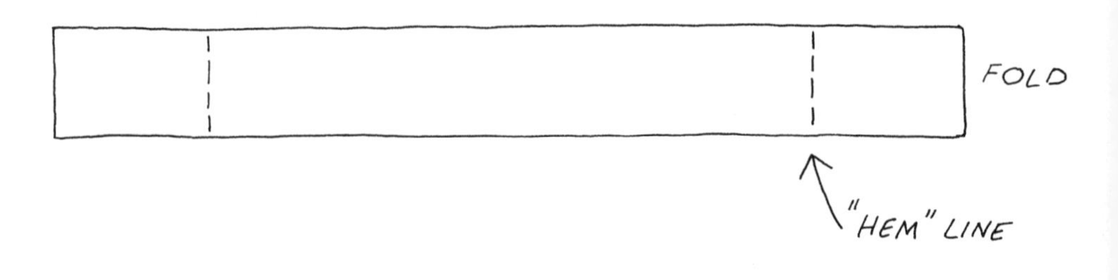

4. Sew the jump ring of a spring-ring closing set to one end of the cording (on the top side, not on the hem side). Sew the spring ring itself to the other end.

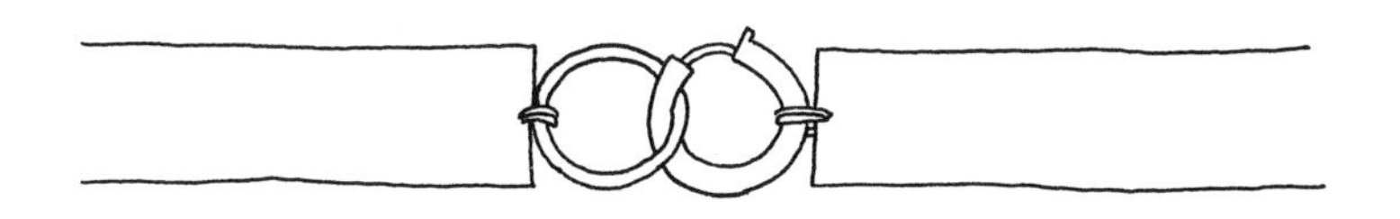

5. Our basic button design calls for the addition of sequins and seed beads that transform the button and complete the design. This is done as you go along, attaching each button to the cording. Start at one end with your first but-

Necklace and earrings made from graduated mother-of-pearl buttons with off-center holes. The buttons were sewn onto narrow cording and seed pearls cover the buttonholes. A spring ring and jump ring close the necklace. The earrings are the largest size of the button with the seed pearls sewn on and the whole glued to screw-back earring bases.

ton. Place it on top of the cording. With your needle coming from underneath, bring your thread up through the end hole of the button. Then thread a sequin over the hole; to secure it in place, thread a seed bead over it. Bring your needle back down through the sequin and the buttonhole. Repeat with the other hole of the button.

6. Sew all the other buttons onto the cording in the same manner, keeping them close together so that no cording shows between them. Work right to the edge of the cording, covering the hem, and meet the edge of the clasp.

BUTTON BRACELET

This is easily made by using elastic ribbon of a color that blends with the buttons. Measure your wrist and cut a length of 1/4-inch-wide elastic to the same size. Sew the ends of the elastic together, overlapping them about 1/2 inch, and making sure they are secure; then sew on the buttons in the same way as you did for the necklace.

You can also use the same type of cording and spring-ring closing that you did for the necklace, sewing the rings on in the same way.

Earrings made with two graduated mother-of-pearl buttons that have off-center holes. The holes are covered with sequins and seed pearls are sewn over them. The finished buttons were then glued onto screw-back earring bases.

You may want to make a wider bracelet, and this is easily done by using wider widths of elastic that will accommodate two or three rows of buttons. If you do this, however, the buttons used should be flat and thin so that they can come very close together and almost overlap. This will prevent the elastic from showing.

BUTTON EARRINGS

These are a little trickier to handle because the elements have to be put together first.

Steps

1. Sew the button, sequin, and seed-bead combination together, and tie the thread at the back as smoothly and neatly as possible.
2. Using contact cement, glue the button to the earring back and let dry.

Remember, just because most buttons are round and have center holes does not mean that you're limited to this type. Many come with off-center holes and are also available in squares, rectangles, ovals and crescents. They may be used alone or in combinations to make exciting patterns and unusual designs, as shown here.

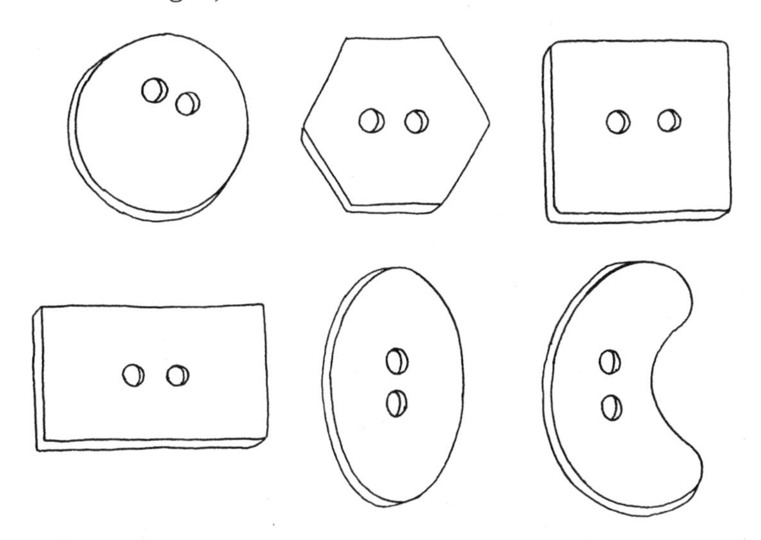

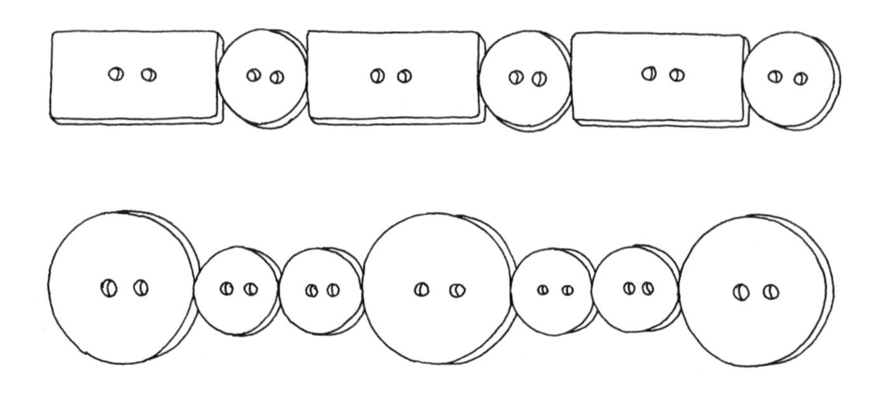

Here are some other ways you can use buttons to make jewelry:

1. You can skip the use of sequins on the buttons and secure them with seed beads or seed pearls alone.
2. You can do the same with sequins—that is, you can use sequins exactly as you do buttons. But remember that they are delicate and will require special handling and care in both making and wearing.
3. You can make necklaces and bracelets from buttons with shank backs simply by sewing them onto the cording or elastic. The flatter the back, the better. In making earrings, however, the shank must be clipped off before the button can be glued to an earring back.

A CIRCLE OF BEADS ON METAL

Beads can also be strung on a circle of metal to make an attractive piece of jewelry. The technique is used in many countries and the style is found in Africa, the Middle East, the Pacific Islands, Asia, and South America as well as in the West. The principal variations are in the type of metal used—anything from a simple and inexpensive iron ring to gold and platinum—and in the kinds of beads and other ornaments hung on and from the collar.

Steps

1. Design your pieces. One style that you might make is shown here.

2. Measure the sizes you want for necklace. The standard necklace size is about 15 inches.
3. Take a piece of 14-gauge wire of gold, silver, or copper color that is approximately 2 inches longer than the neck measurement you want. With your pliers, make a loop at one end. The loop should be about 1/4 inch in diameter.
4. Curve the wire to a circular shape, following the directions in step 11, page 156.
5. Thread your beads directly on the wire according to your design pattern.

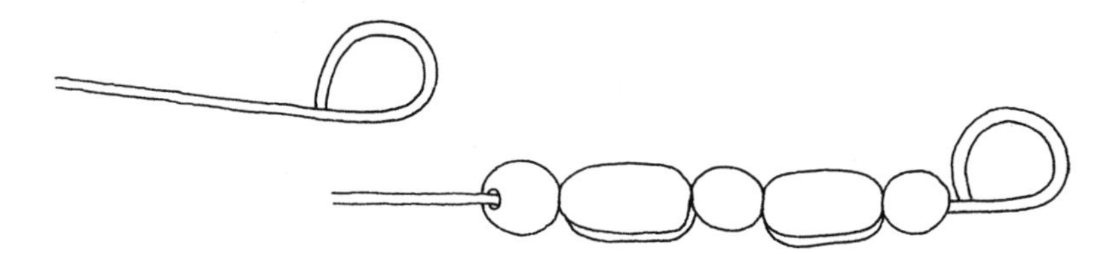

6. Allow 1/2 inch beyond the end of the beads, and cut the excess off with a wire cutter. With your pliers, curve the extra 1/2 inch of wire around to make a hook. This hook will fit into the loop you made in step 3, and the necklace will close in this way. If you find that the necklace is too

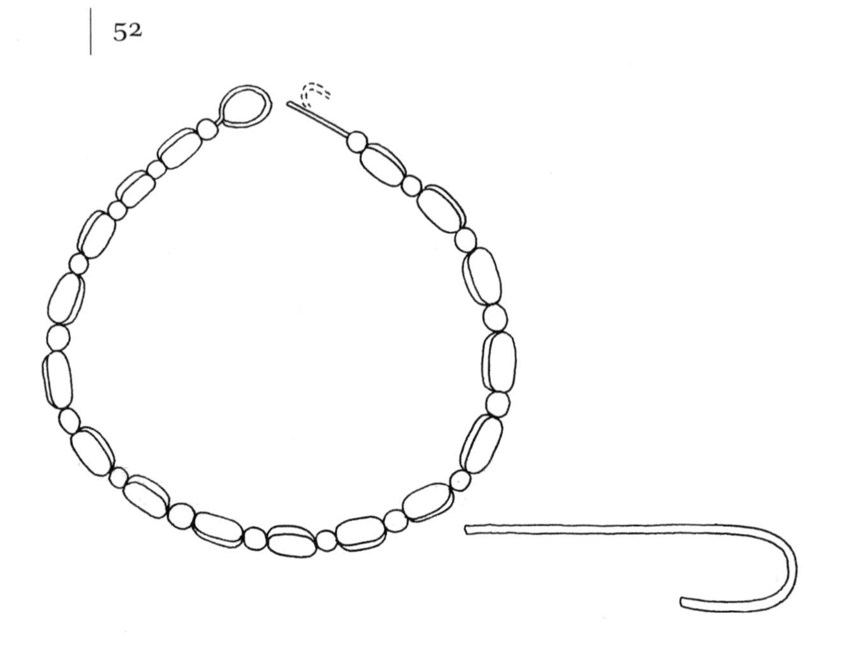

large, you may want to hook above one of the beads (same principle as the hook closing in step 2 on page 31).

7. Finish shaping your necklace to make sure that it is circular.

Variations

1. A bracelet can be made in exactly the same way, the only difference being size. The bracelet should fit your wrist measurement, with an allowance of about 1/2 inch for movement and closing. You might want to make a pair of bracelets to go with a necklace like this.
2. Select any one of the beads to make earrings in any one of the styles already described.

JEWELRY WITH FABRIC

You can individualize an outfit with strips of matching or contrasting felt to which design elements have been sewn or glued. These felt pieces, snapped onto a metal neck wire of the type we have just described, can be interchanged and the basic collar used with as many design pieces as you wish.

The drawings give some ideas for felt jewelry designs. In

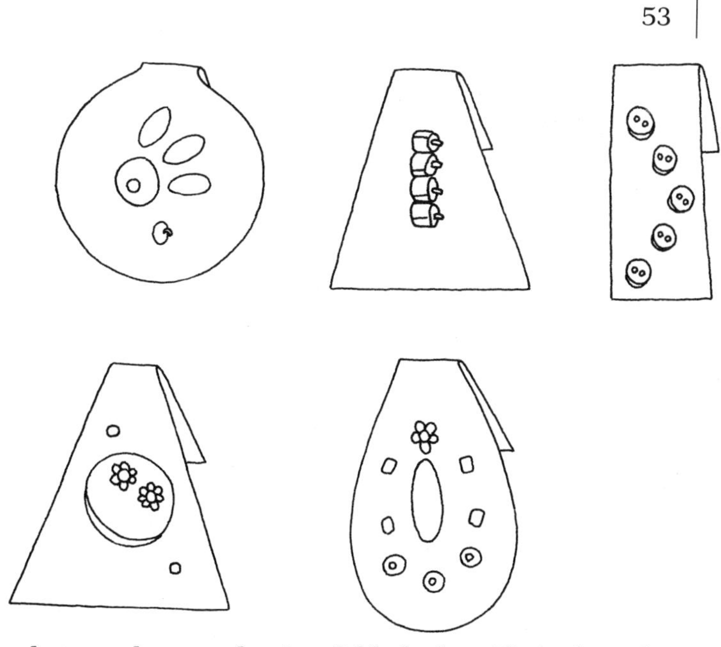

each case, the top edge is a folded edge. The other edges are straight. Design elements are glued or sewn on the felt.

Steps

1. Make a paper pattern for your design. Remember that the folded top part has to fit around the metal collar; if it is too wide, it will not fall smoothly over the circular wire. Two inches is about the maximum suitable width, and narrower is even better. And, unless you are looking for a bib effect, 6 inches is about the longest your piece should be.
2. Cut out the shape you want in a double thickness of felt, with the folded edge at the place where it will fit over the metal collar.
3. Sew or glue the buttons, sequins, pieces of contrasting felt or fabric, beads, metal rings, tassels—whatever you like!—onto the top side of the felt. Heavier objects like buttons should be sewn on for permanence. Lighter ones like sequins may be glued on. Some elements, such as heavy beads, cannot be glued on because they haven't enough surface to make proper contact with the felt. If you are planning to use beads, you might want to add beads to the metal collar to pick up the accent.

4. Depending on the size and shape of the felt, sew three or more snaps to the inner side of the layers of felt. Try to sew them under a spot where you have put a fairly large design element, like a button, so that your stitches will not show. Two of the snaps should be high up near the fold, to hold the piece firm.
5. Snap the felt onto a metal collar. If you want beads on the collar, move them around so that they fall properly in place on either side of the felt, in a pattern you have selected. If you have sewn the snaps up high, as directed in step 4, the beads will not slip under the felt.

Using these techniques or combinations of the techniques described in this chapter, it is possible to make almost any kind of beaded necklace and matching bracelet, earrings, rings, and belts. Here are some additional designs that you can try.

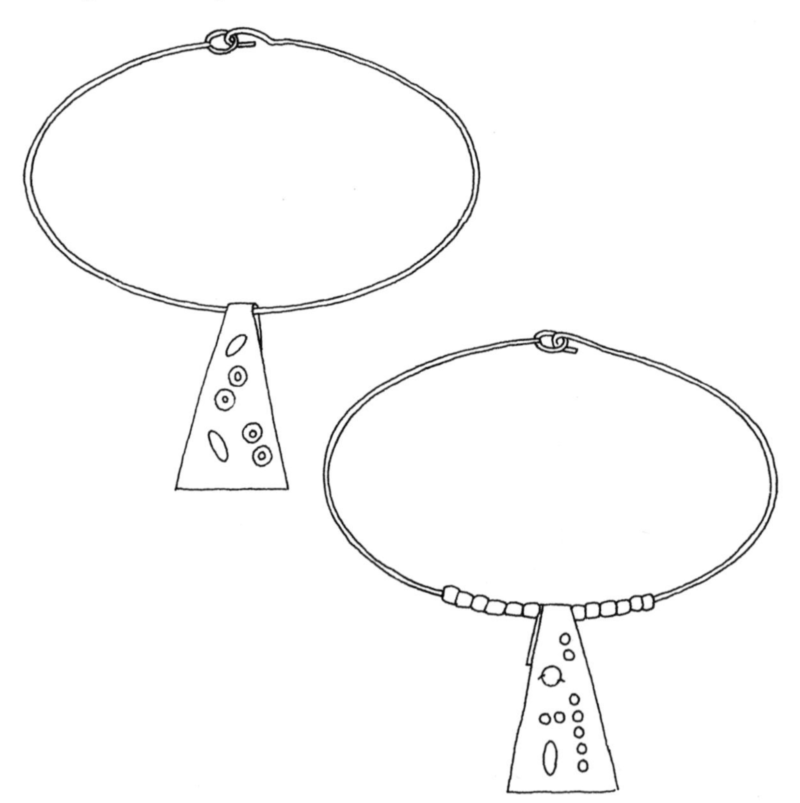

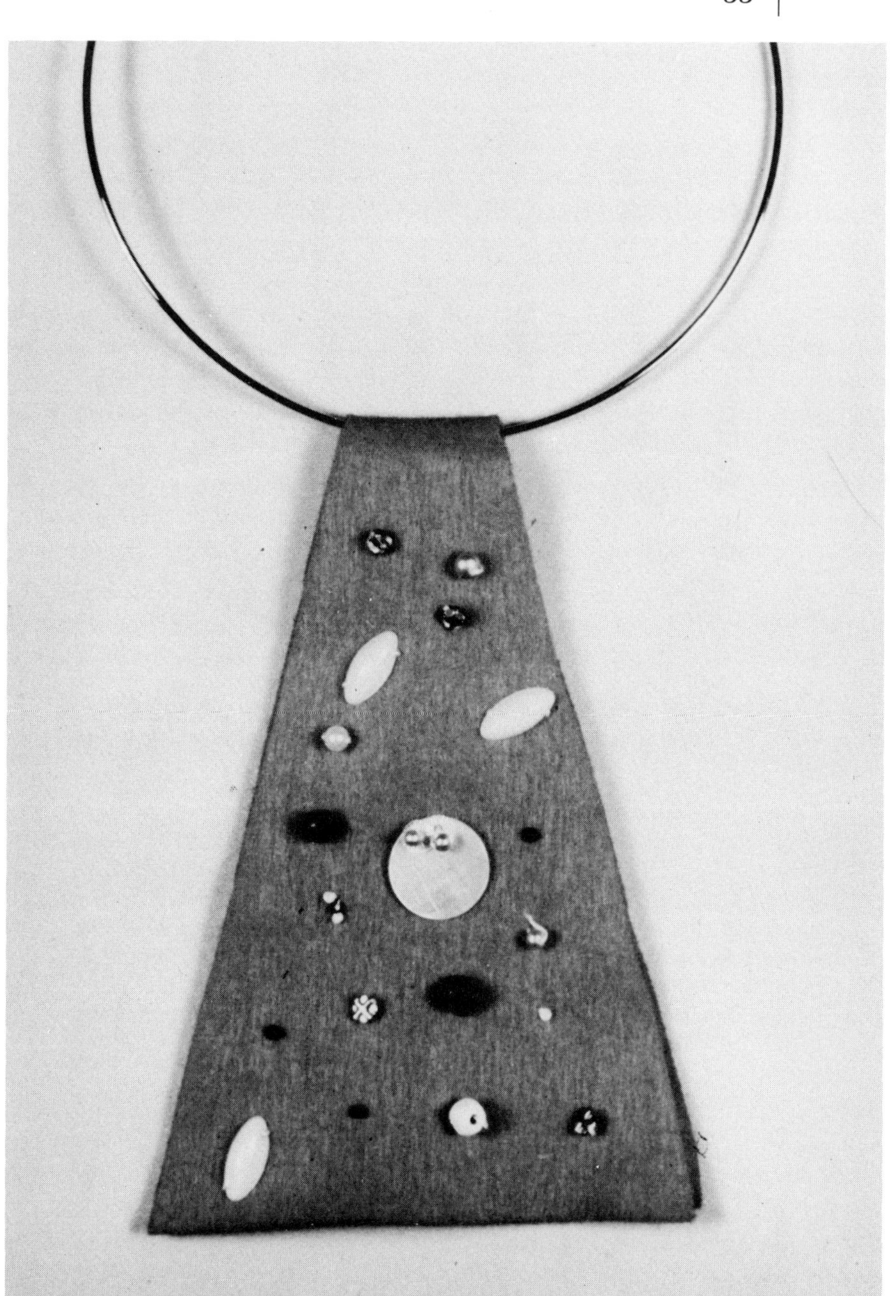

A piece of felt and old buttons and beads make this bib on a wire collar. These bibs are so easily made that they can be created to match an unlimited number of outfits.

Three necklaces on thread, showing variety in design and use of different colors, sizes, and shapes of beads to achieve pleasing effects.

Three necklaces on thread. Left, small jet beads are mixed with elongated ones to make an interesting long necklace that fits over the head. The three tassel strands are made separately and joined through the large center bead to the main part of the necklace. Right, a loop of seed crystal beads joins each of the three brown hanging pieces to the necklace, which is made of beads of two other shades of brown. Above, blue Venetian glass beads form the center of this necklace; the small yellow crystal beads pick up one of the colors in the larger beads.

3. Beads Combined with Wood, Metal and Wire

AS we have seen, needle and thread make possible the creation of a wide range of beaded jewelry. We can expand this range even more by using wire and chain in addition to thread for beading, and adding other nonbeaded materials as design elements.

The basic principles presented in Chapter 2 with regard to joining design elements, measurement, design, and so on also apply to the projects in this chapter. An important difference, however, is that the thread was usually a hidden element in the earlier projects, whereas in many of the wire, metal, and wood creations the links are a part of the design.

TOOLS

Once again, you'll be using *needles* of various sizes, *cosmetic tweezers*, *chain-nose pliers*, a *wire cutter*, and *embroidery scissors*. You will also want a *hand drill* with a fine bit (for instructions on use, see Chapter 5, page 146).

MATERIALS

For these new projects, you'll be working with many of the same elements you used in the designs already completed—beads, of course, and string, laces, thongs, and elastic in various colors and thicknesses. You will also need the usual assortment of jewelry findings—pin backs, earring backs, cuff-link backs, jump rings, catches—as well as clear contact cement for gluing them to your design elements. You will be using wire in copper, gold and silver color, 14-gauge as well as finer weights.

New elements include rings of wood or metal (obtainable in craft shops or lumberyards), plus other findings of wood and metal such as odd-shaped bits of wood, dowel ends, plumbing washers, pipe fittings, wire brads, and so on. (Again, poking around in a hardware store or lumberyard may produce new inspirations.) You can use coins, too, old or new, foreign or American, as elements in these pieces.

To complete some projects, you may want wood stain or paint, as well as metal chains and tassels, which you can get in crafts shops and notions departments. Once again, though, decide on a project and work out a preliminary design before you go shopping for supplies.

GOING-AROUND-IN-CIRCLES NECKLACE

For this first project you will need a simple wooden ring about 2 inches in diameter and ½ inch wide, cut from hollow wooden tubing obtainable at a lumberyard. Or you can use sections of metal pipe, once you have mastered the art of cutting metal described in Chapter 6. Combined with beads and string, the rings make attractive, easily assembled jewelry.

Steps

1. Design your piece for the neck. Keep in mind that if you want matching pieces they will probably have to be modified for the smaller dimensions of the wrist and ear. One possible design is illustrated here.
2. Measure the length of your neckpiece. This type of ornament hangs well when matinee length (24 inches) or opera length (30 inches)—or slightly longer or shorter, according to your taste. Measure also the lengths of side cords you will need, and figure the number of beads.

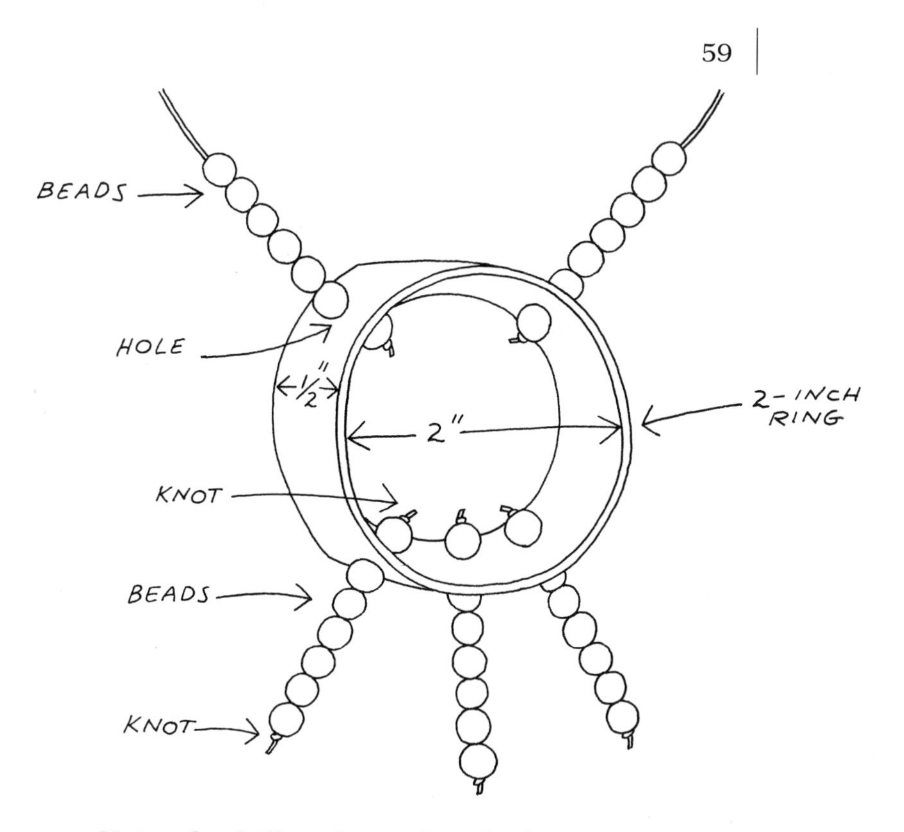

3. Using the drill as directed in the beginning of Chapter 5, drill holes in the wood (or metal) ring at the places where the beads are to be added. Make sure the holes are large enough for the string or leather you are planning to use. But don't make them too much larger, or you will have slipping and sliding.

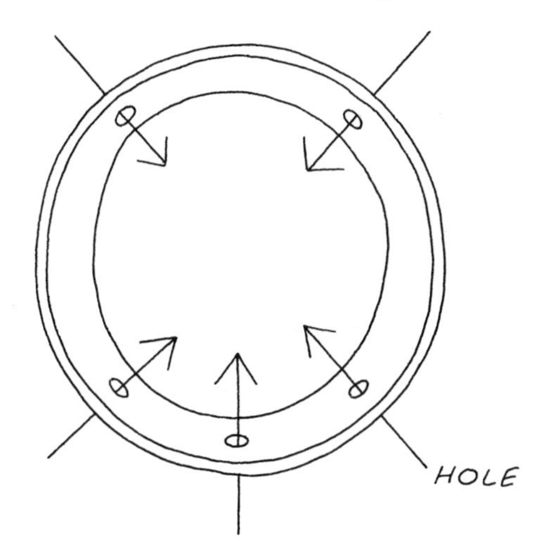

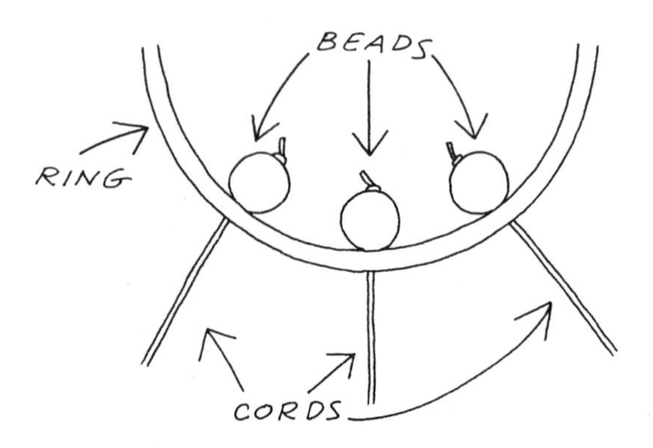

4. If you are using a wooden ring, you may want to stain or paint it another color. Now is the time to do so. Make sure it is dry before proceeding with your work. (Note: if you want a stain with a sheen, shellac or lacquer the wood after staining.)
5. Cut three 6-inch pieces of leather thong or colored package twine. Make a knot at one end of each piece. Add one bead to each strand.
6. Pull each strand through one of the three holes from the inside, so that the beads are on the inside of the circle, as shown.
7. Add the other beads to each of the three strands, securing them tightly onto the cord with knots. Trim the excess cord. To make sure it does not ravel, apply a drop of clear contact cement to the knot. If you use leather thong, this is not necessary, as leather does not ravel and leather knots tend to stay "locked in" once they are made and pulled tightly.
8. Your center ring is now ready to be joined to the neckpiece. Since this piece is large enough to slip over the head, you can make the neckpiece from one piece of leather thong or cord. Take the measured length, make a knot at one end, and add a bead to it, just as you did in step 5.

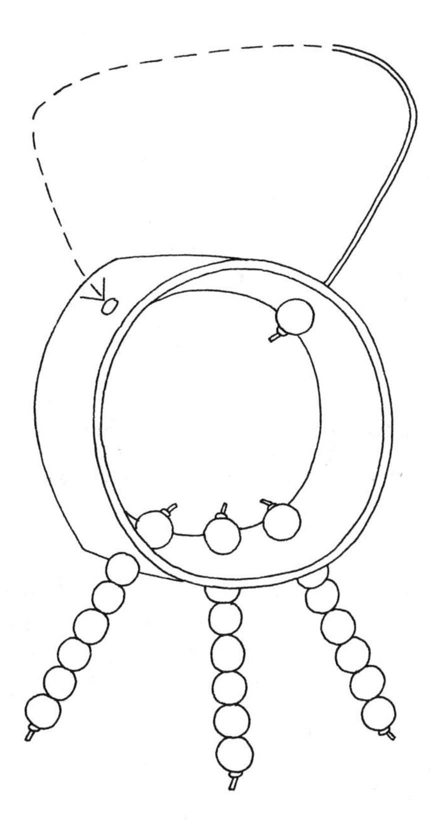

9. String the cord or thong through one of the top holes of the ring, going from inside out. Add beads to the rest of the neckpiece, then pass the end of the string through the top hole on the other side of the ring, outside to inside.
10. Add one last bead to the neckpiece string inside the ring. Before knotting it off, of course, try on your necklace and adjust the length as necessary. Then make a knot and trim it as before. Again, if you have used string to make the necklace, the knots can be glued down with clear contact cement to prevent raveling.

Variations

This design can also be executed using wire instead of string for the neckpiece and the bead attachments. It lends itself to infinite variations, including use as a belt with

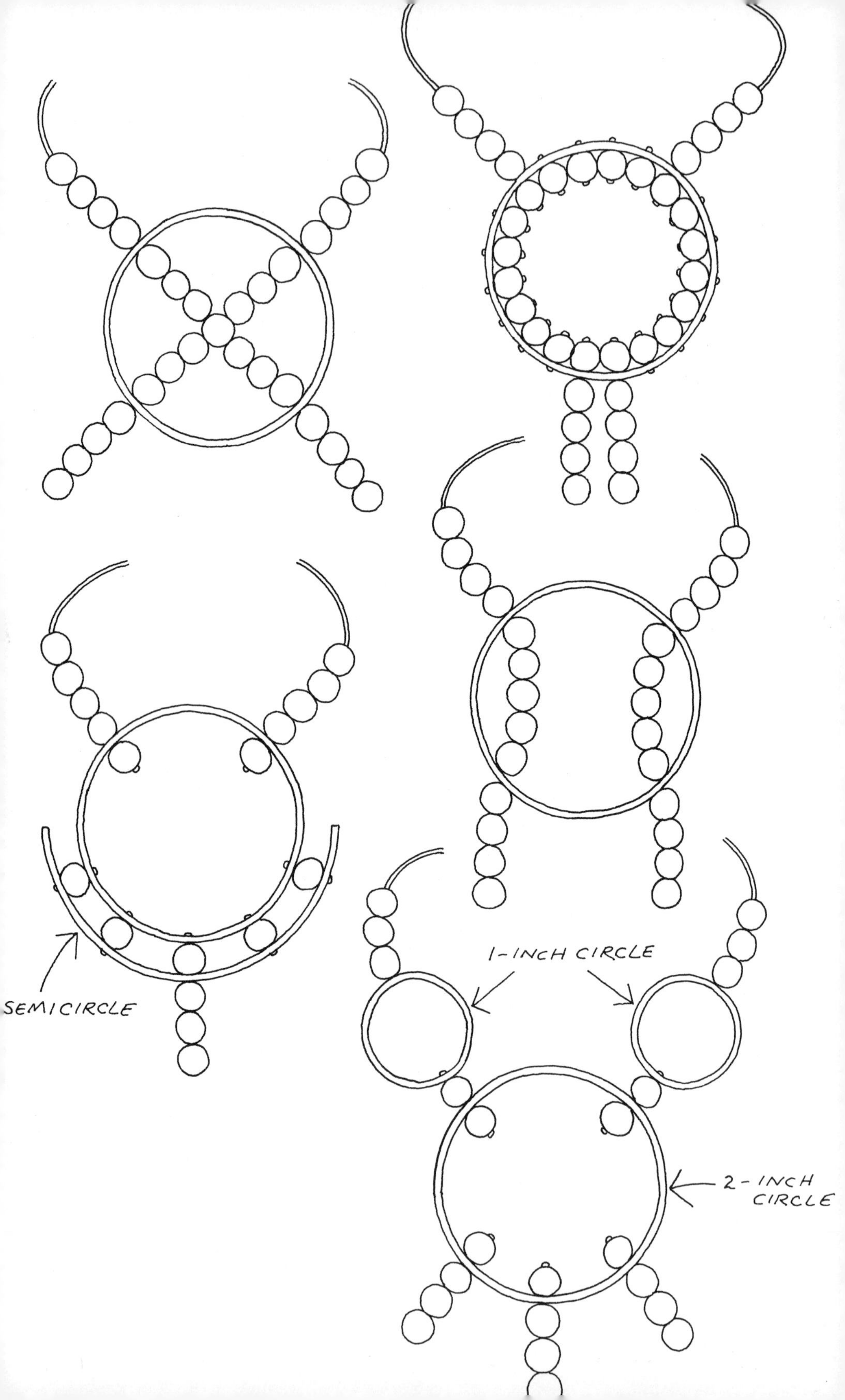
SEMICIRCLE
1-INCH CIRCLE
2-INCH CIRCLE

circles of about 1 inch in diameter. The drawings show some of the alternate patterns you can use for "going around in circles."

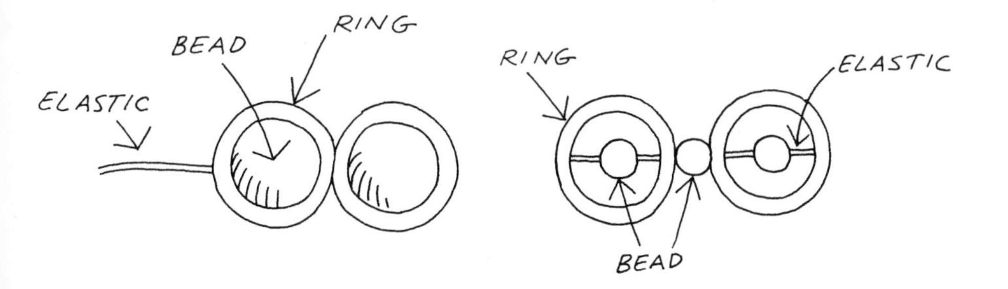

RING BRACELET

One large ring such as that used for the necklace does not make a very attractive bracelet. You can, however, use the basic idea of the necklace to make a bracelet that will go well with it. For instance, you might use a series of smaller rings held together with round elastic or elastic thread. The beads can be big enough to fill the center of the rings, or they can be smaller and "float" in the center openings, suspended by the elastic.

Steps

1. Measure your wrist and do the necessary arithmetic to figure out how much elastic and how many rings and beads you will need.
2. Drill two holes in each ring, directly opposite each other, as indicated in the drawing.

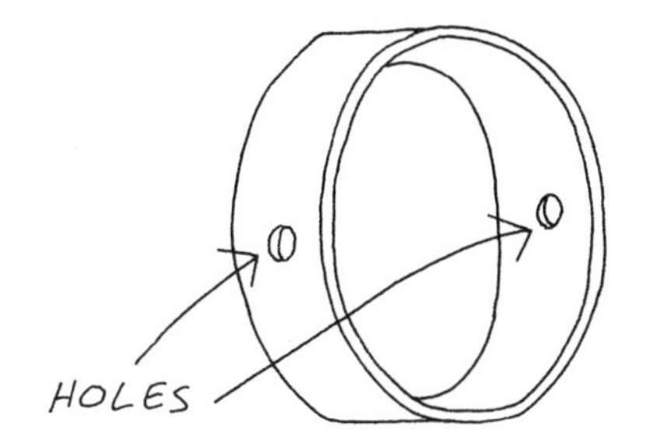

3. If you painted or stained the wooden neck ring, now is the time to do the same for the bracelet rings.
4. String the beads and wooden rings in the pattern selected onto the elastic, tie the ends with a small knot, and cut off the excess thread. Remember that your elastic should end up exactly the same size as your wrist. In this way the bracelet does not sag (as it will if it is too large) and the elastic does not show (as it will if it is too small and must be stretched to fit).

Variations

1. If you want the wooden rings on the bracelet to be larger, and to use string as you did in the necklace, follow this design through step 3, but string the rings as you did the necklace. You will then need to sew a spring ring to one end of the string and a jump ring to the other. You will find it tricky to sew string onto the rings. It can be done, however, with careful, fine, overlapping stitches. Again, the use of clear contact cement will help to prevent raveling and slipping.
2. You can make a simple button-type earring using any of the beads from your main piece. Simply glue it onto the earring back.

RING EARRINGS

This ring style lends itself well to hanging earrings.

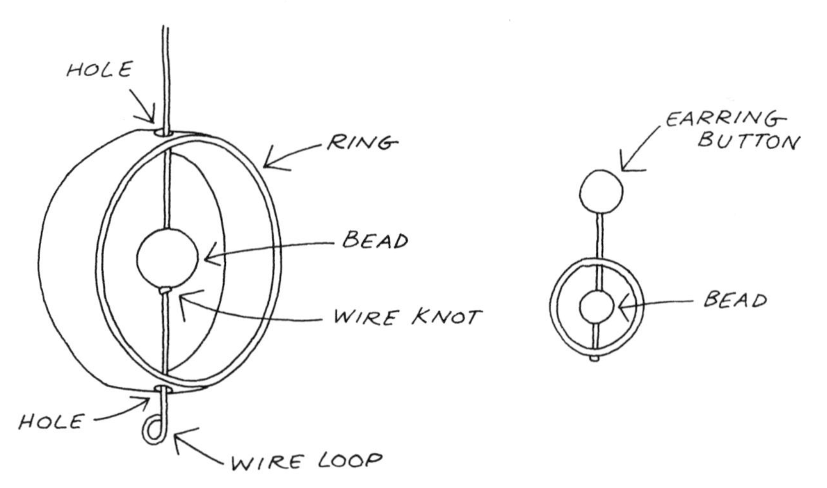

Steps

1. Select a ring of the size you want for the earring drop—about 1 inch in diameter is good. Paint or stain it to match if necessary.
2. Drill two holes at opposite ends of the ring.
3. Take a 4-inch piece of 22-gauge wire and make a knot in it about 1½ inches from one end. Thread your bead onto the wire so that it rests on the knot.
4. Thread the short end (the 1½ inches) into one hole of the ring from the inside out, so that the bead is inside the ring.
5. Make a loop at the end of the wire so that the bead is held in the *middle* of the ring. Cut off any excess wire from the loop.
6. Thread the wire through the other hole in the ring, again from the inside out.
7. Make the wire as taut as possible and make a loop at the end of it (on the outside of the ring). Trim the excess wire with a wire cutter or heavy scissors.
8. Attach the loop to the ring on the earring base.

A CHOKER STRUNG ON WIRE

Steps

1. Design your collar either with a random assortment of bead colors and shapes, or with a design worked into the bead arrangement (see drawings). In designing the piece, decide on the size of the bead you want to use, as this will influence the pattern and the type of materials you get.
2. Measure your neck size, allowing for the closing (see step 9 for the various possibilities for closing).

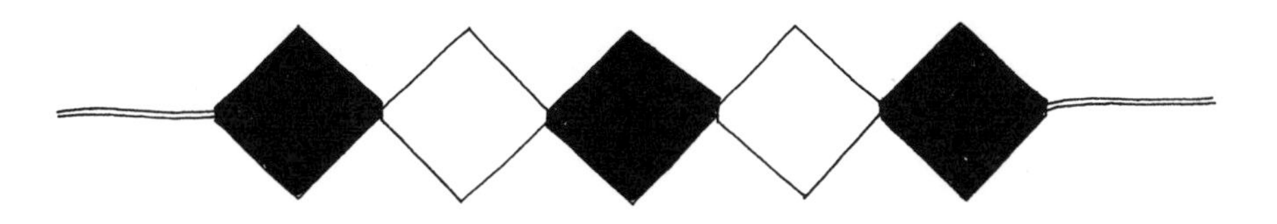

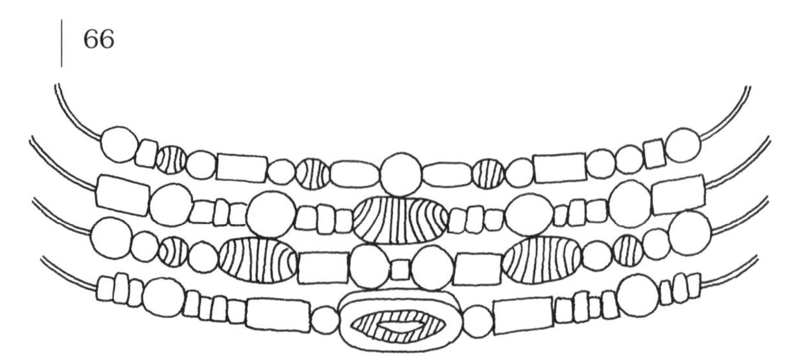

3. Using 20-gauge wire, cut enough pieces to make the number of strands you want. Allow an additional 2 inches for working each strand.
4. With your pliers, make a small loop about 1/8 inch in diameter at one end of each of the wire strands.
5. Shape each strand into a circle with your hands, holding it around your neck.
6. Thread the beads onto the wires. Even if you are using a random assortment of beads, it is wise to lay them out in advance to see how they will look together. If you have made a bead pattern, you must lay them out in advance to make sure you are putting them on in the right order. Work one strand at a time, matching your patterns where necessary. When all your strands are done place them together to make sure that you have put the beads on in the right sequence, and rebead if needed.
7. Making sure the beads are as close as possible, end each strand with another 1/8 inch loop. Cut off the excess wire with scissors or wire cutter.
8. Cut two 2-inch pieces of the same wire. Run one piece through the end loops on one side of the strands, and the other piece through the loops on the other side. This joins the strands at the two ends. Turn the wire around the top and bottom loops of the joined strands so that they cannot slip apart, and cut off the excess wire as before.
9. The necklace can be closed in several different ways. You can attach a spring ring to the middle of the wire joining the strands at one end, and a jump ring to catch it on at the other. Or you can attach a jewelry hook to one side and let it hook onto the vertical wire bar at the end of the strands, or onto a wire loop attached there. You can also attach a button to one side and a loop of cording or wire to the other (for directions see page 41).

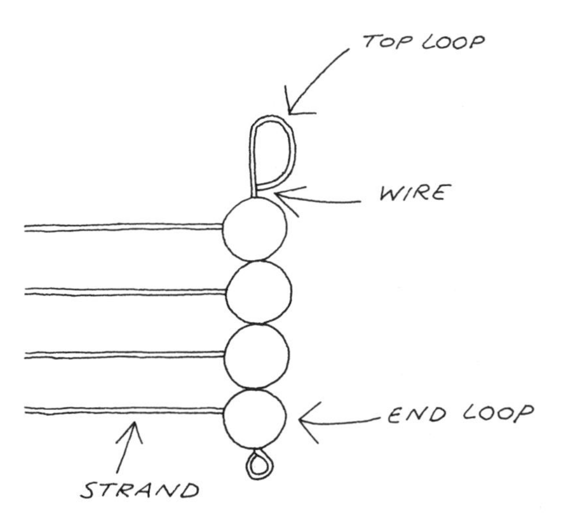

Variations

1. A matching bracelet can be made in exactly the same manner, but it needs no clasp. The spring action of the wire makes it possible to slip the bracelet onto the wrist and to reshape it on the arm afterward.
2. Matching earrings can be made in any of the variations already described.

HALF-CIRCLE CHOKER

This and the following project are variations on the wire-strung choker. Both are interesting to make and can also be used in bracelet and earring form. This one uses strands that go halfway around the neck and are joined in the front with a centerpiece of contrasting beads.

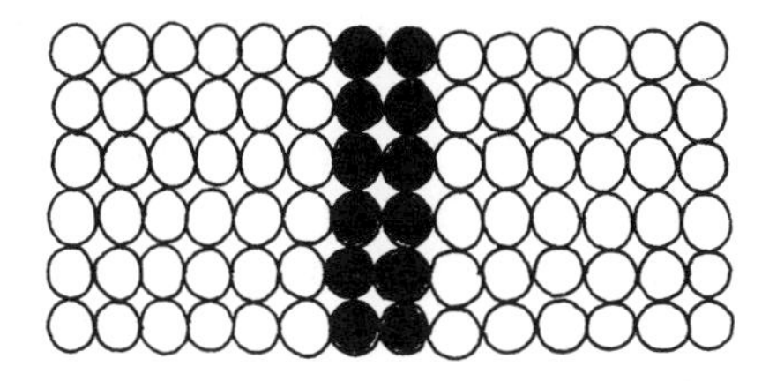

Steps

1. Decide on the bead and color patterns you wish to use in the choker.
2. Using the neck measurements you already have, divide in half to figure the sizes of the strands you are going to use.
3. Cut wire for the number of half-circle strands you will need, then shape the wire into half circles.

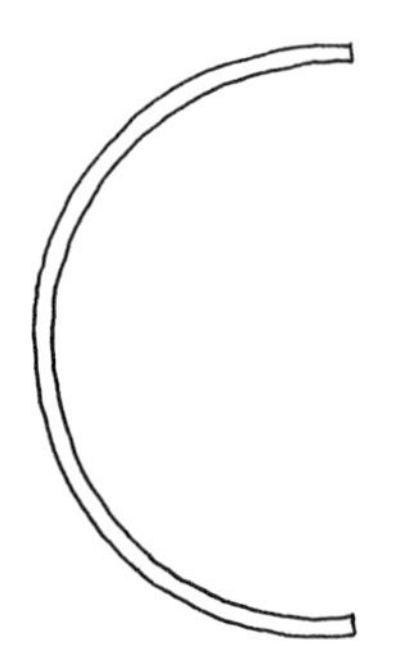

4. Bead the strands in exactly the same way that you beaded the wire-strung choker, with the same end loops and all.

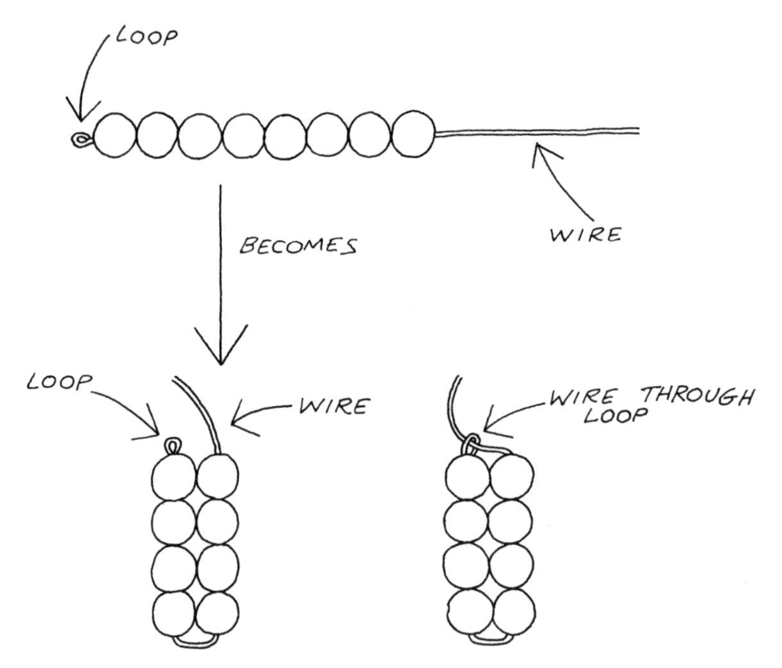

5. Make a small loop at one end of a 4-inch piece of wire. Put onto it twice as many beads as there will be strands in the final necklace. Bend in half. This will make two vertical strands that are the same height as the choker. Attach the free end of the wire through the loop already made and draw the two halves tightly together. Twist the wire through the loop several times, pass it through one bead, and clip off any excess that remains.
6. Use the loop ends made on the half-circle strands to attach each strand to the center vertical bars of beads.
7. Finish off the back following steps 7, 8, and 9 of the preceding project.

DANGLING-BEAD CHOKER

Using one of the two chokers just described as your base, hang other shaped beads or decorative elements from the bottom strand.

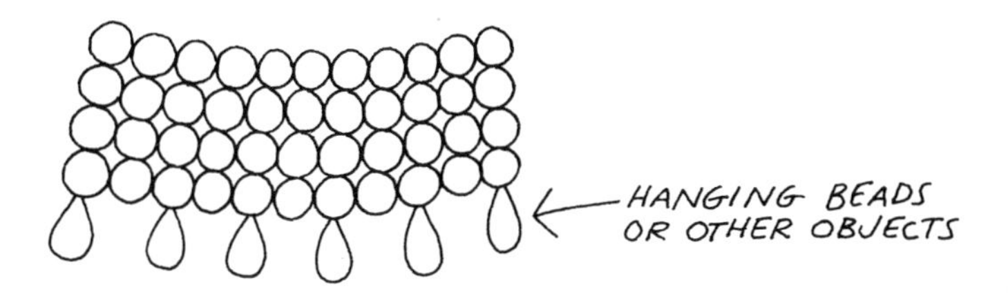

Steps

1. Decide on how many and what kind of hanging pieces you want.
2. If you are using beads, the easiest way to attach them is with wire loops that you make yourself. Take a length of wire several inches long, and loop it at the end; add your bead, then turn the free end of the wire around the bottom strand of the choker, between two beads, as close to the hanging bead as possible. Make a closed loop and cut the wire. Repeat as many times as you wish, all around the base of the choker.

Instead of wire, you can take a thin wire brad (a straight nail with a small head that will serve to hold the bead) about

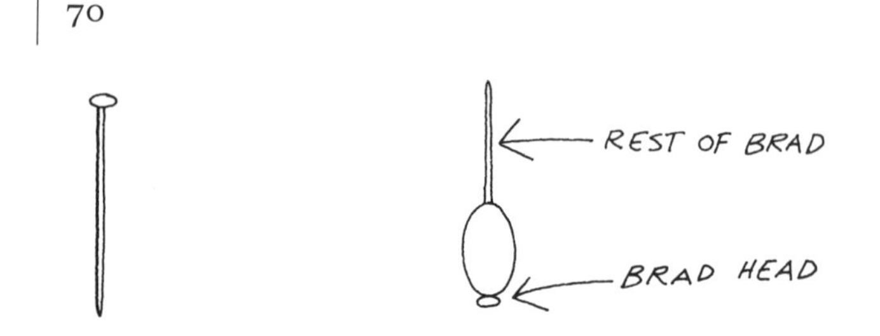

¼ inch longer than the bead. Add your bead; then turn up the end of the brad and loop it around the bottom strand of the choker, between two beads. Repeat as often as your design requires.

If you use shells, pierced metal pieces, or odd-shaped wood pieces painted and stained, attach them to the bottom strand of the choker by using jump rings between beads.

WIRE-STRUNG COLLAR WITH BIB

Wire strands covered with beads can make necklaces of varying sizes. For instance, a flat collar of beads can be made in the same way as the choker. Only you must allow for the fact that each strand must be smaller than the one below it if the necklace is to fit properly at the neckline.

Remember that this heavier piece will need a stronger clasp. A jewelry hook, which is also adjustable, is preferable to a spring-ring closing for this reason.

As with the choker, you can add dangling beads or a decorative centerpiece. You can build on it in other ways, too, because the collar allows for longer additions than the choker. You might try a bib effect of more beads, hooked on as were the individual beads. Or you might hook on individual tassels of beads. Or you might have a long streamer of beads added directly to the necklace, or to the bib.

Steps

1. Take a piece of 18- or 20-gauge wire that is equal to the length and two widths of the bib you are making, plus 1 inch.
2. Shape the wire into the form you want for the bib, leaving it open at the top. Some possible shapes are shown here.

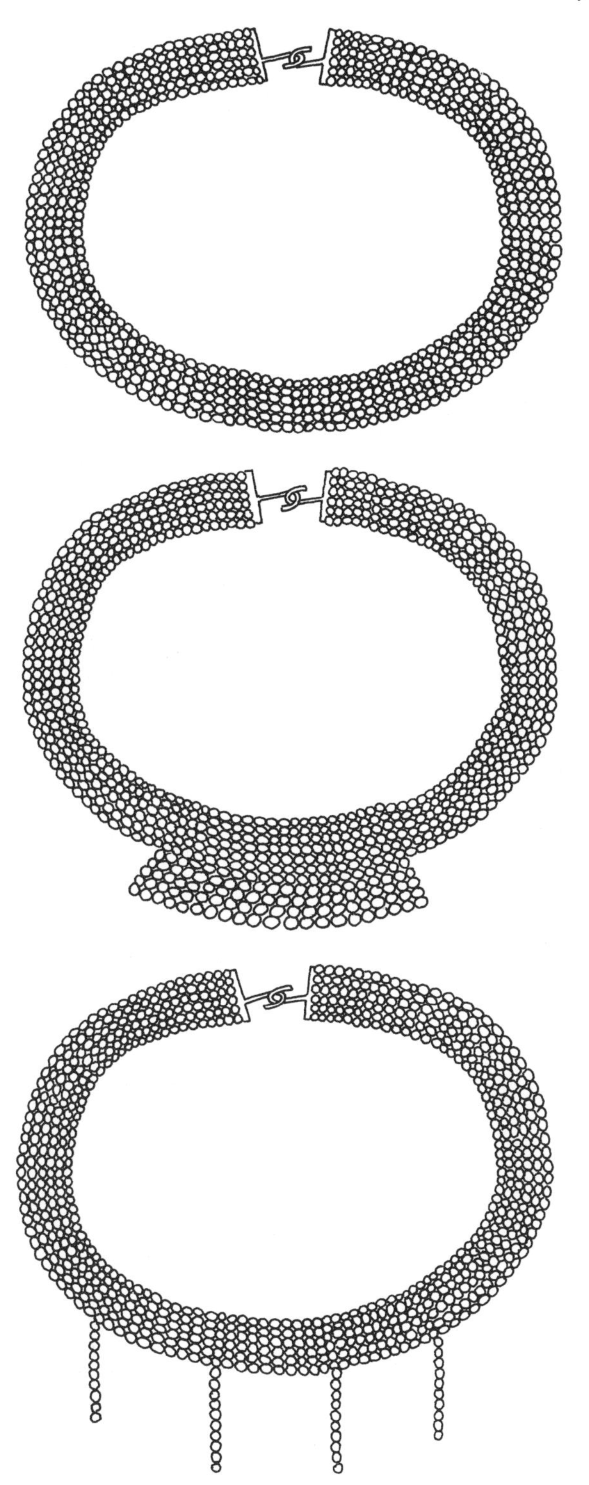

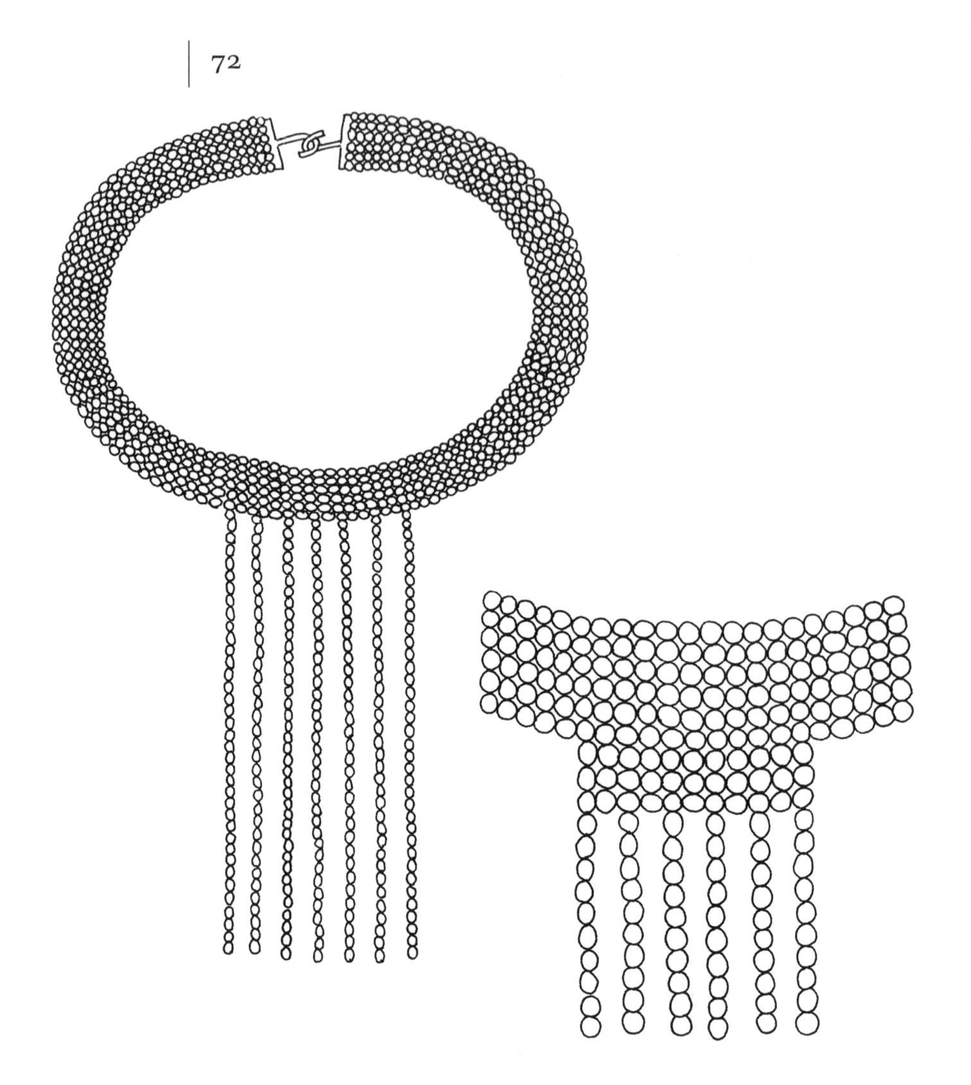

3. Turn up one end of the wire slightly, just enough to hold the beads on, and add all your outer beads in the pattern you have selected. Shape as desired and turn up the other end to hold beads on.

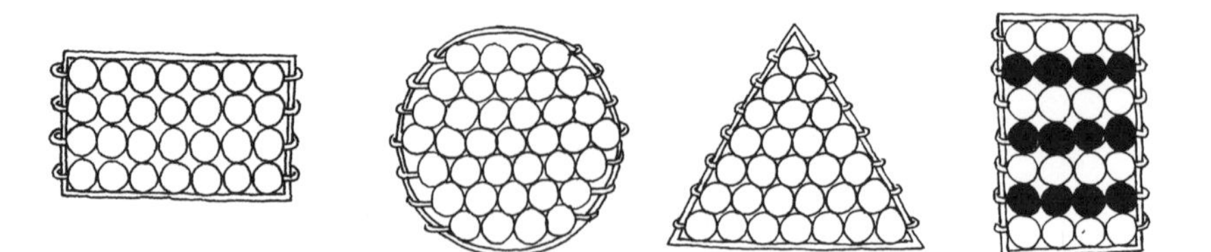

4. Cut wire for the number of horizontal strands you want. String all the strands in the bead pattern selected, making small loops at the ends of each strand.
5. Attach the horizontal strands to the outer strand by looping their end wires between the beads.
6. Attach the bib by looping the ends of the wire of the outer strand around the bottom strand of the piece to which the bib is being added. The piece might be a single strand of beads, a wire collar, a beaded collar, and so on. A few of the possible end products are shown here.

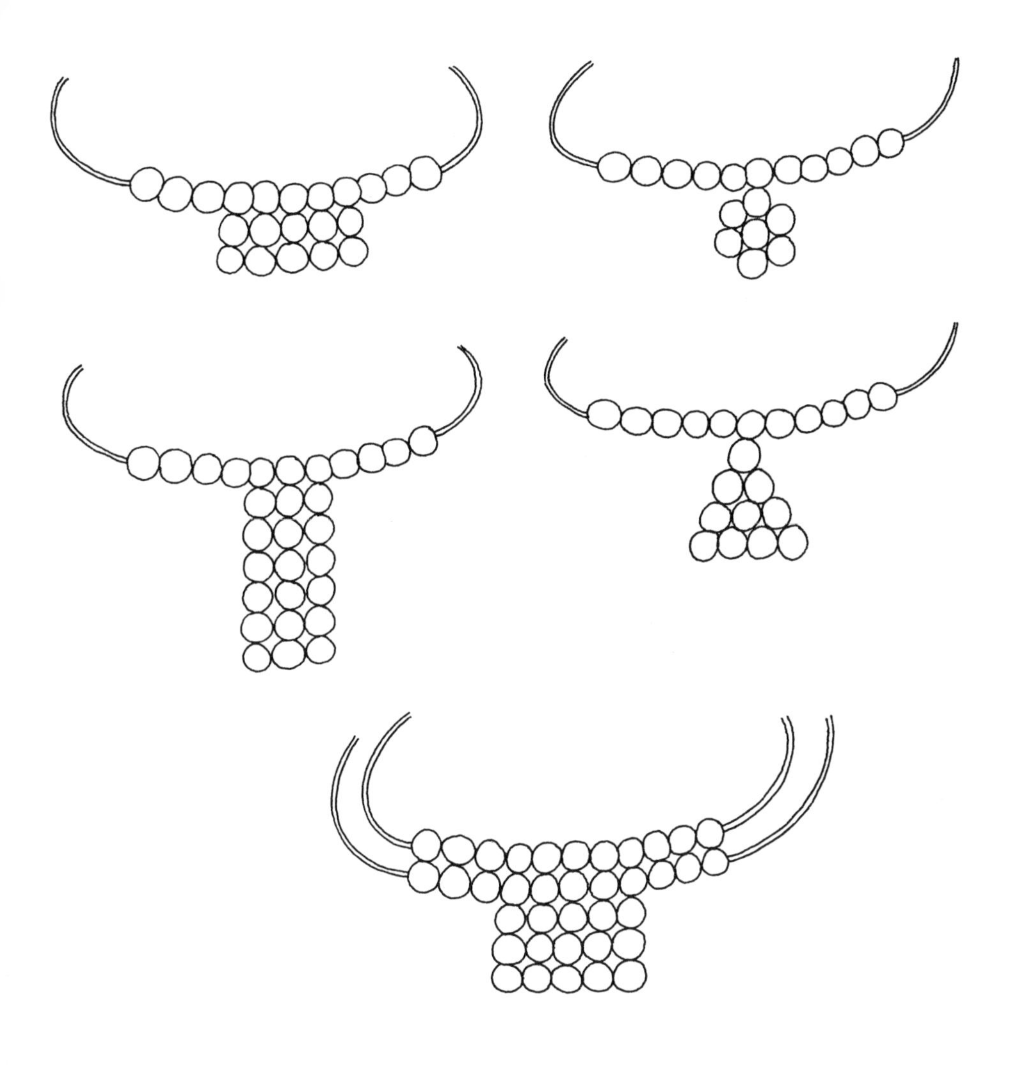

BEADS ON A WIRE CHAIN

Stringing beads on wire chains that you make yourself has a number of advantages. The links themselves are a decorative element. The wire is stronger than most threads so that you can work with heavy beads and metal accent pieces. And you can shape the wire in ways that you cannot do with thread.

The wire chain is essentially pieces of wire bent and hooked onto each other in a continuous fashion, with decorative elements in between.

For practice, you might start with a simple single-strand necklace of beads (see illustration).

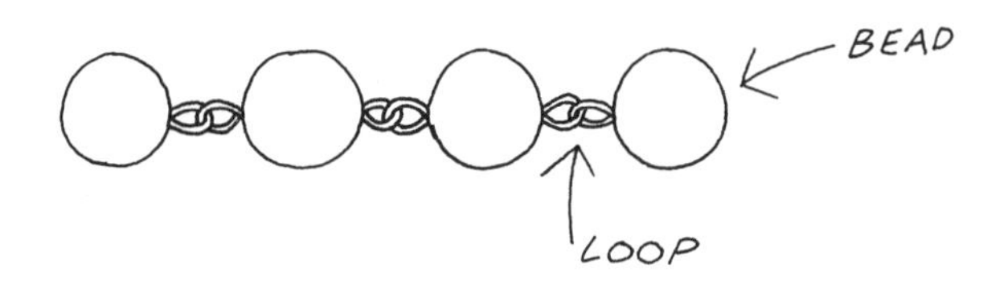

Steps

1. Sketch your design and select the beads you want to use. Decide if you want gold- or silver-color wire.
2. Measure off the length of your necklace with a piece of soft package string. You will have to measure your work against this, as you go along, since you will not be beading on a straight piece of thread.
3. Lay out your beads so that they appear in exactly the order that you want them to have in the finished piece.
4. Use 24-gauge wire on a spool. Attach the wire to a spring ring by looping it over securely.
5. Add your first bead, push it down to the loop, make a loop against it, and cut off the wire.
6. Insert the end of the wire into the loop you have just made, and loop it so that it is secure. Cut the wire from the spool, thread on the next bead, and loop and trim the wire as you did in step 5.
7. Repeat this process until you have strung all your beads. End by attaching the wire to the jump ring of the spring-ring closing.

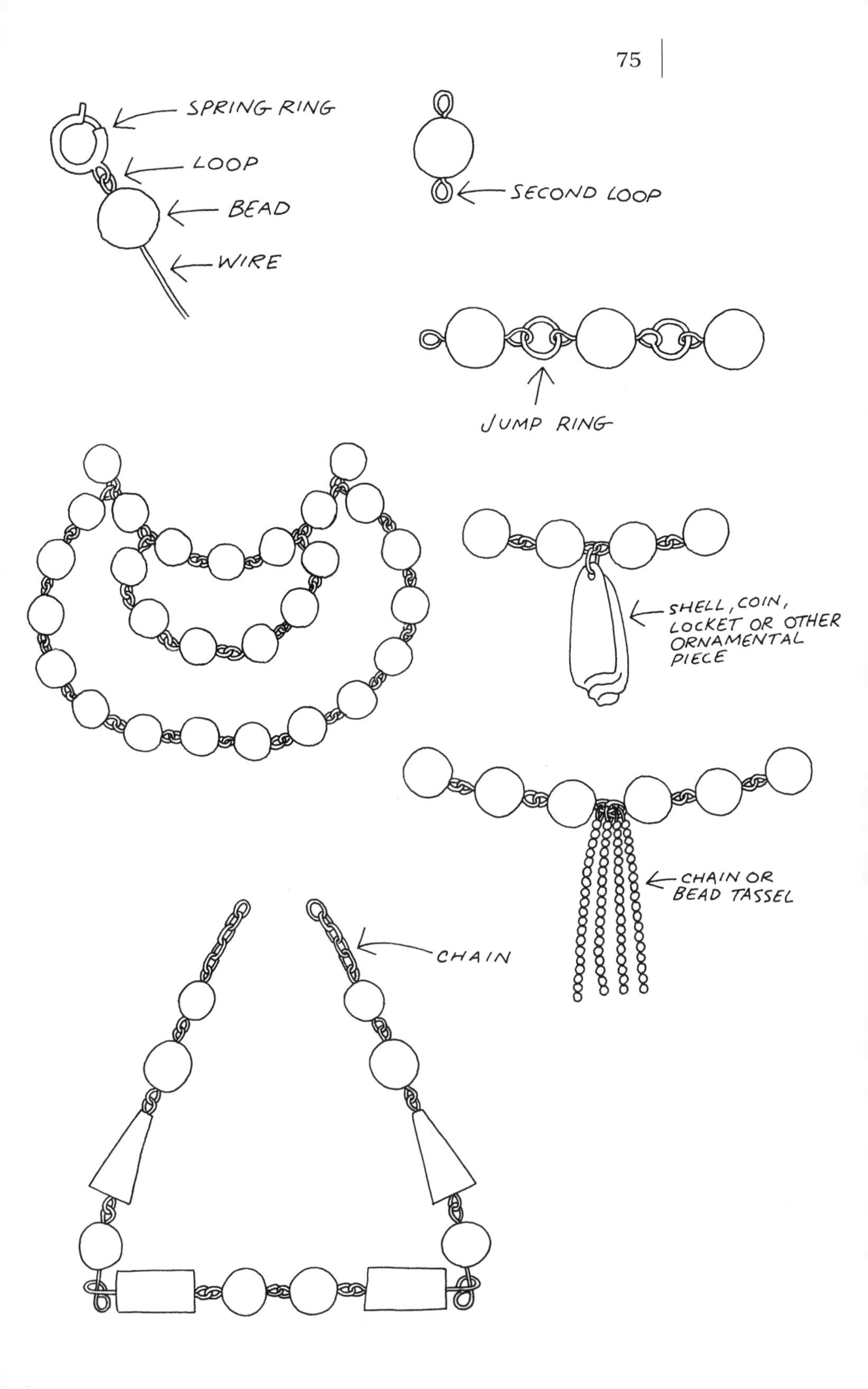
SPRING RING
LOOP
BEAD
WIRE
SECOND LOOP
JUMP RING
SHELL, COIN, LOCKET OR OTHER ORNAMENTAL PIECE
CHAIN OR BEAD TASSEL
CHAIN

Variations

1. You may vary the necklace by adding matching jump rings between the loops.
2. You may add extra loops of beads to the front of the necklace.
3. Add tassels, metal pieces, or shells, so that your necklace looks like one of the designs shown here.

CHAIN NECKLACE

You may want to use your self-made wire chains in conjunction with chains purchased in craft shops or notions departments to get variety of design and additional strength. For instance, for a necklace like the one shown here, you would not want to make the entire chain yourself. It wouldn't be pretty enough for your nice piece, nor would

Black beads of different sizes and shapes, strung on wire and joined with jump rings in two sizes, make an interesting bracelet and necklace. Note that flat gold-colored discs cover the holes of the beads to create an interesting professionally finished effect.

it be strong enough to hold its weight. Directions for making the piece are simple.

Steps

1. Choose the color and design elements you want, and decide if you want gold or silver chain. You'll also need wire and jump rings.
2. Measure the length of the necklace with string, then lay out your beads in the pattern you want for the finished piece.
3. Starting at one end of the beaded portion of the necklace, string your beads by making a wire chain. Use wire that is heavy enough to hold them and also heavy enough to go with the purchased chain. It need not be as heavy as the chain (it would be too hard to loop and work with), but it should not be flimsy-looking in comparison. Continue to the corner where you want the beads to angle. Make a second vertical piece for the other side.
4. Make your horizontal piece, stringing the beads on a single piece of wire.
5. Link the horizontal piece to the vertical strands so that the loops form an angle. You do this by hooking the horizontal loop to the wire *above* the vertical loop, rather than through it (see drawing). Make sure that the loop at the vertical end is a very firm and secure one as it must hold the weight of the horizontal piece.

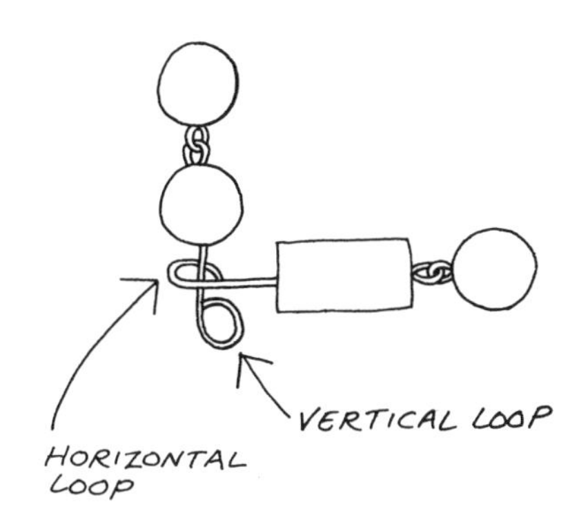

6. Using jump rings, attach the commercial chain to each side of the design portion of the necklace. If it is going to be large enough to fit over your head, you can use one piece of chain and eliminate the clasp. If it is going to be short, your chain will have to add the appropriate closing for the piece. A jewelry hook is probably best because it can support the heavy weight and also allows for adjusting the length of the piece. Finished necklace is shown at bottom of page 75.

Variations

1. You can change the character of this piece by adding other decorative elements of metal or wood, and having them hang from the center.
2. Metal and wood may also be used as integral design elements instead of as added decorations. For instance, you can use all sorts of shapes between your beads to create unusual effects. An attractive necklace with the large piece made of metal is shown in the photograph.

All of the separate parts are made on wires and chains as already described. The holes are drilled in the wood or metal piece with the drill. All of the various parts are joined by matching jump rings. Again, if you use wood, stain or paint it *after* you have drilled the holes, but *before* you add the attachments.

Necklace strung on wire with a center ornament made from a brass pin. The tassels and beads are joined with jump rings.

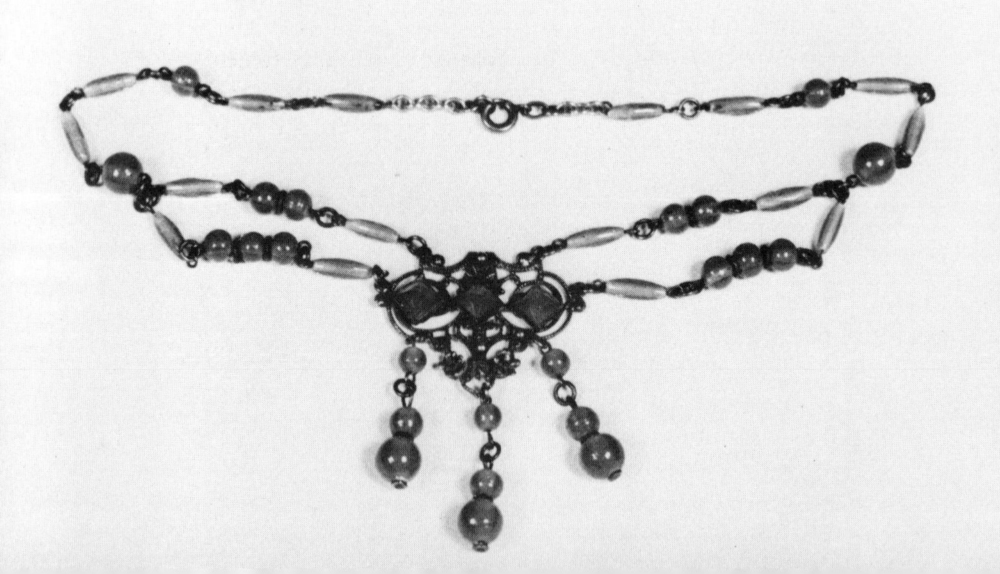

A glass-bead necklace strung on wire has a collar of hanging glass-bead tassels. Each graduated tassel is strung on wire and attached to the main neckpiece with wire. Even the chain for the hook closing has beads, which act as anchors for the hook.

3. Another design using this same principle, equally easy to make, is this necklace and pendant combination.
4. You can use beads in combination with small pieces of metal or wood to make unusual designs. For instance, the two top designs on page 80 are neck wires to which have been added coins, plumbing washers, or hardware washers attached to beads. Holes are drilled in the pieces and the beads are attached to them with wire (or wire brads), with or without jump rings. The pieces are then threaded onto the neck wire by means of the jump rings.
5. You can also make a long, hanging necklace in the same way. The jump rings are attached directly to the neck wire.

Bracelets, pendants, and earrings can all be made from these same designs, using the principles described previously. Style modifications and clasps will be a matter of personal preference.

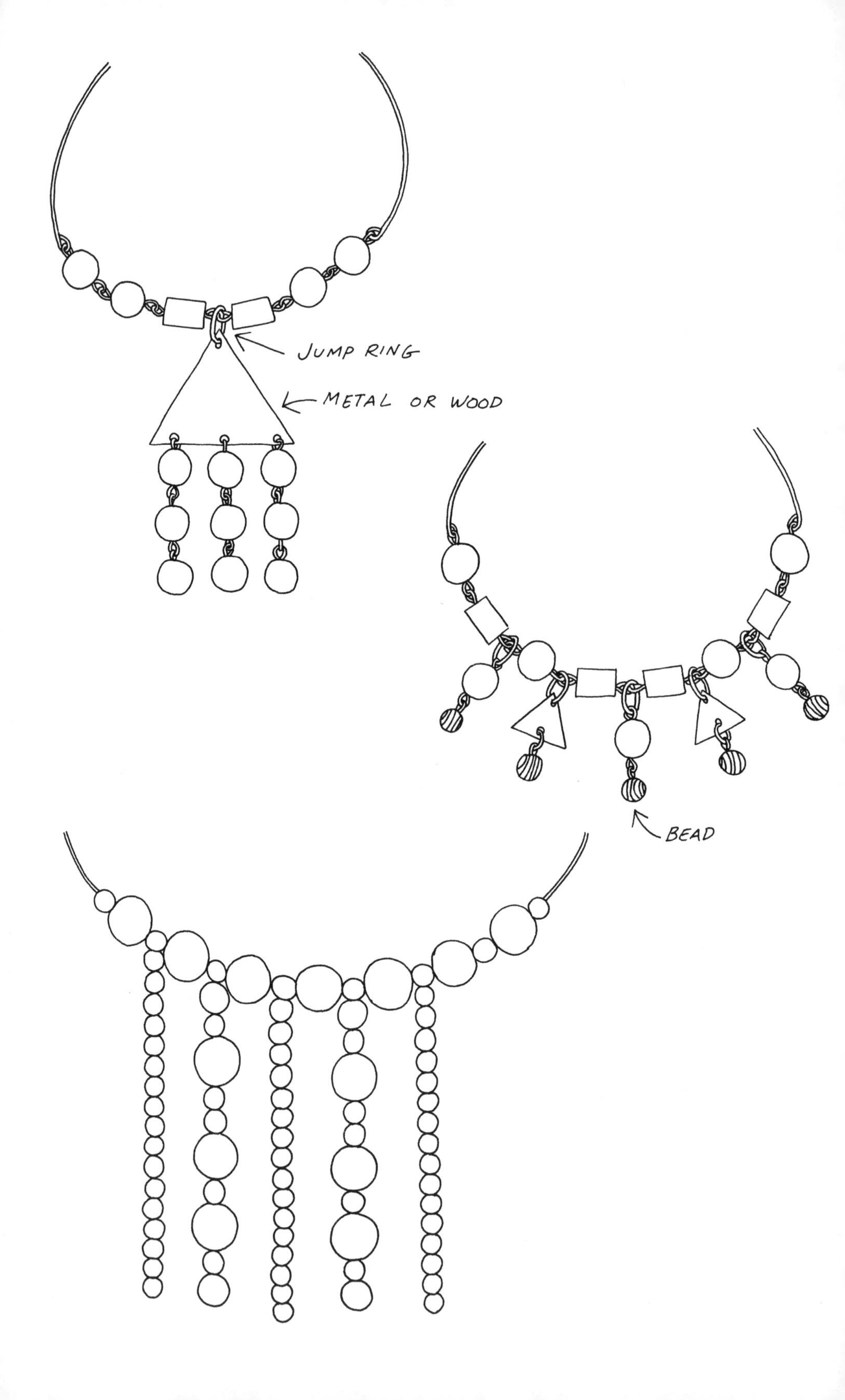
JUMP RING
METAL OR WOOD
BEAD

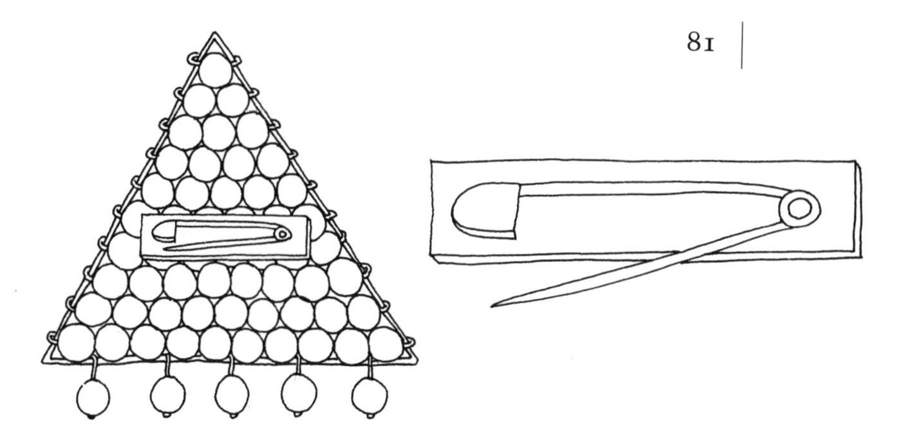

An advantage of working with wire and chains is that you can make pins with them, which is almost impossible to do with needle-and-thread beading alone. Beads do not, in general, lend themselves to use in pin form, but with imagination you can create some unique pieces. For instance, you can make a simple shape like a triangle, constructing it in the same way you made the bib on page 70. Then attach small washers to the bottom. The pin back is wired onto the strands of the beads, and is quite firm. The drawing shows what it looks like from behind.

You can do this with any number of shapes and with your beads going in all directions and varying in color, shape, contour and plane. Some styles are pictured here.

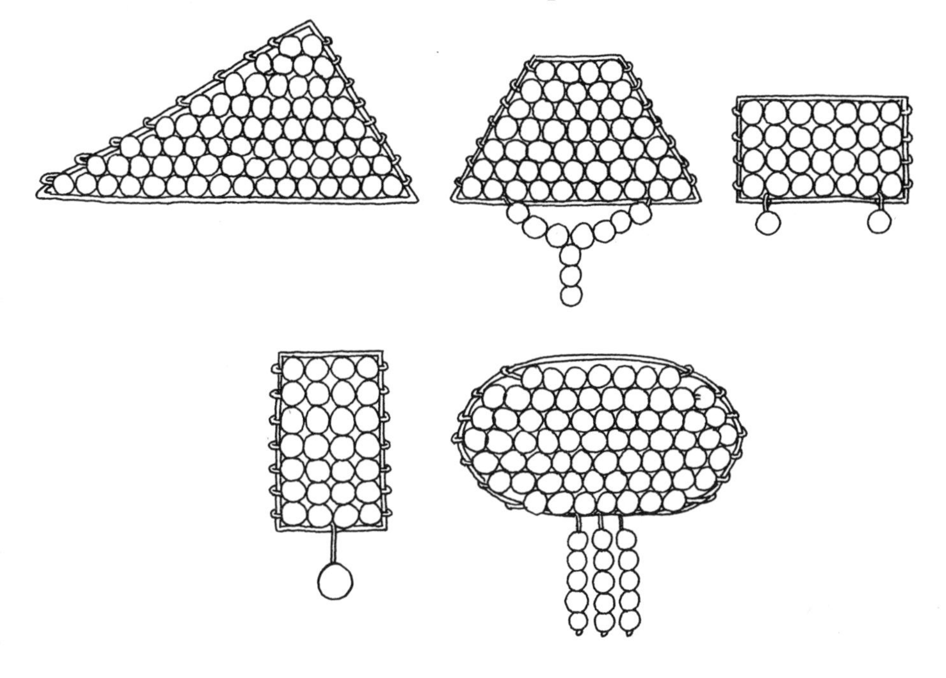

Old Chinese coins, small pearls, and striped beads of varied shapes are combined to make a long necklace or belt. The coins have holes drilled in them and all elements are joined with wire and jump rings, which also serve as decorative elements. A purchased gold-colored metal tassel completes the piece, which is closed with a large spring ring that fits over the chain.

Holes drilled in an old coin are threaded with heavy wire to which beads, also threaded on wire, are added. The piece is worn on a neck wire, which may also be strung with matching beads.

CLAY jewelry is fun to make, and most of the tools required come from the kitchen cabinets. With the new clays you do not need a kiln, the special high-heat oven traditionally used for firing clay. Instead, the clays are baked in the kitchen oven, set at 250 degrees. And the glazes can be baked at the same temperature or air dried. Beads, pendants, earrings, pins, and cuff links can all be made very quickly. (It is not wise to make rings or bracelets because of the brittleness of the material.)

Jewelry is made from two basic clay-handling techniques—flat slabs and rolled coils.

TOOLS

Collect your tools for these projects from the kitchen cabinets and drawers. What you don't find there you can buy in variety or hardware stores.

First, you will need a *plastic rolling pin* and a *wooden pastry* or *chopping board* for rolling out the clay. As tracks you can use two *rulers*, 1/4 inch thick, or two similar *strips of wood* bought at a lumberyard or hobby shop. A plain, *plastic place mat* will serve as a working surface, and a

Tools for ceramic jewelry. On the plastic-covered wooden block: plastic bowl and skewer, two cooky cutters, small and large sponge, 1/4-inch-thick wooden tracks, sculptor's looped-wire tool, paring knife, small and large brush, kitchen cake turner, rolling pin, and wedging tool made of thread spools and wire.

Materials for glazing ceramic jewelry. Back row: undercoat, an empty jar for mixing, several bottle sizes of glaze, hardener. Front: measuring spoons, aluminum and paper cups for mixing glazes, brushes, star stilts, and two nails used in place of stilts.

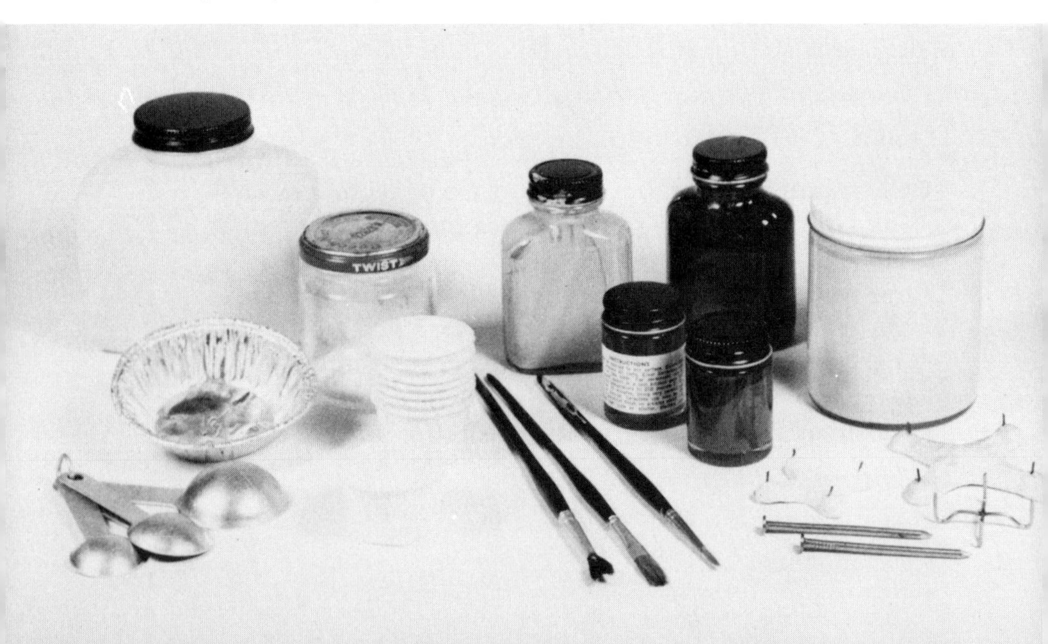

plastic garment bag from the dry cleaner's will protect your table or board.

To cut the ball of clay, you will need about 15 inches of thin *copper wire* or *picture hanging wire,* as well as two empty *thread spools* to serve as handles for the wire.

Other tools useful in forming the clay are: a small *paring knife,* a cellulose kitchen *sponge,* a small *plastic bowl,* a hot-plate ceramic *tile,* a *skewer,* a *fork,* a *cake turner,* small *cooky cutters,* a shallow *cake pan,* a square of *sandpaper,* and an *oven thermometer.* At an art or craft store buy a *sculptor's looped-wire tool,* which is two loops of wire fitted to either end of a round wooden handle, the whole thing about 6 or 7 inches long.

The glazing process will require pointed small- and medium-size *camel's hair brushes* (student quality), disposable *foil cupcake pans* or *paper cups* (not plastic) for mixing the glaze, *paper towels,* and a set of *metal measuring spoons.* Not necessary but useful are *star stilts,* which you can buy at a craft shop. These are made of hard-fired clay and have small metal points set upright in four flat arms.

MATERIALS

The materials, too, are simple and inexpensive, and the quantities required are small. Among the firms making *oven-baked clay* are Sculpture House, makers of Della Robbia Miracle Clay, and Stewart Clay Company, makers of Ceraclay. These two products are available in most art stores and craft shops, or they can be ordered by mail from the manufacturers, who also have complete catalogs of clay supplies. (See Supplies listing at the end of this book.)

Della Robbia Miracle Clay is a reddish brown that dries to a light, warm tan color. It has some grit in it, which makes it more porous and easier to handle.

Ceraclay is gray in color, quite dense in texture with a slippery surface. It is heavy for its bulk – the 5-pound package is about the same size as the 3½-pound package of Della Robbia Miracle Clay.

Both companies supply color glazes for their clays that can be air dried or baked in the oven. The opaque glazes come in $^3/_4$-ounce jars in red, blue, green, orange, yellow and purple plus black, white, and brown. There are several shades of each color available, and there is a clear transparent glaze as well. Colors can be mixed with each other to make other shades and tones. If a colored glaze is mixed with a clear glaze, you get a transparent color.

Sculpture House also has a reducer for cleaning brushes, wiping off baked clay, and thinning the glaze; an undercoat to be applied before glazing; and a drier to be added to the glaze for air drying. All three are sold in $^3/_4$-ounce and pint jars. Ceraglaze is thinned with turpentine.

You will be using the same types of findings you've already used in making jewelry—pin backs, earring backs, cuff link-backs, catches, cord, leather thongs, colored hemp rope for necklaces or pendants. These are all available at variety stores and hobby shops, or by mail order from jewelry supply companies. You will also need epoxy cement—its great strength makes it more reliable than contact cement for attaching pin backs or earring backs to the heavier clay pieces.

PREPARATION OF THE WORKING SURFACE AND TOOLS

If you use a pastry or chopping board as the surface for rolling out your clay, put it on a newspaper-covered table. Put a clear, plastic garment bag from the cleaner's around the board. This protects the board from the clay and forms a nonsticking surface, making it easier to lift up the clay pieces.

If you use a table top as a working surface, cover it first with several layers of newspaper, and cover these in turn with a plastic garment bag.

Cut an oblong $3^1/_2$-by-6-inch cellulose kitchen sponge in half. Then split the thickness of one of the halves with a knife or scissors into two equal-size sponges, so that you have one thick and two thin pieces.

Next, make the *wedging*, or clay-cutting tool. Take the 15-inch length of wire and put one end through the center hole of an empty wooden spool. Bring it around, and with a few turns fasten it tightly to the rest of the wire, close to the spool. Repeat on the other end. You now have a cutting wire with two spools for handles. These will fit into the palms of your clenched fists, the wire coming out between the second and third fingers.

This is the classic tool for cutting sections of clay from the main lump, or cutting a ball of clay in half during the wedging process (explained in the following section).

PREPARING THE CLAY

Oven-baked clay is sold premixed, wrapped in plastic, and protected by a cardboard carton. The manufacturer advises that this is bubble-free, already wedged, and ready to use. The clay can be a bit stiff to handle, however, and the addition of a little water to the piece you cut off is necessary.

Open up the plastic bag, slip out the rectangle of clay, and cut off one-third. Put this piece in a clean plastic bag, and add about 2 tablespoons of water. Close the bag with twister seals and let it sit for about half an hour. Then, with the bag still closed, knead the clay until the water is absorbed. Form into a ball inside the bag, then turn out onto the covered work surface.

Now proceed with the *wedging*. Wedging is a potter's term for the process that removes air bubbles from the clay and makes it more workable and malleable. (Air holes could cause your design to explode in the oven, when the air expands in the heat.) It's a good way to work off aggressions, too.

Cut the ball of clay in half with your wire, putting the cut side of one half face down on the working surface. Then slap the other half, cut side *up*, on top of the first half. With the heel of your hand press the two halves together, punching them hard. Cut in half again, and wedge the two pieces together. Repeat the routine several times until you cannot see holes in a cut surface.

ROLLING OUT SLABS

Pendants, buttons, bib necklaces, earrings, and other flat designs are cut out of a rolled slab of clay.

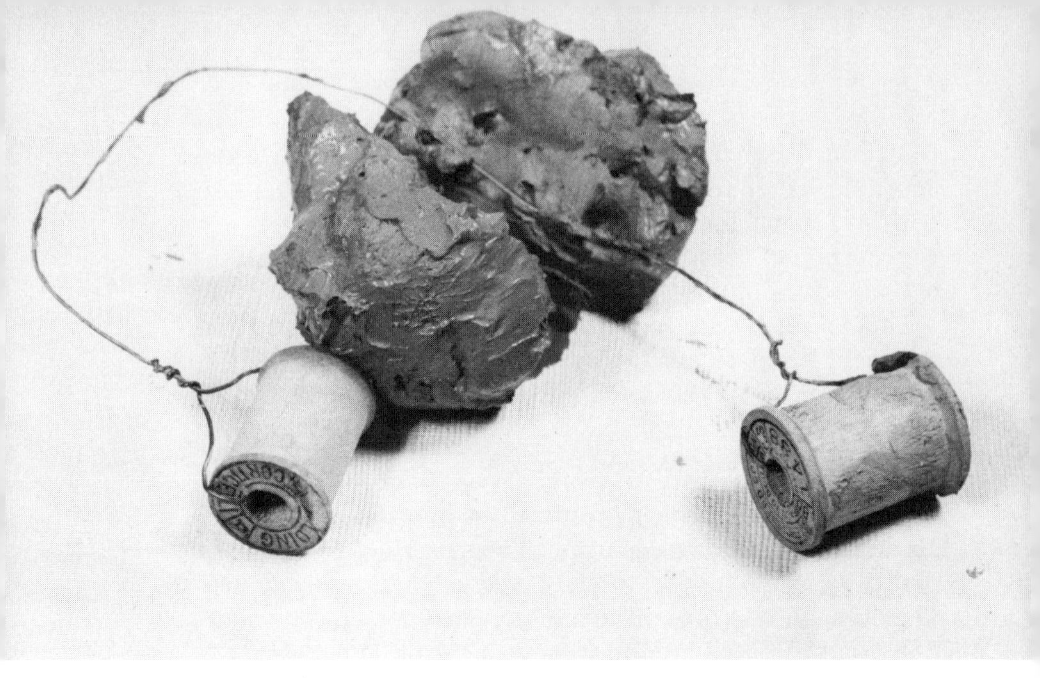

Cutting a ball of clay with the wedging tool, exposing the air bubbles in the center.

A slab of clay, level with the wooden tracks, can now be cut into shapes with a cooky cutter.

Fill a bowl with water and wipe off the plastic cover of the working surface, using the largest sponge. Put the ball of wedged clay in the middle of this area, and place the two 1/4-inch thick strips of wood on each side of the clay, 6 inches apart. These are the tracks on which the rolling pin will run when the ball is flattened. They insure that the slab will be an even 1/4 inch thick.

Wipe the rolling pin with water and start rolling. Each stroke forward and back should be made clockwise around the circle, so the clay fills a rectangular area bounded by the strips left and right. Keep moistening the surface of the clay to prevent sticking to the rolling pin. If any cracks develop along the edges while you are rolling, moisten each side of the crack with the wet sponge, and squeeze the edges together.

When the rolling pin rolls comfortably along the wooden strips, the slab is finished. The clay is now ready to be stamped out with small decorative cooky cutters or cut with a pointed knife around your own paper patterns. You may also press a design into the surface of the clay.

MAKING CLAY COILS

Thin rolls of clay, called coils, are used in making beads, coiled pendants, and raised decorations on flat slab shapes.

Break off a piece approximately 3/4 inches square from the wedged clay ball. Form it into a short round roll. Moisten your hands so they will not stick to the clay, and moisten the working surface.

Start rolling the clay back and forth with the palm and heel of one hand. Keep an even, light pressure on the clay so it will stay round and not flatten anywhere. This is the secret of rolling clay.

As the coil lengthens use both hands, moving them back and forth so the clay does not develop thick and thin spots. If the coil gets too long, cut it in half and continue to roll one half until it is the thickness you want for your design. Keep the other coil in a closed plastic bag until ready to use; otherwise it will dry out.

MAKING SLIP

Slip is a syrupy mixture of clay and water. The old description of its consistency was "like heavy cream"—but cream was heavier in those days. It's made by mixing small pieces of clay with water, mashing and smoothing until you have a liquid that is thick but not stiff. Keep in a covered container so the water will not evaporate.

Slip is used to bind separate pieces of clay together. Coiled clay designs placed on the top of flat surfaces are stuck on with slip. If the strip to be added is very broad or thick, the base area is scored with crisscross lines and slip is smeared over the scratches. Then the separate piece of clay is put into position. The joining edges are smoothed down with a blunt knife point and the fingers until no crack remains.

A joining is best done when the clay base has stiffened a bit. Designs to be added should be made at the same time as the base, so that both reach the same stage of stiffness at the same time. A joint made of stiff clay and soft clay may spring apart in baking.

Slip is also used in conjunction with a stencil to make a raised design on a flat or curved base of clay.

DRYING AND BAKING CLAY

Once a design has been made from a clay slab or coil, it has to be well dried before it is put in the oven to bake. If any moisture is left in the clay, the heat will turn the water into steam, and the pressure of escaping steam will cause the clay to crack or explode, ruining the design.

There are two stages in drying. The first is called *leather hard*. This is the point midway between limp, wet clay and hard, dry material. This partially moist clay can be picked up, and any rough areas smoothed with a loop-wire tool, a wet sponge, or a paint brush. If there are any carved decorations to be made, this is the time to do them, as edges will stay sharp and clear and not sink back into softness.

The second stage is a totally dry piece. Your design is left on a flat tile until no water remains in the clay. The time

A coil of clay being rolled on the working surface.

Applying slip to the base shape through holes in a stencil.

depends on the size of the object and weather conditions. Clay dries faster in a heated house in the winter than during humid summer days.

When all is dry, put the clay object on a small baking pan, along with the oven thermometer. The throwaway aluminum pans supplied with some frozen products are recommended, but be sure they are clean with no grease on the surface. Light the oven and set the pan on the middle shelf. Leave the door open and let the oven warm up slowly, for about 10 minutes. This will remove the last bits of moisture from the clay.

Now, almost close the oven door, leaving an opening 1½ to 2 inches wide. If you have a door that snaps closed, wedge a pot holder between the door and the stove to hold it open. Watch the oven and check on the heat every 15 minutes or so. The heat should not rise above 250 degrees. Bake at this temperature for 1 hour. Turn off the heat, open door fully, and let the clay cool down before removing from the oven.

Your design is now *bisque ware*, and is ready to be glazed.

Oven thermometer and pressed clay pendant on an aluminum baking pan, ready to go into the oven.

DECORATING WITH GLAZES

As we have seen, there are several glazes on the market. Some can be air dried after the addition of a special drying liquid (hardener); otherwise, they are oven-baked at 250 degrees for 1/2 to 1 hour. The air-dried glazes are easiest to use, since there are no problems with overbaking, or possible impurities on the surface of the clay that will cause bubbling in the glaze. The final air drying takes about a week to ten days in damp humid weather—less time in a dry, heated house. The piece is dry when the surface is no longer tacky and feels hard to the touch.

After the clay design has been baked and cooled, wipe with reducer to remove all loose particles of clay and any oil which may have come from your hands. Let the surface dry.

If you are using Della Robbia Miracle Glaze, cover the piece with two coats of the undercoat, and let dry between each coat. If the undercoat liquid is too thick, thin it out with reducer.

The Ceraglaze colors go directly on the clay.

Applying Glaze

When it comes to colors, it's up to you. Some tips on application:

Two to three thin layers of glaze are better than one thick coat, with a drying time between each glaze of an hour or two.

For a transparent glaze, add opaque glaze a few drops at a time to the clear glaze until the right color is achieved. You may have to thin this out with the reducer if the glaze is too thick.

Put the glaze on in even strokes, using a fully loaded brush, so that the liquid flows on. As soon as the brush drags, dip it into the glaze again. Try not to go back over areas already glazed, unless there is a bare spot. Remember, your second coat will take care of any irregularities. And a few irregularities make an interesting natural finish, in contrast to a manufacturer's cold perfection.

Pieces of jewelry are glazed front and back, and this

Decorating a baked clay pendant with a mixture of gold and transparent glaze, applied over the dry undercoat.

means that each side has to dry. It is usually best to do the back first. In this way no support marks will show on the front. Turn over, placing your piece on a star stilt, on two long nails laid flat, or on half a cork with small nails or pins poking up through the surface as supports.

If you are air drying, a fifth of your glaze should be hardener, that is, 1/2 teaspoon of hardener to 2 teaspoons of glaze. This proportion will change depending on weather, so test out the glaze on a sample square. Thin out with reducer if necessary, but watch your proportions as you may have to add more hardener.

The glaze colors can be mixed with each other and with white to achieve various colors and tones. The colors in the bottles do not change in drying, so a dry mixed color will be the same as when you mixed it.

General Precautions

If you are baking a color, test-bake it on a small square of clay. If there is bubbling, change to an air-dried mixture.

Use paper or aluminum foil cupcake pans for mixing the glazes. Plastic-surfaced cups will disintegrate. You can also use empty baby food jars, or other small glass jars. These have the advantage of having covers, which will keep glaze from hardening before you put on the second or third coat. Cover other containers with tightly stretched clear plastic food wrap when not in use.

Wipe brushes and other tools with reducer-soaked pieces of paper toweling after every use. For Ceraglaze use turpentine. This keeps your colors clean and your brushes soft.

Always let each coat of glaze dry until the surface loses its tackiness, probably about an hour, before adding the next coat. Final drying of all the coats takes much longer.

Special Effects

Many design effects can be achieved with these glazes: a solid color as a background with another color painted over it in a design; a thinned-out transparent color over a solid background of color; a transparent color put directly over the clay base; an opaque color decorating the base in a design and covered by a clear or transparent color glaze. The possibilities are endless, and you will think of many more.

Most of the glazes dry to a gloss finish, and those that do not can be covered with a final coat of clear transparent glaze.

The following designs include all of the clay techniques, and they will start you off making new designs of your own.

HOLIDAY FAVORS

These are pins, or bib-type necklaces, made of shapes cut out of 1/8- or 1/4-inch thick slabs of clay. Tree-shaped cooky cutters make pins or necklaces for Christmas time, and are great as favors at a festive table. It's a good pre-Christmas project. Heart pins for Valentine's Day can be personalized

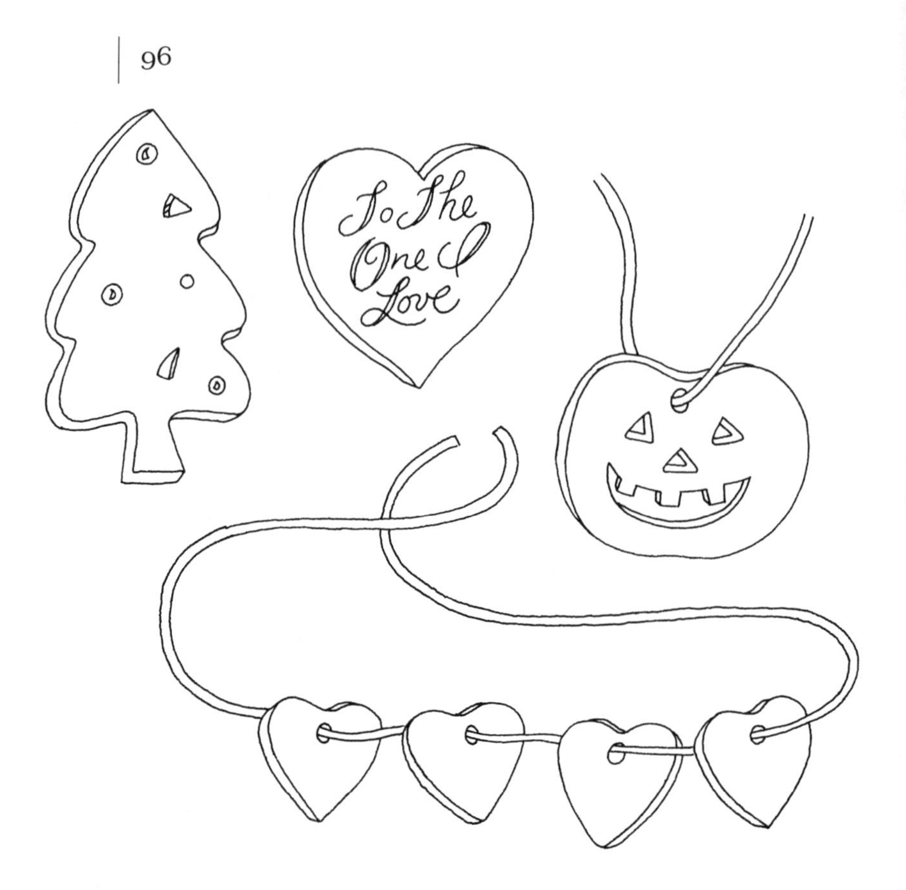

as fun gifts in place of a card. The cutouts are a surprise, too, at children's parties. You can make hatchets for Washington's Birthday, turkeys for Thanksgiving, ducks for Easter, and pumpkins for Halloween trick-or-treat.

Materials

Small cooky cutters, bought in sets or separately, are ideal for this project. Various assortments contain hearts, trees, ducks, hatchets, bells, farm animals, and so forth. You will also need clay, the appropriate color glazes, plastic or leather thongs or ribbon for the necklaces, bar-type pin backs, and epoxy glue for attaching the pin backs.

Steps

1. Roll out the clay into a slab following directions at the beginning of this chapter. The overall size depends on what you are making and how many pieces you want.

Roughly plan the layout on a piece of paper, tracing around the cooky cutters.

2. Dip the cutter into water before stamping out the clay. Dip in water before each cut. Make as many shapes as you need.
3. Carefully transfer each shape to a plastic place mat, using a wet cake turner or broad spatula. If any shapes have been damaged, straighten them out or recut. Let dry until they have begun to stiffen a bit and can be handled.
4. If the cutouts are to be hung on a cord as a necklace, punch holes at the top of each piece large enough so that the cord can be threaded through them. Allow for clay shrinkage. Smooth all the pieces using a small wet sponge, knife, and your fingers.
5. Dry for several days, then bake in the oven at 250 degrees, following the directions at the beginning of this chapter.
6. Now decorate with glaze. Use a pink or red or gold glaze for the hearts, green for the Christmas trees, with other colors for little spots of ornaments. Or you might try a gold tree with red ornaments. Use yellow for the ducks and brown for the turkeys, with white, black, and red trim. Pumpkins, of course, are orange, with black marking the face. In all cases follow the directions for glazing given earlier in this chapter. Pins can be left unglazed on the back, but cover the clay with two coats of underglaze to protect it.
7. Now for the finishing details. String the pendants or necklace pieces on cord or thongs, and tie at the back of the neck.

Mark a straight horizontal line across the back of the pin design, just as long as the pin back and above the center, so the design will lie flat when worn. Mix epoxy glue according to directions on the package and apply thickly over your pencil mark. Let dry a bit, then press pin back into the epoxy, allowing the epoxy to come up through the holes in the back. But be careful that no glue gets into the catch or the pin swivel or you're in trouble. Do not distrub for 24 hours.

A SQUARE-MAZE PENDANT

This design combines a flat slab and thin coils of clay.

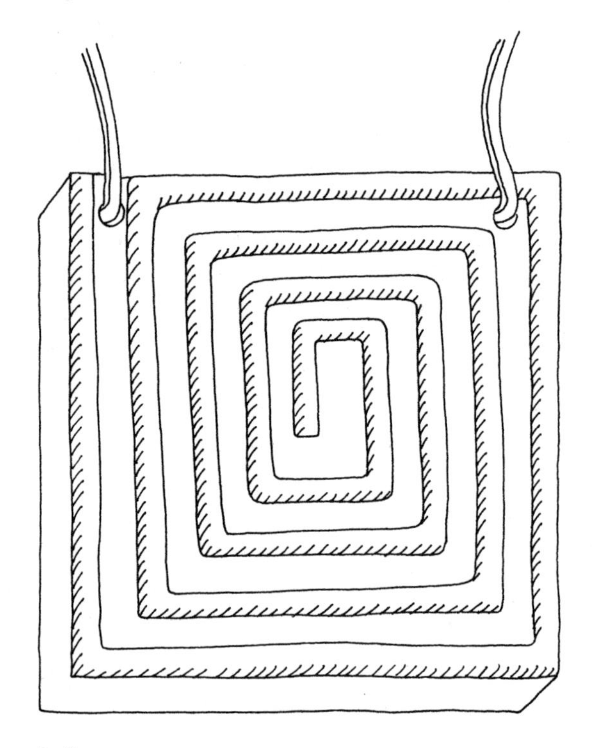

Materials

Wedged clay and slip; undercoat and glazes in the colors of your choice; thong or cord for hanging.

Steps

1. Make a pattern on typewriter paper, $2^3/_4$ by $2^3/_4$ inches square. This includes an allowance for shrinkage of the clay in drying. If you prefer a larger pendant, change the size.
2. Roll out a small piece of clay into a slab $^1/_4$ inch thick, following directions at the beginning of this chapter. Lay the paper pattern over the clay and, with a wet knife, cut out the square following the outlines. Transfer to a tile with a wet cake turner. Correct any distortions caused by the moving.

3. Make a ball of the leftover rolled clay. Make it into a thin coil 1/8 inch in diameter. If the square has dried enough to be a little stiff, you can proceed with your design. If not, store the leftover ball of clay in a small plastic bag to keep it moist until the clay square is slightly stiff. Then make the thin coil.
4. Smooth the top of the square with the dampened small sponge. Take out any irregularities on the sides. Turn over and smooth back. Then turn again with the design side facing upward.
5. Cover the whole surface of the square with a thin coat of slip. Dip or smear coil with slip as you go along.

   Starting at the upper left corner and working clockwise, outline the top edge of the square with the coil. You will have to patch the coil as you go along. Try to make the joinings at the corners, though, as they will be less obvious. Be sure to smooth a joint carefully with fingers and the knife point, using slip.

   As the coil is laid down on the slipped surface, smooth the length of juncture with the knife and your fingers so that no air spaces remain. Also press lightly on the top of the coil, but do not spoil its roundness. Be sure the whole thing is secure; otherwise the design will loosen in the drying.

   Carry the continuous coil in decreasing squares until you reach the center. Cut off the clay at the top of a left-side downward line.

   Punch out two holes, one in each upper corner, between the first and second lines of coils.
6. When the clay is leather hard, go over the whole design, smoothing any rough areas with a wet sponge and fingers, and sharpening up the raised strips with a knife or looped-wire tool. Make sure the outside edge is smooth and solid with no joining cracks showing. Go over the back with the wet sponge.
7. After the maze pendant is dry, bake at 250 degrees, following the procedure described at the beginning of this chapter.
8. The glaze colors are your own choice. A pendant can be one solid color, or a background color with the maze in

another color. The background can be a transparent color and the maze a solid one. It's all up to you. Just follow the directions for glazing given in the first part of this chapter.

9. Bring each end of the thong through a hole, from back to front. Equalize ends, and bring around to the back of the neck and tie. You may want to make a knot above each hole.

Variations

1. Start the first row of coils ½ inch in from the edge, then continue on into the middle in the same square design. This will leave a plain border all around the edge.
2. A circle or a triangle can be substituted as the basic shape.
3. The coil technique can be used to form two straight lines on the left, and two across the top, the two sets of lines crossing at the top left corner. The free space on the right contains an initial in raised coils. Hang this either as a square or as a diamond shape.
4. An in-and-out design can be made around the edge of a circle, with a snail design in the center.
5. All of these can be worn as pins with the addition of a pin back, and the elimination of the corner holes.
6. Smaller versions make button or hanging earrings.

PERSIAN DONKEY BEADS

Materials

A piece of wedged clay about 2 inches square; turquoise-blue glaze, undercoat, reducer, hardener, clear glaze; a drinking straw or lollipop stick; leather or plastic thong.

Steps

1. Measure your neck, using limp package string. Cut string, and put the length flat on a plastic mat on your working surface.
2. From wedged clay, make a coil approximately ⅝ inch in diameter.

A
A

A Persian donkey bead made from coiled clay (see page 89).

3. Roll one end of the coil around a drinking straw or stick, until you have completed the circle. Cut off clay. Moisten each end with slip and press together, smoothing the joint. Slide fingers up each end of the straw, and simultaneously press each side of the clay. This will slightly flatten the bead at the top and bottom.

   You can press in the bead surface here and there to give it a slightly irregular appearance, as it should not be smooth and globular.
4. Remove the bead from the straw or stick, and set it aside to dry. It can be set down off the perpendicular so that the air can circulate through the center hole–this means that the tube opening is at a 45-degree angle to the working surface. The originals are all done this way.

   Repeat process until you have enough beads to go around your neck. As each bead is finished, put it in line beside the measured string. When you have reached the end, make two or three more beads, as clay shrinks in drying, and you will need these extra beads. Or you may spoil a bead in the making.
5. Let the beads dry to leather hard. Now prick them all over with a sewing pin. Make the pricks quite close. This will simulate the surface created by the glaze used in Persia.

Check the center opening to be sure it is large enough for the thong on which the beads will be strung. Remember that the opening will shrink even more in the final drying and baking. If necessary, carefully enlarge the hole using the stick or an opened-up paper clip or a skewer.

6. Let the beads dry completely. Bake in the oven on a flat pan at 250 degrees for one hour. Let cool and take out.
7. If using air-dried glaze, wipe off beads with reducer. Dry, and cover with two coats of undercoat, letting the undercoat dry between applications. Let dry overnight after final coat to be sure the surface is hard.
8. Using a mixing cup, add turquoise-blue glaze to the clear glaze until a semitransparent effect is reached. This should not be an opaque glaze, nor should it be too transparent. Add the right amount of hardener—1 part hardener to 4 parts glaze. If you do not have a turquoise glaze, mix some of the clear green with blue to make a blue-green color. Add a little reducer if the glaze seems too thick.
9. Cut a length of thin picture wire, longer than your necklace by quite a bit. Find a place to stretch it, as the glazed beads will be strung on this to dry. As each bead is glazed it will be slipped on, then a little hump of wire squeezed up so the beads will not touch each other.
10. Apply a thin coat of glaze to the clay beads. The glaze does not have to be even, as donkey bead glazes are always mottled with light and dark areas. Push a glaze brush down through the tube opening to glaze the inside lightly.

    Put each bead on the wire and let dry. When ready, apply a second coat to each bead, and in turn slip on the wire for final drying.
11. When the glaze is fully hard—this could be a week—slip the beads off the wire. Cut a length of thong long enough to go around your neck and tie in a bow in the back.

    String the beads, put around your neck, tie the bow—and admire your handiwork.

PAPER PATTERN PENDANTS

These are pendants cut from paper patterns you have made yourself. To make the patterns, all you need is typewriter paper, tracing paper, carbon paper, and a pencil.

Copy simple, natural shapes from books or magazines—shells, fish, flowers. Or put a piece of tracing paper over the drawing or photograph and trace lightly. Transfer your tracing to typewriter paper using carbon paper.

If your drawing is too large or too small for a pendant, reduce or enlarge it by the square method. Make a grid of equally spaced horizontal and vertical lines over your drawing. Now make another grid with the spaces between the lines narrower or wider, depending on whether you need to reduce or enlarge your drawing. Copy the lines of your first drawing onto the new grid, following your design through each square and across each line. Even though the new drawing is larger or smaller, the proportions will be the same as the first one.

Freeform shapes are interesting, either left solid or with holes punched in them.

Initial letters or numbers can be cut and used separately, or added on top of a shape.

The variations are endless, and you'll find yourself seeing shapes and designs everywhere.

Materials

Wedged clay, thongs or cord, typewriter paper, tracing paper, pencil, carbon paper, ruler, scissors, glazes, reducer, undercoat, hardener.

Steps

1. Make patterns by drawing a bold, simple design, or tracing one in a book or magazine. Transfer to typewriter paper, and cut out with small scissors.
2. Roll out enough clay into a ¼-inch-thick slab to make your design. You might want to cut out several designs at once, since they are so easy and quick to make.

   Smooth the paper pattern over the wet clay. Cut

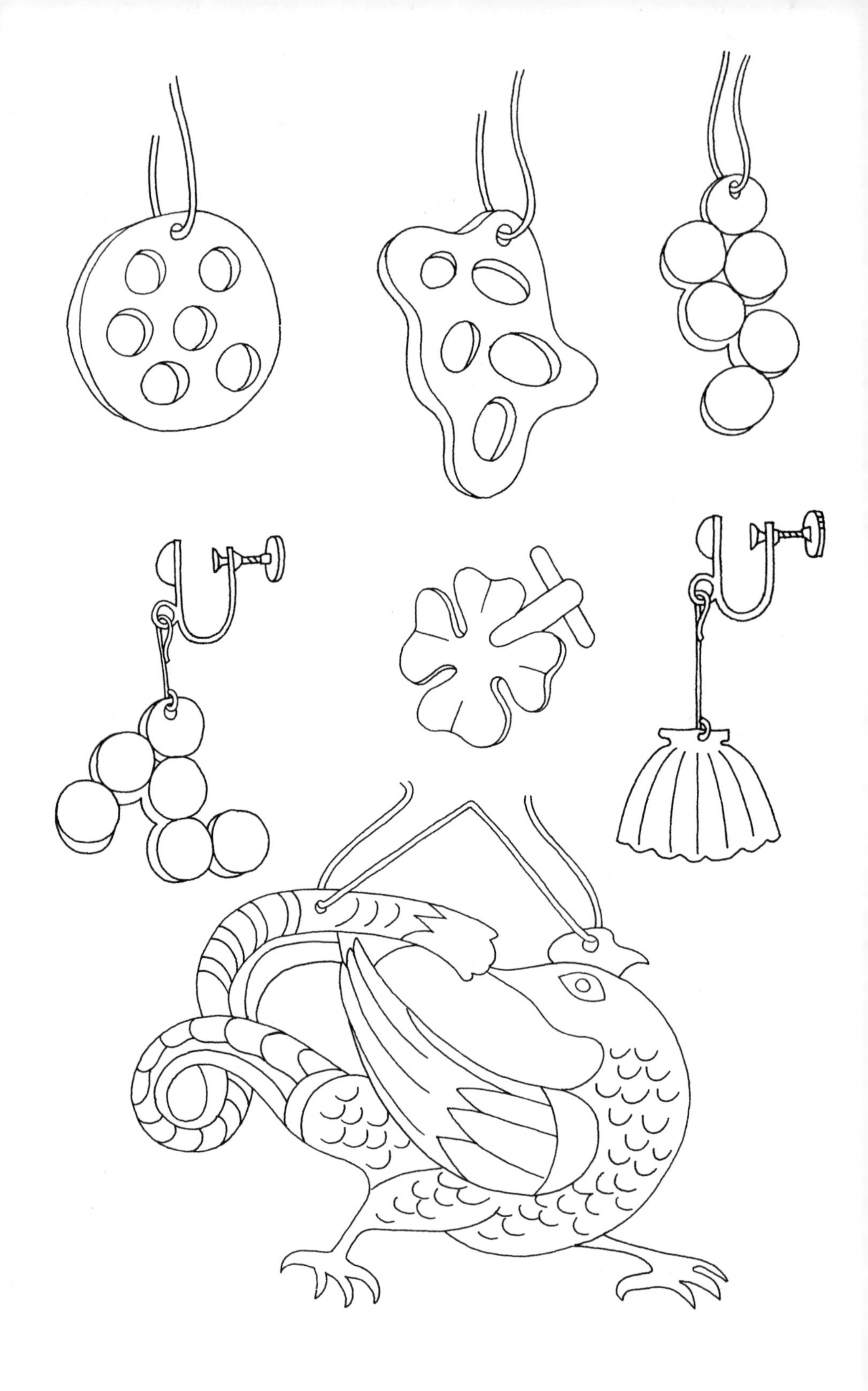

around the edges with a wet, pointed knife, going right down to the plastic covering of the working surface. Keep wetting the knife so it cuts easily. Remove pieces of excess clay as you work.

3. Carefully transfer your design to a tile for drying. Lift it up with a wet cake turner, easing the plastic away from the bottom. Re-form the clay if it has been pulled out of shape. Let dry until it has begun to stiffen.
4. When clay is a bit stiff but not leather hard, cut a hole in the top large enough for the thong or cord. If design is long horizontally, you will need a hole at either end. If design is to have larger cutout holes do them now. Ball-point pen caps are good hole makers. Also smooth out the marks left by the knife around the edges.

   This is also the time to add any surface decorations.
5. If you want a domed shape, or want to change the level of any one part of your pendant, test the feel of the clay. If it is stiff enough to hold in the hand, but not rigid and not limp, then this is the right time for molding into a final shape.

   Sometimes shell designs can be rounded to look natural, or flower petals curved a bit forward or back.

   Smooth any rough areas with a damp sponge and the wire-loop tool. Let dry.
6. When your design is dry, bake it in a 250-degree oven, following directions at the beginning of this chapter.
7. After the clay has been baked and cooled it is ready to glaze. Follow the regular procedure for glazing given at the beginning of this chapter.

The choice of color or colors is a very personal thing, and you are on your own!

When all is finished, slip cord or thong through the top hole or holes, knot just above the upper outline of the pendant, and tie at the back of the neck.

Variations

1. Smaller designs can be epoxy-glued to earring backs, or hung by a fine cord as dangling earrings. You could use a very fine chain.

2. The same small designs make good cuff links, epoxied onto the right findings.
3. Instead of a hole at the top of a design, put a pin back on with epoxy glue, and use the design as a pin.

A SWAG NECKLACE

This is a necklace made of a quarter-moon shape cut from a slab of clay and decorated with raised slip designs. It is hung from a cord or thong knotted through holes at each end, and tied at the back of the neck in a bow.

Materials

Clay, wedged and ready to roll out; container of very thick slip; typewriter paper, small scissors, pencil, brushes; glazes in your choice of colors and all the glaze supplies; thong or cord for hanging. A commercial catch for the cord is optional.

Steps

1. Cut out a quarter-moon shape from typewriter paper, curving the top line down a bit so it is not a straight line. Try it against your neck for length and depth. An average finished size is 6 inches long and 2¼ inches deep in the center. Clay shrinks in the drying, so you will want to add an extra ½ inch to each measurement.
2. Now make the stencil pattern. Within the swag shape, draw two facing fish, or two large and two small petaled flower forms, or two butterflies, or a row of mushrooms. Any design is suitable that is a simple, recognizable shape and can be cut out as a solid form. Transfer your design to a fresh paper pattern of the swag shape. Cut out the design with small scissors.
3. Roll out a ¼-inch-thick slab of clay, 7 inches long and 3 inches wide (or whatever size is large enough for your quarter-moon shape). Lay the swag pattern on the clay, and cut out around the outline with a wet, pointed knife. Clear away the excess clay.
4. While the swag design is drying, mix up a *very thick* slip, using some of the excess clay. The slip will be

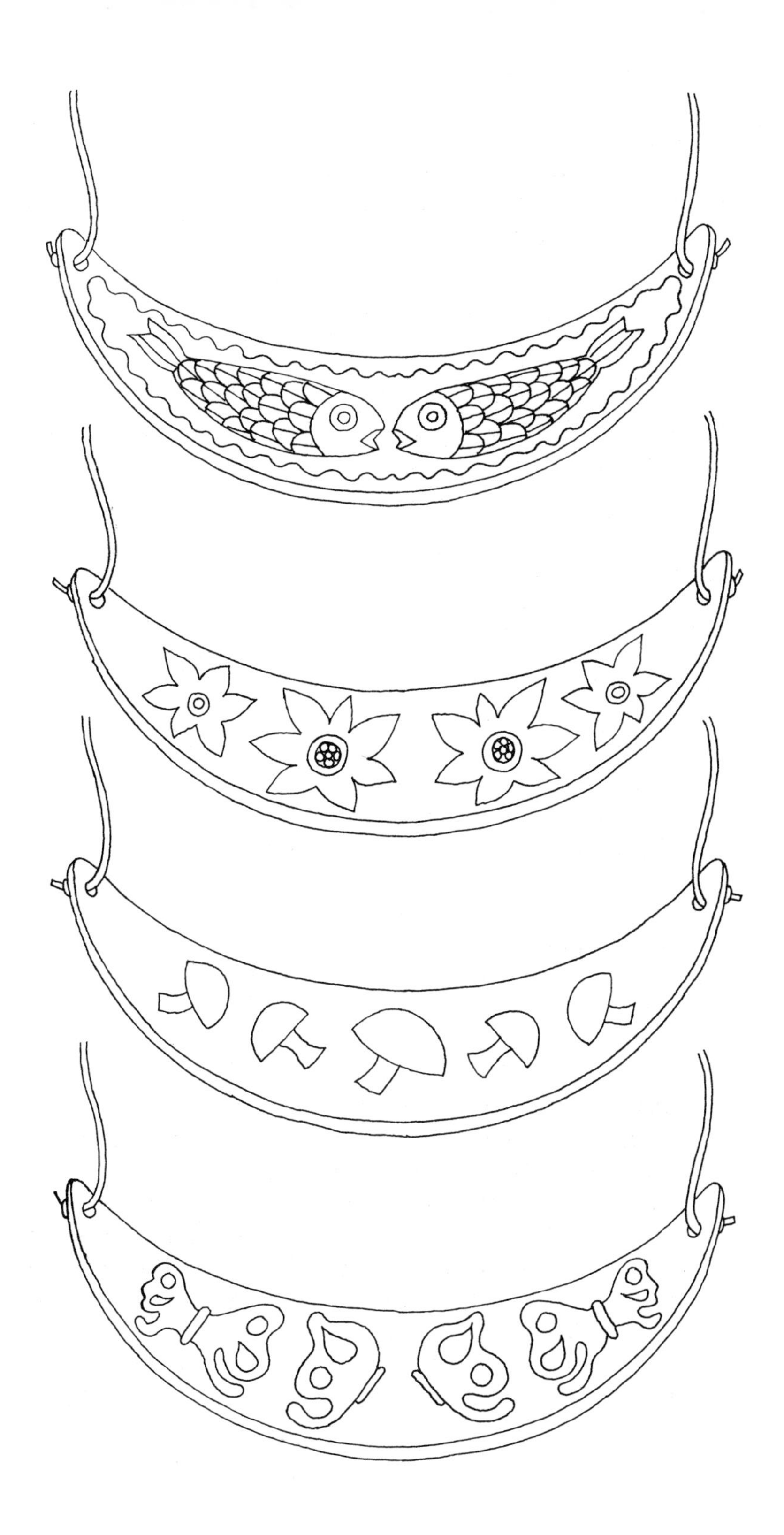

painted on the swag necklace, filling in the cutout area of the stencil, and so building up a relief pattern. Put the cover on the slip container to keep the water from evaporating.

5. When the swag shape has begun to stiffen a bit, just enough so that it can be handled, transfer it to the plastic place mat with a wet cake turner. Smooth the top surface and sides with a damp sponge and a wet finger, removing any irregularities left by the cutting knife.
6. Smooth the stencil pattern over the clay. The clay should be just stiff enough to absorb some of the water from the slip, drying it out as it is applied. In this way you get a sharp-edged design that keeps its form. Try a few drops of slip first to see if the water is absorbed. If not, wait half an hour and try again.

   With a brush, put on the slip in thin layers, letting it dry a bit. Gradually you will build up the design so it is higher than the background. Some clay will spread over the edges of the stencil, no matter how careful you are, but this will be lifted off when the paper is finally removed. The clay slip will build up to 1/16 inch or more in the center, gradually curving down to the edge of each cutout.
7. Let the decoration dry a bit so it is stiff, and then very carefully peel off the stencil, trying not to disturb the slip design. If there is any resistance, gently use the point of the knife to cut away the overlapping clay.

   Put a hole at each end of the swag shape for the thong or cord. Make it large enough to hold the cord when the clay has shrunk in drying.
8. This is an optional step, depending on your design. Make very thin coils of clay, and outline the quarter-moon shape, putting the thin roll of clay on with slip.
9. Let the necklace dry to leather hard. Turn over and smooth the back with the wire-loop tool and the damp sponge. Check the edges and top of the stencil design, and make any necessary repairs.
10. Allow the necklace to dry for several days before baking. Then bake in a 250-degree oven, following directions at the beginning of this chapter.

11. The quarter moon can be glazed in one color, either opaque or semitransparent. Or the raised design can be one color and the background a lighter or deeper shade, or a totally different color. This is your choice! Follow directions at the beginning of this chapter for glazing, covering both sides of the quarter-moon shape.
12. Dry necklace well (a week or two weeks, depending on the weather).

Cut the thong or cord in half and slip one end through one hole. It can be tied with the knot facing outward, or looped through with a knot tied just above the hole. If cord is used, the end can be sewn with thread to the main cord, forming a loop at the end. Repeat on the other side. Bring each end to the back of the neck, and tie in a bow to fasten.

A BIG GOLD PENDANT

Materials

Oven-baked clay that has been wedged; clear glaze plus gold glaze, as well as reducer, undercoat, hardener; leather or plastic thong, nylon cord, or colored hemp rope to hang the pendant on.

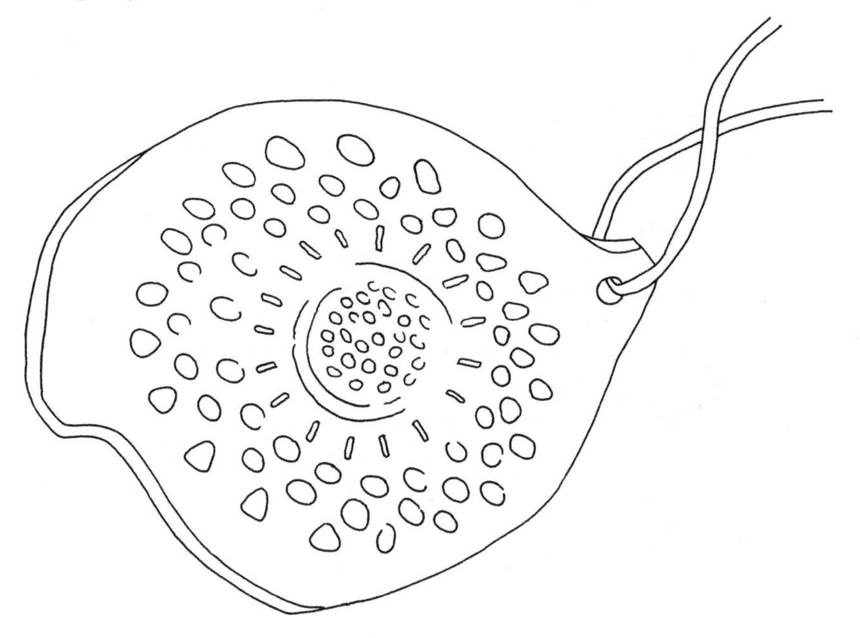

Steps

1. Roll out a 4-by-5-inch slab of clay, 1/4 inch thick, following directions at the beginning of this chapter.
2. While clay is still wet, press a wet cut glass dessert dish into the clay, leaving a clear impression of the bottom design. You may have to experiment several times before you can determine just how deep to press, how wet the dish should be, and how to lift up the dish to leave a clear design. But clay can always be squeezed into a ball and rerolled.
3. With a sharp knife dipped in water, cut around the design, making either a circle or a round shape that is pointed at either end. Lift away the excess clay.

   Punch a hole with a stick or pencil in the top of the pendant, large enough for the hanging thong. Don't forget to allow for clay shrinkage in drying and baking.
4. Slip a wide spatula or cake turner dipped in water under the clay pendant, being careful not to crease it or disturb the outline or the pressed design. Transfer to a tile where it will stay until dry. Smooth the edges with a wet finger and the side of a knife.
5. When the design is leather hard, turn over so the underside will dry. Smooth the back with the wire-loop tool and a wet sponge. Also use the sponge on the front of the pendant if there are any rough spots. Open up the hole at the top if needed.

   Now let the pendant dry until ready to bake—maybe four days.
6. Bake the clay in a 250-degree oven, following directions at the beginning of this chapter.
7. Wipe off pendant with reducer and let dry for 15 minutes. Cover back with the first coat of undercoat, and let dry for an hour. Cover with second coat and let dry overnight.

   Turn over pendant after putting on the second coat, prop up on a star stilt, and cover front and sides with undercoat. When dry put on second coat and allow to dry overnight.
8. Mix a small amount of gold glaze into clear glaze, ad-

Pendant and glass dish used to press pattern into clay.

Pottery pendant, covered with a gold glaze, and hung on a thin, black thong.

ding hardener and, if glaze is too thick, reducer. Cover pendant back with the gold glaze. Let it dry until it is no longer tacky. Cover the glaze container so the liquid will not harden.

9. Turn over the pendant, balancing it on two star stilts or on long nails laid flat. Stir up the glaze and cover the front surface. This is tricky, as you will want to glaze in all the holes that form the pattern, but not let them fill up with liquid. Put on only a thin coat. Set aside to dry. Cover glaze jar.
10. Put on the second coat of glaze, following the procedures in steps 8 and 9. Let the piece dry until it is no longer tacky–approximately a week.
11. Hang the pendant on the thong or cord, twisting the material into a knot just above the hole, or an inch or two up the length, so it will lie flat when worn. Tie in a bow at the back of the neck.

5.

Go Metal, Go Simple

THE jewelry designs described in this chapter are made from stamped-out sterling silver and copper shapes, or brass, copper, or silver wire, or chains. All can be bought at art stores, craft shops, or by mail order from craft-supply houses.

Working with the commercial metal shapes is a first step toward making your own metal designs, and will give you the feel of metalwork, as well as creating very wearable jewelry. Some of these same shapes will be used later as the basis for enamel designs (see Chapter 9).

The techniques of putting the shapes together are simple, and many of them you know already from earlier chapters. But the variations in designs are infinite, and you will develop far more combinations than we are able to show in this book.

TOOLS

You will be using two of the tools already described in the previous chapters: *chain-nose pliers* and the small *wire cutter.* In addition you will buy a medium *needle file* (which is flat on one side and half round on the other), as well as *metal tongs* with a heat-proof handle. For polishing the metal, you'll need one sheet of medium *emery paper* or cloth, and one sheet of fine *crocus cloth,* which is dull red in color and is used as a final polish.

For the projects in this chapter, plus all future ones, you will need a *V-board* or a *bench pin.* These are standard jeweler's equipment from time immemorial, as basic as a table and chair. A V-board is the best, being more versatile than a bench pin. It is a wooden board 7 inches long, 2½ inches wide, and ⅜ inch thick. The working end has a cutout keyhole shape about 2¾ inches long. The other end has a metal C-clamp that screws onto a table edge.

The board projects out from the table and is used as a working surface for filing, sawing, and polishing metal. The top of the metal clamp fits snugly into the board's surface and is a good place on which to tap flat a piece of metal, substituting for a steel block or anvil. The V-board can be put on the edge of any table, then stored away in a drawer when not in use. You can buy it in any craft shop or order it by mail. It costs under four dollars.

If you buy only metal shapes with a top hole already drilled in them, a small *hand drill* is not essential for the projects in this chapter. But if you do see a shape that you want to use and it does not have a hole for attaching to your design, then the drill is a necessity. And for the projects in the following chapters it is a must. Drills can be bought at a hardware, variety, or craft store, or by mail order, and cost from three to five dollars. They operate on the same principle as a mechanical, hand-operated egg beater, with a small turning handle at the side attached to a large, cogged wheel. The drilling points, called *bits,* are available in a number of sizes. For most of your projects you will need small-size holes, so check the bit sizes against the wire or jump rings you will be using.

You will need a small *hammer* with one round end and one flat face. You can buy this type at a craft or jeweler's supply store, and it is called a *chasing hammer.* It has a ball-style handle and a 1⅛ inch face. Cost is about four dollars. The standard hardware store *ball peen hammer* will also serve the purpose.

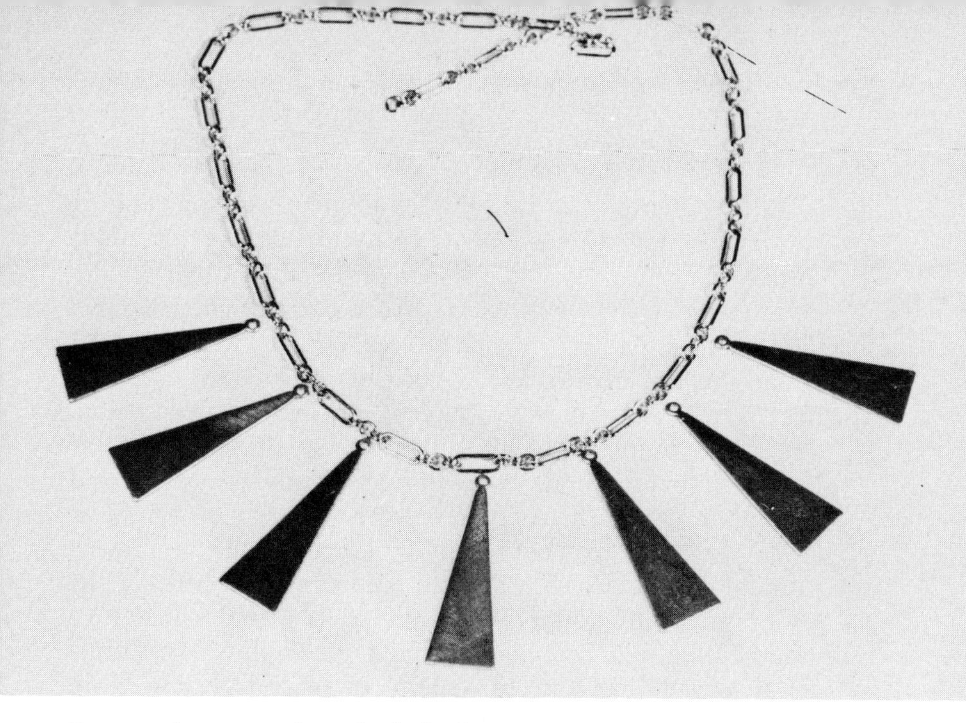

Copper shapes ready to be linked to a copper chain for a necklace.

The two parts of a V-board. The wooden working surface is on the left. The C-clamp is on the right.

MATERIALS

Stamped shapes are small, flat shapes of metal, ranging in size from 1/2 to 2 7/8 inches in diameter. Commercially stamped or cut from 18- or 20-gauge sheets of silver or copper, they are sold in various sizes and shapes—squares, rectangles, triangles, diamonds, circles, cutout circles, domed circles, ovals, cutout ovals, domed ovals, hearts, cutout hearts, free forms, palettes, leaves, four-leaf clovers, curled, sea horses. Some of the shapes have a small hole drilled at the top so that a round or oval jump ring can be inserted and the metal hung from a chain or wire.

Metal chains are sold by the foot, come in an incredible number of designs with all sizes and shapes of links. They are brass, sterling silver, white and yellow gold (usually 12 carat), filled gold, copperplate, and nickelplate. The links are arranged so that there is plenty of space to attach jump rings along a length. Chains can be bought at jewelry supply stores, craft shops, and by mail order. Most mail order catalogs have actual size photographs of their chains. Prices vary from under fifty cents to five dollars a foot, depending on the metal used, the weight of the chain, the size of the links, and the fluctuating metal market.

Wire is used to make hooks for modern necklace fastenings, and for short and long hooked hangers for necklaces and earrings. Thicker wire makes a neck circle or band, worn alone or with a center pendant. Wire can be formed into spiral designs and twisted in several patterns. It can be bought in thicknesses ranging from 9 to 24 gauge, and in round, half-round, rectangular, and square shapes. It is sold in lengths as short as a foot, and most supply shops list a price per foot.

The *metals* used for wire are brass, copper, silver, gold, and filled gold. Copper and brass can be bought in hardware and variety stores in a limited number of gauges wrapped around a wooden spool, or as a smaller coil in a cardboard and plastic package. Many railroad hobby shops carry copper and brass wire in 18-, 24-, and 30-inch lengths. Silver and gold are bought at jewelry craft shops or ordered by mail.

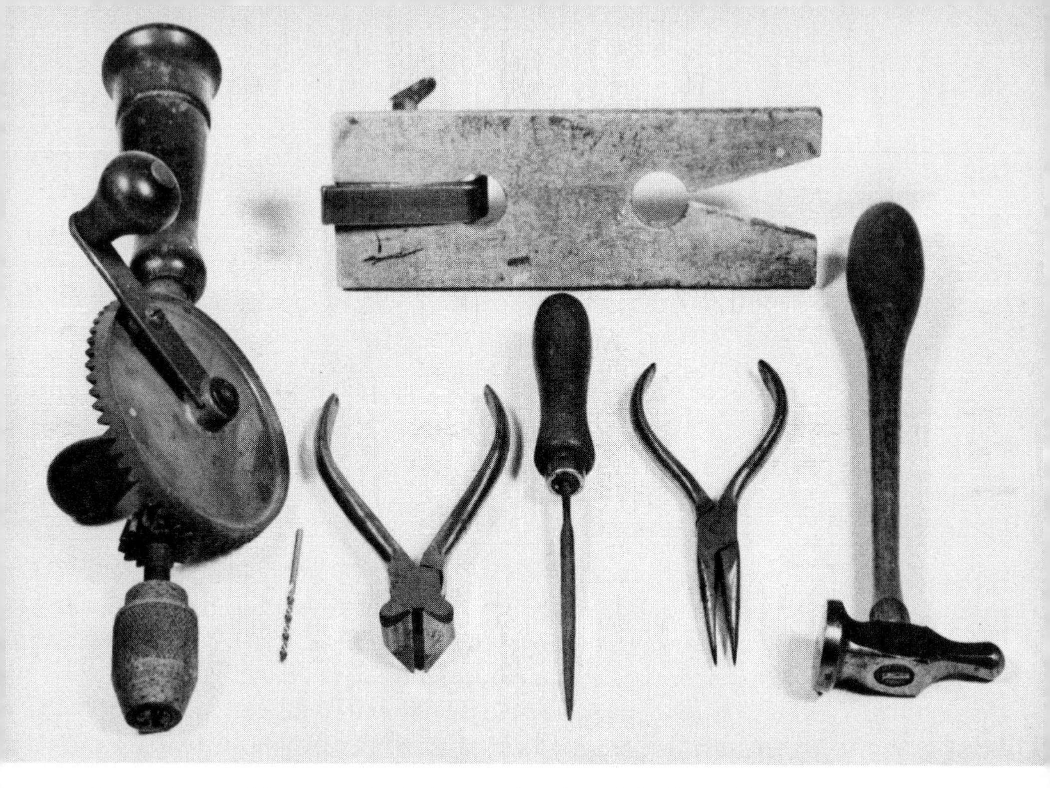

Tools for working metal. Left to right: hand drill and bit, wire cutter, needle file, chain-nose pliers, and chasing hammer; in the back, an assembled V-board.

An assortment of stamped copper shapes.

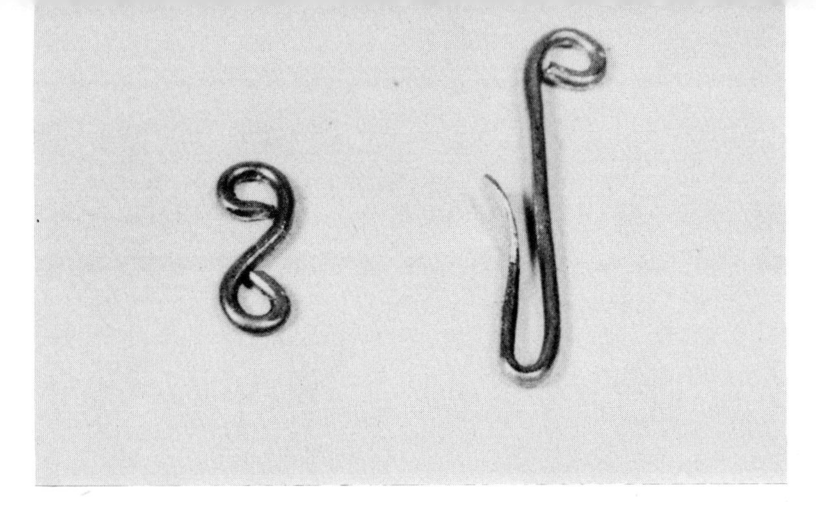

Figure-8 link and hook, formed from wire.

Findings such as pin backs, earring backs, cuff link-backs, catches, and jump rings, described in the previous chapters, are used in these projects, too.

Clear lacquer used as a final coat over polished metal will prevent tarnish from forming on the surface. A jeweler's clear lacquer is sold in craft shops and jewelry supply stores, but *clear nail polish* is equally good and available in smaller quantities at drug and variety stores.

If you are softening metal for a particular project (see next section), you should have on hand a box of *Sparex*. This is a commercial powder that, when dissolved in water, removes fire stains from metal. It saves you the work of cleaning and polishing by hand, and it is much safer than the acids that are sometimes used for the same purpose.

HOW TO ANNEAL METAL

Softening metal is a basic and necessary skill, as most sheet metal and wire is sold as hardened metal. For most projects that involve sawing, filing, and soldering, you can use the metal just as you buy it; this applies, too, to the stamped shapes. However, if you want to dome the metal, or beat one part flatter, or twist wire into a shape, then the metal has to be softened in a heating process called *annealing*. The piece to be worked on is annealed after it is cut from your larger supply of sheet or wire.

When you have worked a piece of metal for a while, it

begins to resist you, and you must anneal it again. Otherwise it may crack or snap in two, or just not bend smoothly.

Only copper, brass, and silver wire are annealed. The plated, gold-filled, and base-metal wires should not be heated, as they will lose their plating or melt. (The stamped shapes do not need softening as you will be using them just as they are.)

The process is very simple, and can be done at your kitchen stove. Fill a pot with cold water and put it on the side of the stove top. Wind copper, silver, or brass wire into a loose coil, about 3 to 4 inches in diameter, depending on how much wire you have to soften.

Light the gas burner or the electric coil of the kitchen stove. Hold the wire with the tongs at the point where the two ends cross. Move the coil slowly back and forth across the heat until it turns red; then drop it immediately into the cold water. If the wire is discolored by heat, drop the hot wire into a bowl or pot of water to which Sparex has been added. That's all there is to it.

Only one warning – watch that the silver wire does not get too hot, as it might melt.

Dry off the wire. If you have not used Sparex, rub copper or brass lightly with emery or crocus cloth to remove fire scale. You can polish copper wire with vinegar and salt or a commercial copper cleaner. Brass responds to ordinary powdered kitchen cleansers. Sterling silver wire will have a light deposit of fine silver on the surface, giving it a frosty look. This will gradually rub off as you work the silver. Or you can take it off with crocus cloth.

The wire is now ready to use in any of the following projects.

BARBARIC TRIANGLES

Materials

You'll need the following:

Nine narrow copper triangles, 1½ inches high with a small hole at the top.

Twelve oval jump rings to attach the triangles and the catch to the neck chain. In buying jump rings, be sure the

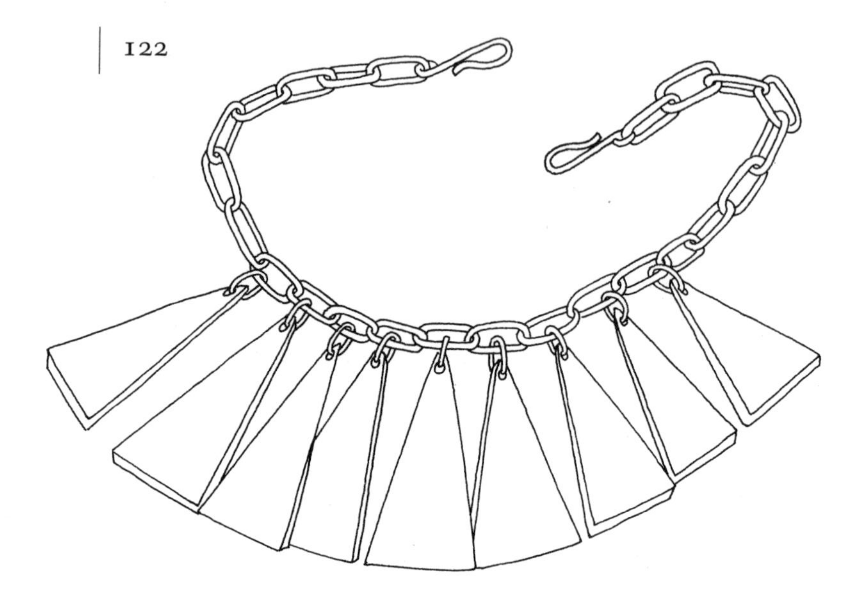

wire is thin enough to be inserted in the drilled hole or the chain link for which it is intended.

A gold plated chain, 18 inches long, in a ladder or rope design.

Commercial minihooks or spring rings for closing the chain at the back. You can make your own hook, which is fun and satisfying, by using about 1 inch of brass wire.

Clear nail polish.

Steps

1. If you are making your own hook, anneal a 1-inch length of brass wire, following directions at the beginning of this chapter. Beat 1/8 inch of one end of the wire to flatten, using the hammer and resting the wire on the V-board's metal strip (the top of the C-clamp). File into a round end, and curl up 1/2 inch to form a hook that curves back to the straight wire and out again. Grasp the other end of the wire with the chain-nose pliers and curl it over into a circle in the same direction as the hook, until the wire touches the straight shank.

   This is the standard procedure for making a hook, and you will use it many times when you do not want a commercial finish to a necklace. Measurements and sizes of hooks vary with each design, so adjust accordingly.
2. Attach the hook to one end of the chain. This is done by

opening one of the jump rings—moving the ends sideways away from each other and spreading them apart until there is enough space to slip the last link of the chain through. Use chain-nose pliers and fingers. Then slip the circle end of your hook (hook end should be on the up side) into this link. Bring ends of the jump ring back to the original position.

In all working with metal, be firm but slow in handling. Quick, sharp pulls or tugs are liable to break the metal, as the molecules do not have time to adjust to a new position.

3. Now hold the chain against your neck, with the catch in the center of the back. Mark the cutoff spot with your finger, allowing for the length of one jump ring at the other end. Bring this marked spot down to the working surface and cut away the extra links with the wire cutter.
4. Insert a jump ring on the end of the last link of the chain, following the directions in step 3. Try on the chain again.
5. Find the center of your chain, and mark the link. Insert a jump ring on this link and place a triangle on the jump ring at the same time.
6. Stretch the chain across your working surface and place the rest of the triangles in position—four on each side of the center triangle. Make sure that they are equal distances apart and that they do not overlap each other at the bottom points. The jump rings will slide to the "corner" of the chain link nearest the center, so take this into consideration when measuring. The triangles should hang in the front area of the chain, across a distance of approximately 7 inches.
7. Open the other eight jump rings and insert at their designated spots on the chain. Slip the triangles on the open jump rings. Close rings.
8. Using the file or crocus cloth, take out any nicks in the jump rings and triangles.
9. Stretch out the necklace and cover the back of each triangle with clear nail polish, being sure that no polish drips over to the front. Let the back dry until hard; then turn over and do the front. Let dry until hard. This may take several hours, as metal is nonabsorbent.

Variations

In place of triangles, use any of the shapes with a small hole at the top—circles, ovals, open ovals, or hearts.

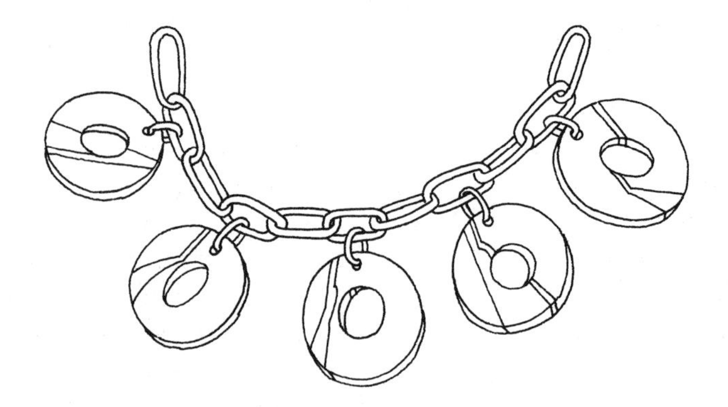

A WIRE-HANGER NECKLACE

In this design the triangles, instead of being held close to the chain by jump rings, are suspended on thin wire $1\frac{1}{4}$ inches long.

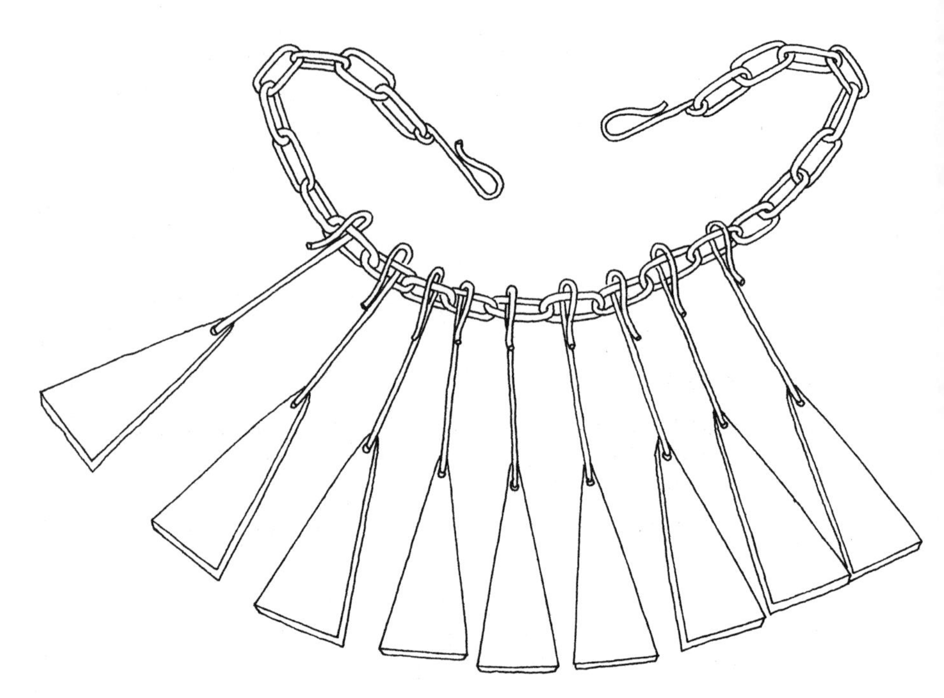

Materials

Nine long triangles of copper; an 18-inch length of brass wire, 18 or 20 gauge in thickness; a gold plated chain, 18 inches long; a piece of wire for a hook, or a spring catch, and two jump rings; clear nail polish.

Steps

1. Cut the chain to size, and attach the clasp or the hook and the jump rings to the ends, following the directions given in steps 2, 3, and 4 of the previous project.
2. The next step is to make the wire hangers. Since the bending will be minimal, do not anneal the wire. With the chain-nose pliers, curl the end of the wire into a tight circle. Measure 1¼ inches from the top of the circle. Put the pliers at this point, and bend the wire at a right angle. Clip off ⅜ inch beyond this point, and bend the short length so that it is parallel with the shank, forming a narrow U. Bend the tip outward, at the same time pushing the wire back toward the shank at the point where the tip curves out. This will produce a hook shape. File end into a smooth round.

   Repeat process until you have formed nine hangers.
3. Now find the front center of the chain. Put the first hanger at this spot by opening the circle a bit and slipping it over the wire of the center link. The hook end faces out, and the triangle is hung on this. Evenly space the eight other hangers and triangles on the chain (see step 6 of the preceding project).
4. Cover back of the triangles with clear nail polish and let dry. Repeat with the front side and dry.

Variations

1. The hanging wires can be made shorter toward the sides of the chain. Make the three center wires 1¼ inches long, and the three on each side 1 inch long.
2. Other shapes than the triangle can be used—circles, squares, ovals, and so forth.
3. Hangers and triangles can be hung by a jump hook to earring backs that have a small loop for this purpose.
4. Use silver shapes instead of copper.

TRIANGLES AND CURLED SHAPES

Here is the first of several suggestions for necklaces that use a combination of shapes, as well as jump rings and wire hooks. You will develop your own exciting combinations, for the possibilities are endless.

Steps

1. Follow the directions for measuring and clasping the chain given in the barbaric triangles project.
2. Make one 1¼-inch wire hanger and two 1-inch hangers (see the preceding project for directions). You will also need to buy four oval jump rings.
3. String the shapes on the chain, putting a triangle in the middle on the 1¼-inch hanger. Attach curled shapes next. You'll need one piece that curls left and one that curls right, so that both curls turn toward the center.

Hang the curls on the 1-inch hangers. Next add two triangles on each side, hung on the oval jump rings. Clear nail polish is painted over all.

HEARTS, DIAMONDS AND TRIANGLES

Steps

1. Follow the directions for measuring and clasping the chain given in the barbaric triangles project.
2. Make five hangers—one 1 inch, two 1½ inches, and two ¾ inch. You will also need two oval jump rings.
3. String the shapes on the chain. At the center place an open heart on a 1-inch hanger. To each side, place a diamond on a 1½-inch hanger. Next add small, solid hearts on ¾-inch hangers. And finally, attach long triangles on the oval jump rings.

THE LONG WAY AROUND

Here's a long chain with four assorted shapes, two of which are arranged in a compound pendant effect.

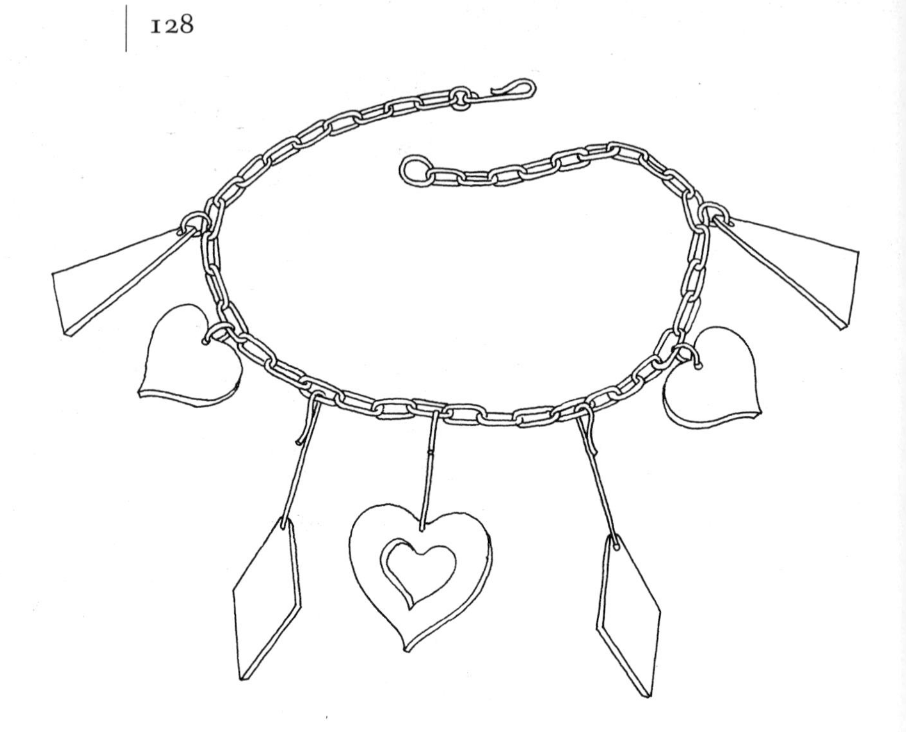

Steps

1. Start with a chain 27 inches long. Connect the ends with a jump ring (no clasp is needed since the chain will fit over the head).
2. Find the front center of the chain, and hang a cutout oval on a 1-inch hanger. The next hanger is a *double-hooked* one, 1 1/4 inches long. Clip one end, at the bottom, over the inside of an oval cutout. The other hook goes through the hole in the top of a round cutout. On each side of this pendant, hang a narrow triangle on an oval jump ring.

Variations

All of the assorted shapes can be mixed or matched on a long chain, following the directions for the short chain.

RING WITH A SPIRAL ENDING

The ever-popular neck wire can be worn just by itself or finished with coiled designs or hanging spirals.

To make the basic shape, you will follow the directions in

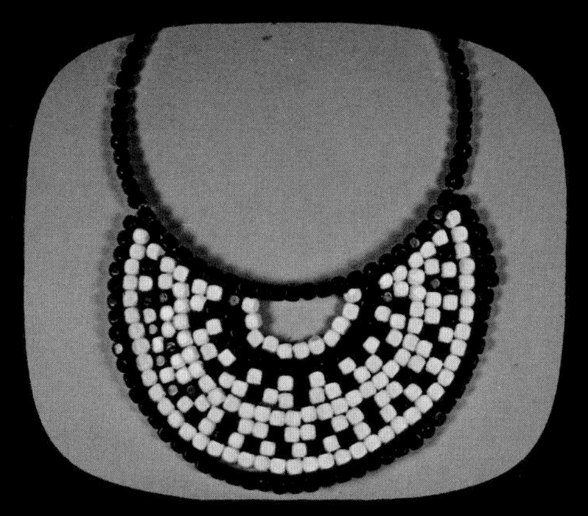

African necklace, page 45

Collection of stones. *Top, left to right:* carnelian cabochon, jadite, azurite with malachite. *Bottom, left to right:* tiger-eye, rhodochrosite, amethyst wrapped with silver wire. Pages 192 to 225

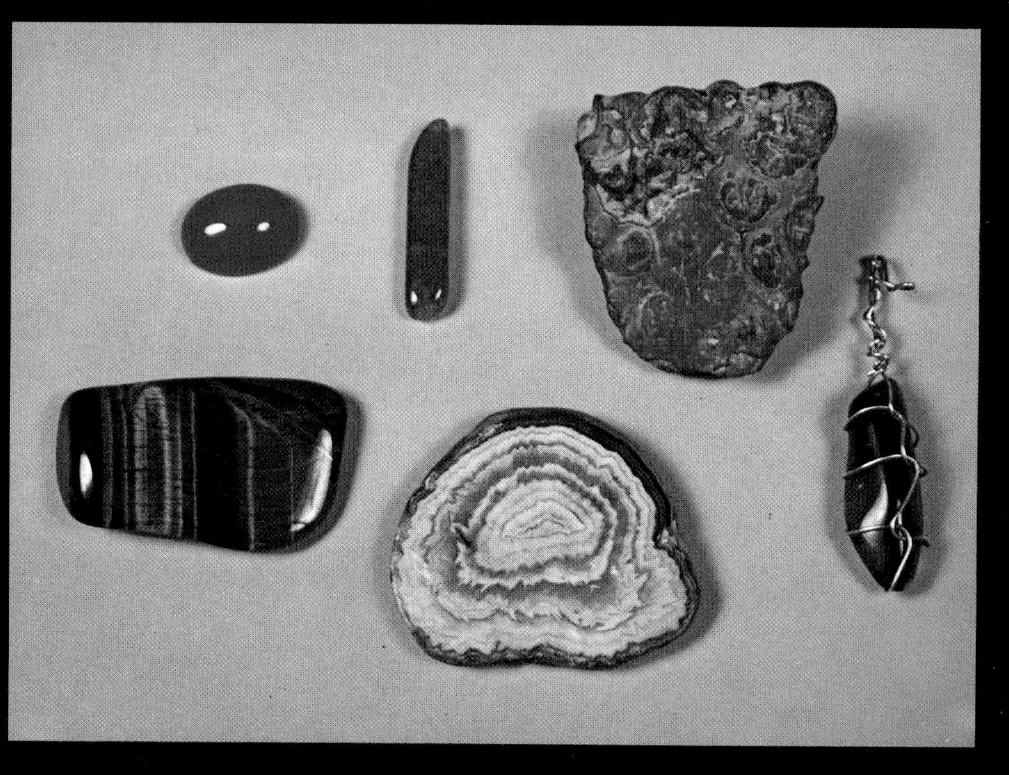

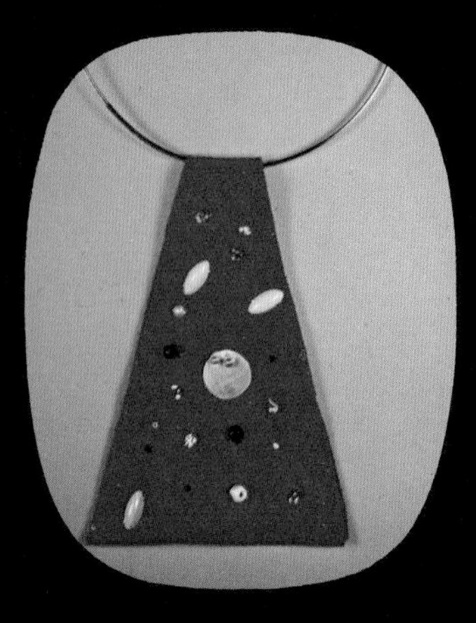

From left to right:
Felt bib necklace, page 55
Hanging spiral necklace, page 131
"Gold" and jade pendant, page 202
Shell necklace, page 21
Decorated silver pendant, page 267
Gold pendant, page 111

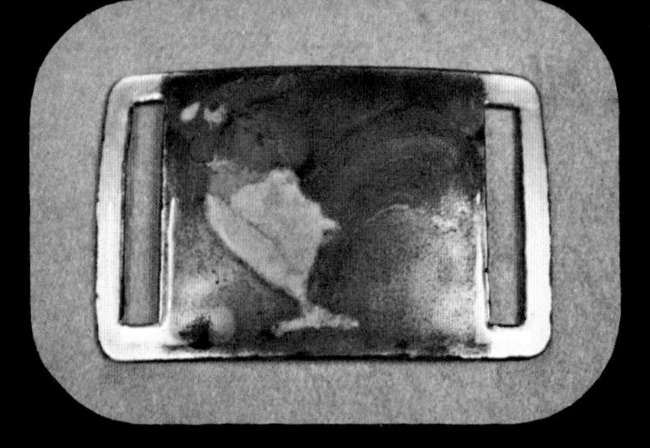

Rooster buckle, page 255

Earrings from found objects, page 259; silver charm pendant, page 264

Various types of enamel, pages 228 to 231

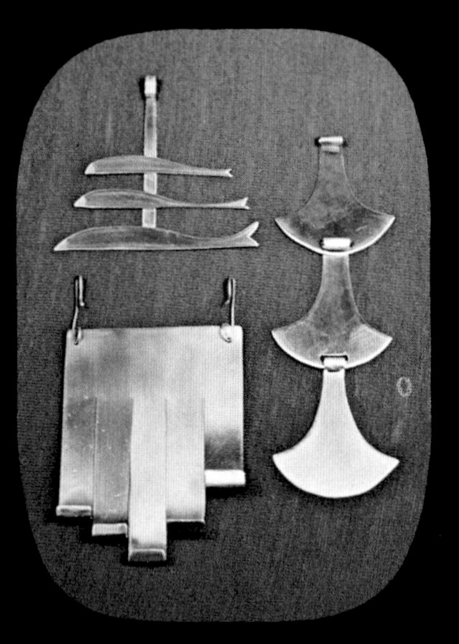

Collection of pendants, pages 157, 176 and 252

Charm bracelet, page 274; enamel buckles turned into pins, page 266

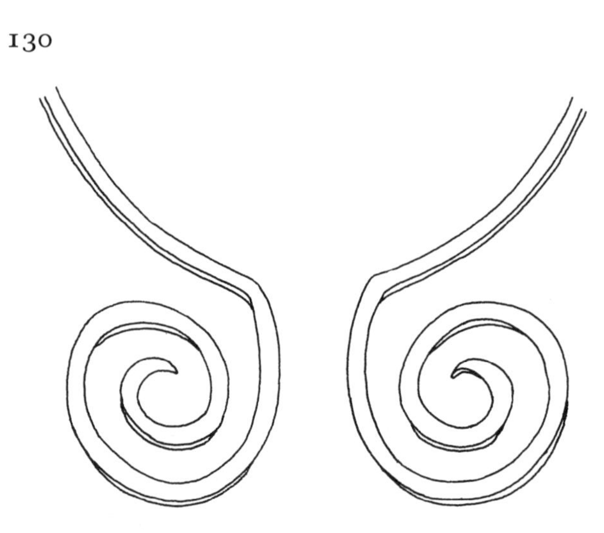

step 11 for the Primitive Neck Ornament in Chapter 6, using 14-gauge brass or silver wire. (For a variation, you can beat the wire with a hammer after the circle has been made. This gives it an irregular surface and outline.)

In this and the following designs, there are no back hooks; the opening is swung around to the front and there is a 3/4 inch gap. In this version the two ends of the neck wire curve into large spirals at each side.

Materials

You will need 31 1/4 inches of brass or silver wire, 14 gauge. Anneal the wire, following the directions at the beginning of this chapter.

Steps

1. Stretch out the wire. Make a center mark, then two marks 7 7/8 inches to each side of the center. This will be the length of your neck wire proper. The additional wire will become the two spirals.
2. Make the neck wire, following directions in step 11 on page 156.
3. Copy each of the spirals onto a piece of tracing paper. The spirals curve in opposite directions.

   Following these patterns, curve the wire ends around the fingers and pliers, first one side, then the other.

   An alternate method: lay the patterns on a soft asbestos tile or a piece of wood, drive small brass nails or

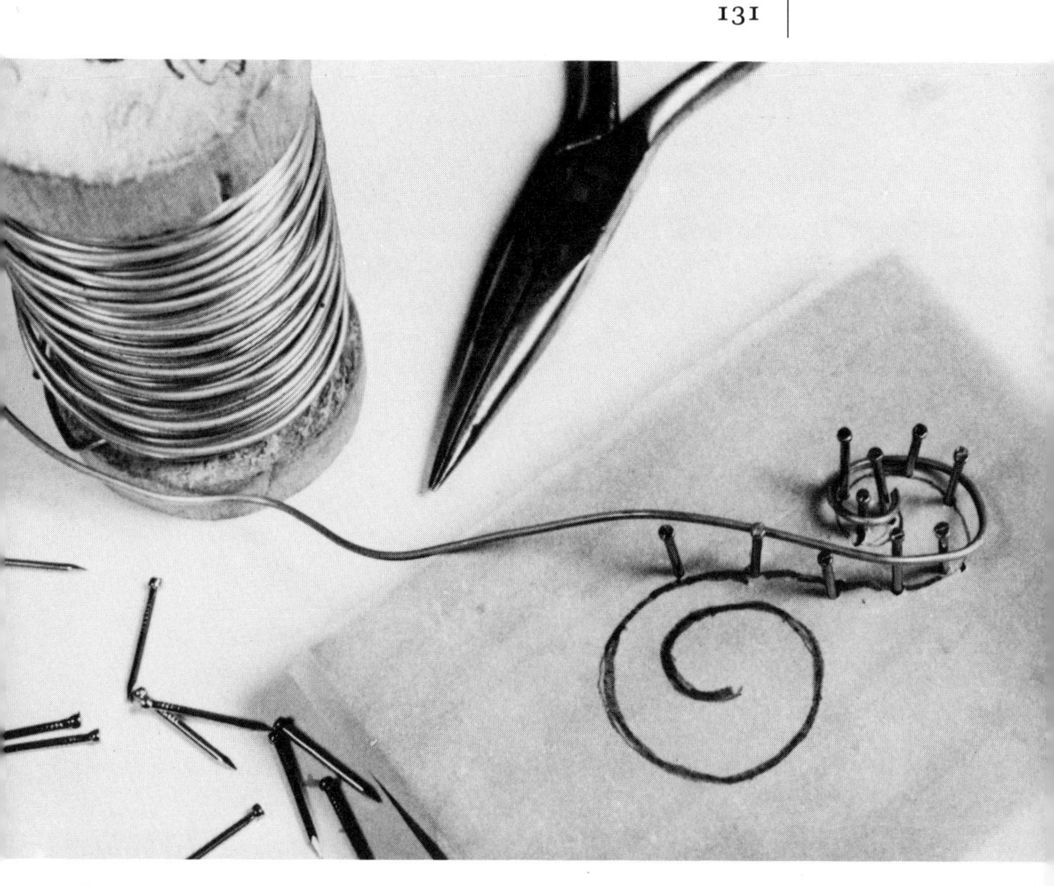

Forming wire into a spiral.

brads along the design, and wrap the wire around, using the nails as guides and braces. Keep adding nails or brads as you bend the metal.

4. The wire necklace should not close at the front of the neck – the gap is approximately 3/4 inch. File off any nicks made by the pliers, and polish the wire first with emery cloth, then crocus cloth. Cover wire with clear nail polish and let dry.

A HANGING SPIRAL

This design has small spirals at the front ends of the neck wire, to which hanging spirals are attached.

Materials

For the neck wire, the two hanging spirals, and the two linking loops, you will need $53\frac{3}{4}$ inches of 14-gauge wire, annealed.

Steps

1. Cut off $24\frac{1}{2}$ inches of wire. Follow directions in step 11, page 156 for measuring and making the basic neck wire. In this case you will be making smaller spirals at each end, and they are each made from $4\frac{3}{8}$ inches of wire. Follow the directions given for the larger spirals in step 3 of the preceding project.
2. Cut the remaining wire into four pieces—two pieces $8\frac{1}{2}$ inches long for the hanging spirals, and two pieces $1\frac{1}{8}$ inches long for the loops.

   Make two tracings of the spirals, as the designs are reversed. Bend the wire, following the patterns.

   Make the oval loops, bringing the ends together in the middle of one long side.
3. File and polish the wire until the surface is smooth and gleaming. Attach the two spirals to the neck wire with the loops. Cover with clear nail polish and dry.

Variations

1. Make only one of the hanging spirals, and hang it by a loop from a plain, hooked-in-the-back neck wire.
2. Small spirals can be made into earrings by hanging the spirals with loops from earring backs.

AN ORIENTAL SNAKE DESIGN

This has a center pendant hung by a hook. The swirl of wire is faintly reminiscent of the classic Eastern snake design.

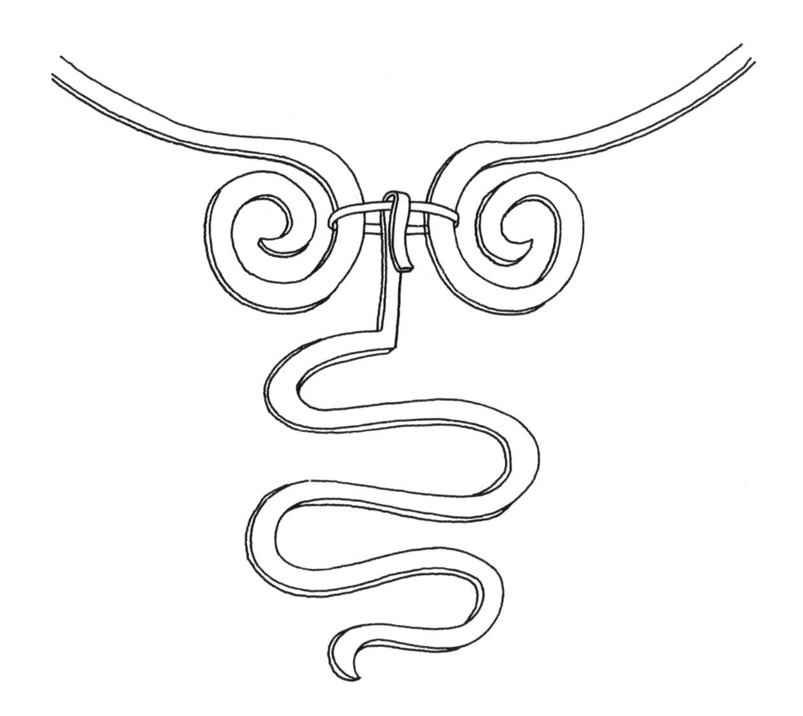

Materials

You will use $35\frac{1}{2}$ inches of 14-gauge wire, annealed.

Steps

1. Cut off $24\frac{1}{2}$ inches for the neck wire and its two side spirals. Follow directions for the hanging spiral neck wire, as this is exactly like it.

2. Cut off $9^1/_4$ inches of wire. Make a hook at the top, curling over the first $^1/_2$ inch. Make an oval ring with the remaining $1^3/_4$ inch wire.
3. Make a tracing of the design. Follow the lines, bending the wire into the pattern.
4. File and polish all the pieces. Slip the loop over the vertical, facing neck wire spirals. Hang the snake design from this loop by the hook. Cover with clear nail polish and let dry.

Variation

Make two snake patterns, in a smaller size, and hang from earring backs.

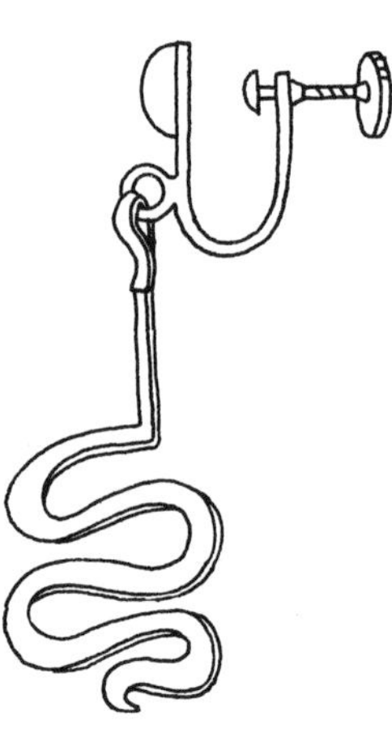

6. Cut It and Heat It

THE jewelry projects in this chapter are the outgrowth of those described in Chapter 5. They are the next exciting step in jewelry making. The techniques are the same as those used by professional jewelers. They also saw, drill, and solder metal. The type of saw you will use is that used throughout the world. The drills may vary slightly. The hammer and sandbag are classic tools. Soldering equipment comes in many varieties, depending on the type of soldering you are doing. The soldering techniques described here are those used for the most basic articles, and they can be easily handled by a beginner.

Interesting jewelry is often not a matter of sophisticated techniques, but of good design. Some of the simplest shapes are the most beautiful and startling. After you have made several pieces of jewelry and acquired the basic skills, you will notice designs in fine stores that are well within your ability to construct.

TOOLS

The tools used in Chapter 5 are the mainstays in the projects given in this chapter. In addition, you will need some other tools that are inexpensive and can be bought in craft shops, hobby departments, and variety and hardware stores, as well as by mail order from craft supply shops. Many of the tools are packaged individually by X-acto Tools. The list of basic tools has been kept to a minimum, and the beginner is advised to buy the cheaper "school" model if more than one model is available.

For Cutting Metal

You will need a *jeweler's saw,* which is similar to a hacksaw in shape, but smaller. We suggest the 8-inch size. The *saw blades* come in several tooth sizes used for various thicknesses of metal, and are numbered accordingly. Numbers 1/0, 1, and 2 are the most useful. We recommend the 5¼-inch blades (saw frame adjusts to fit). These are sold in small bundles of twelve blades. You will also need a small piece of *wax candle* for lubricating the blades.

A small *hand drill* and *bits* for drilling holes in metal are again needed. These are sold in hardware, variety, and craft shops.

You will also need a *riffle file,* a double-ended file that comes in many versions. Get the type with one end shaped like the bowl of a spoon, the other end shaped like an elongated, curved triangle (good for getting into cracks and right angles).

For Soldering Metal

You can begin with the tools for soft soldering—a small *electric soldering iron* or *soldering gun,* both of which can be bought in hardware stores. If later on you decide you want to use medium or hard solder, you will need a handheld *propane* or *butane torch* obtainable at both hardware and hobby shops.

You will, of course, need silver-color *soft solder,* which comes in wire form, *sheet medium* and *hard solder, liquid flux* for both soft and medium soldering, and a *borax cone* for hard soldering. (We'll say more about these materials a bit further on, when we describe soldering techniques.)

To hold a piece of hot metal while it is being soldered, you will need *stainless steel tweezers* with an insulated handle

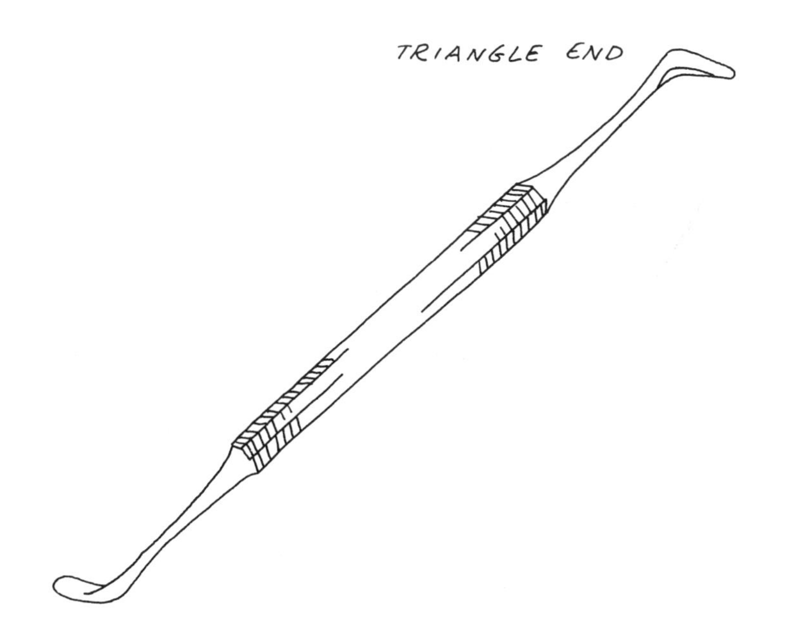

and a bent tip. Other equipment for holding things steady when the heat is on include *cotter pins*, small *brass nails* or *brads*, and *paper clips*, all obtainable in hardware and variety stores.

For protecting the table top while you are soldering, a hard *asbestos pad* (called *transite*) is invaluable. The 12-by-12 inch size is ample for any work. You can solder directly on this surface. A small *asbestos tile* is also useful. An additional softer material is needed, and you have the choice of two types. One is a *charcoal block*, and the size depends on your designs—either 4¾ by 3 inches, or 7 by 4 inches. But what we find even more useful is a *coiled asbestos circle* made of a thin 1-inch strip coiled around and around a small open center, and set in a 5½ inch tin pan.

For Transferring A Design

After the paper design is ready it has to be transferred to metal. For this you will use the standard means—*carbon paper* and a hard, sharp-pointed *pencil* or a *mimeograph*

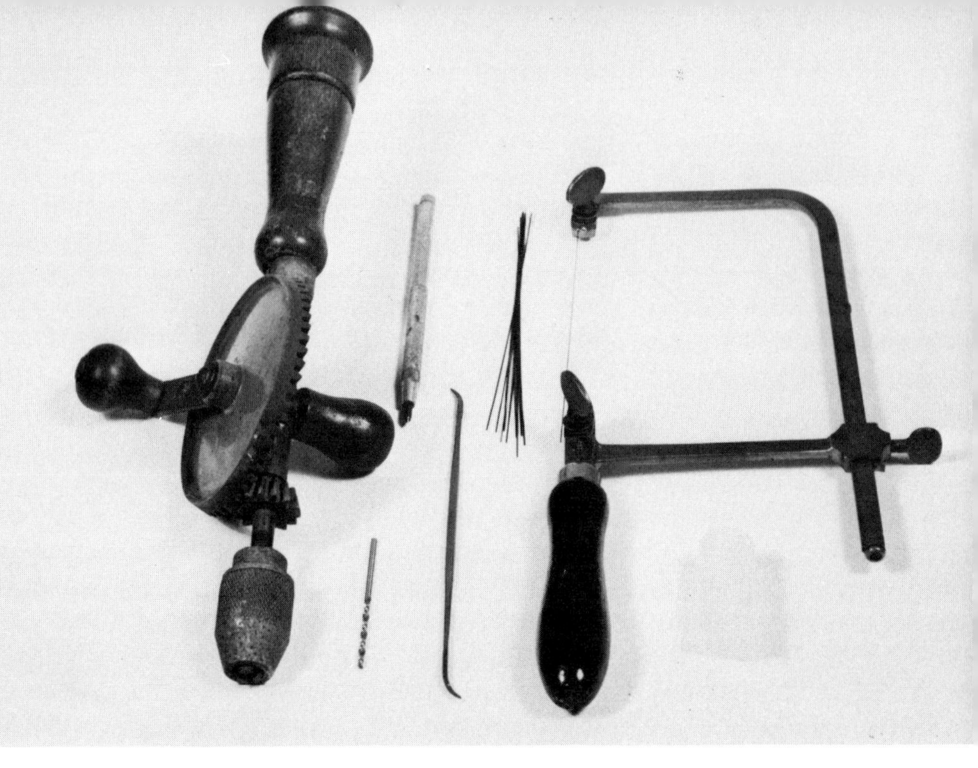

Tools for cutting metal. Left to right: hand drill and bit, scriber, riffle file, saw blades, jeweler's saw, and a piece of candle.

Tools for heating metal. The tools, laid out on a transite asbestos pad, are (left to right): soldering gun, bottle of flux, borax cone, coiled asbestos circle, propane torch, charcoal block, butane torch. On the small asbestos square: stainless-steel tweezers, cotter pins, paper clips, and brads.

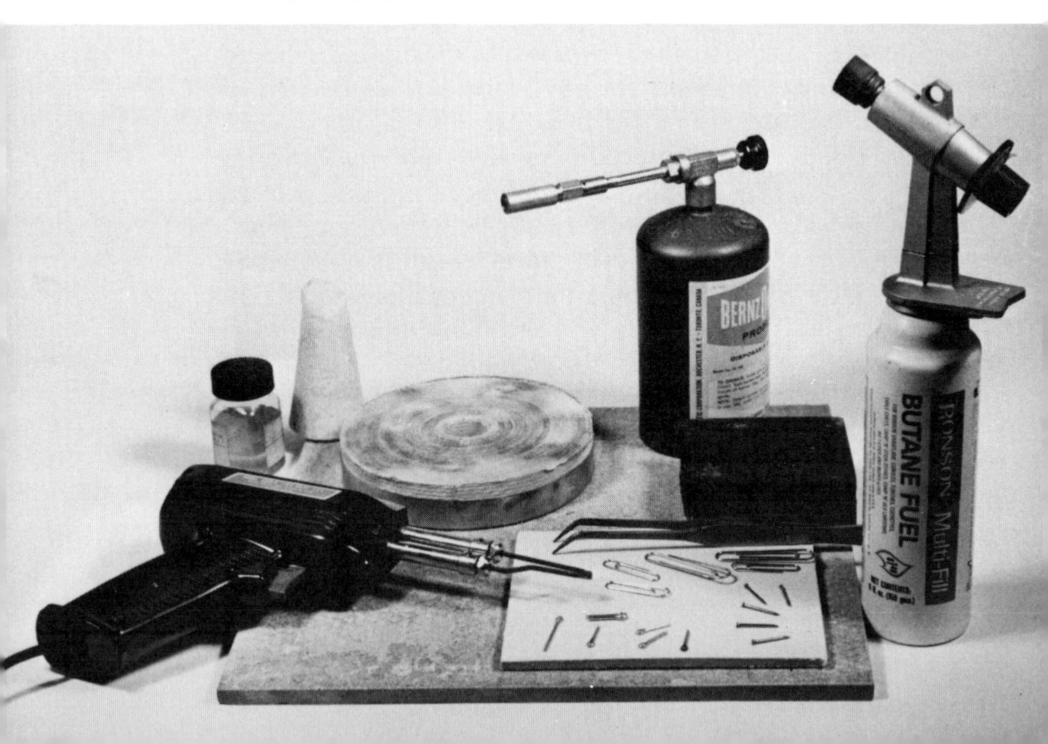

stylus. One additional tool is needed. This is a metal *scriber,* which you use to make a sharp line in metal, following the carbon line. Afterwards the black line is taken off with *rubbing alcohol,* leaving a scratched line that cannot be destroyed or smudged while working.

For Forming Metal

An all-purpose tool is a type of small *hammer* that goes by several names. In hardware stores it is called a *ball peen hammer,* and in craft shops it is a *chasing hammer.* Any small hammer that has a steel head flat on one side and rounded on the other will serve the purpose. If you can buy the chasing hammer, it is a better tool.

For any slight forming of metal into concave or convex surfaces, you use a small *sandbag* as a support. This you can make yourself. Take two 6-inch squares of heavy, tightly woven material like canvas and machine-stitch them together with an overlapped seam, leaving a small opening on part of the seam. Fill with sand through a funnel so the bag is firm but not too hard and resistant. If sand eludes you, and machine stitching is not your thing, the bags can be bought at a craft shop. Usually the size is 7½ by 11 inches, and the bag is made of heavy canvas.

The alternate is a small *lead block,* also available at craft shops. The size is 3 by 3½ inches.

For flattening metal edges, a steel block known as a *bench block,* measuring 2½ by 2½ by ¾ inches, is useful. But one can just as easily use the narrow metal center of the V-board—the top of the C-clamp—for small pieces of jewelry. Large objects do need the larger square of hard metal.

For Cleaning Metal

Metal that has been heated will need a stronger cleaning and polishing agent than emery paper. For this you need a box of Sparex. You just mix the Sparex powder with water, in a glass bowl large enough to hold your design. It is perfectly clean and safe, and you do not need to take all the precautions necessary in handling acids.

Copper tongs, 9 inches long with bent tips, are always used to lift work in and out of a pickling solution such as

Tools for forming metal. In the rear: homemade sandbag, steel block, lead block. In front: ball peen hammer and chasing hammer with ball handle.

A metal shape on a sandbag being formed into a concave surface by the chasing hammer.

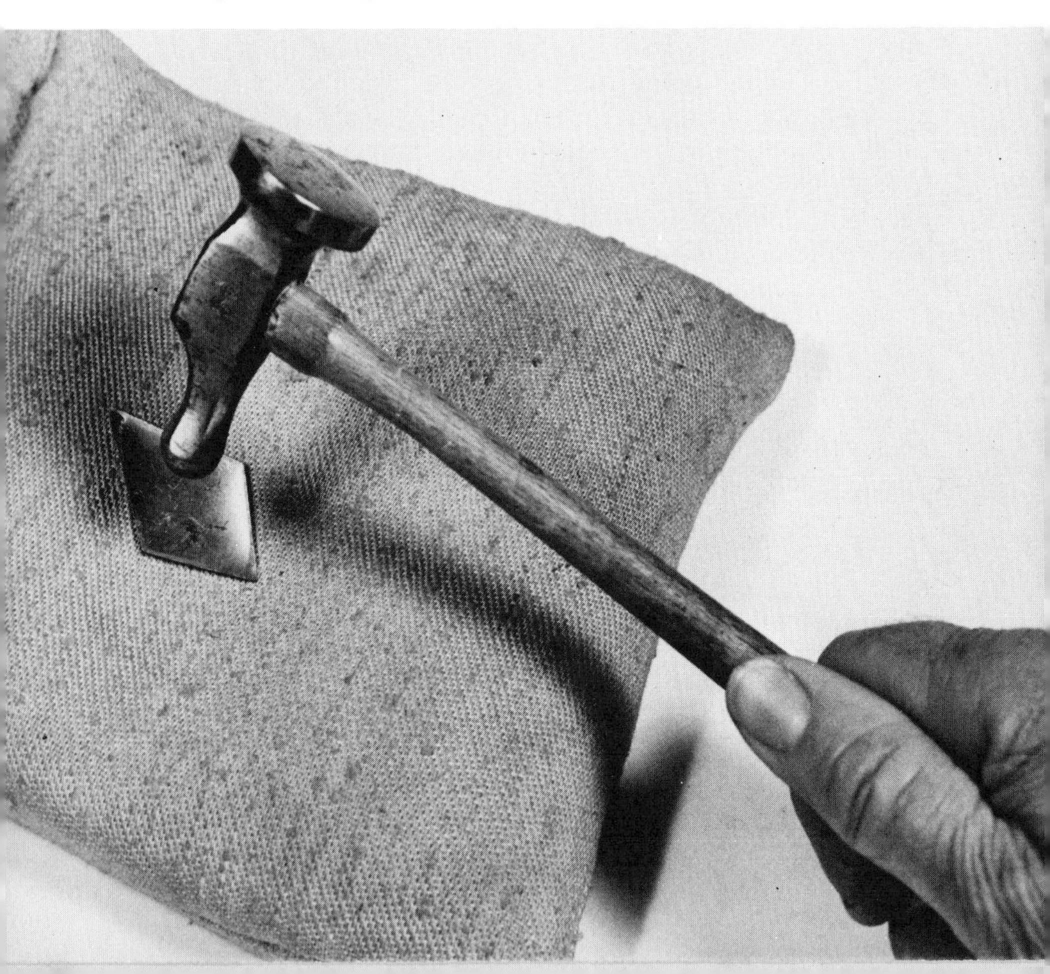

Sparex because they will not rust, nor will they affect the metals being worked on.

Odds and Ends

Finally, there is that general list of everyday articles—*pencils, scissors, ruler,* sheets of *white paper,* a pad of *tracing paper*—all things you have at home or can buy at the stationery store.

MATERIALS

In Chapter 5 the jewelry was made with preformed shapes of 18-gauge copper and silver. In this chapter you are going to make your own shapes from wire, tubes, and small sheets of metal. The choice of metals will include not only copper and silver, but brass and pewter as well. Also available is a combination of copper and brass called Nu-Gold.

Prices of metals fluctuate daily on the world markets, but at the retail outlets the prices usually remain stable for a few months at a time. Since prices on these commodities are changing all the time, we can only indicate roughly what costs will be.

Brass, copper, pewter and Nu-Gold can be bought in sheets measuring 6 by 6 and 6 by 12 inches. In gauges of 16 to 20, the prices for a 6-by-6-inch sheet is under two dollars. A comparable size sterling silver sheet is three to five times that much, and may go higher. That is one reason why pewter, which has been used so much by the Scandinavian jewelers, is becoming very popular. Silver can be bought in many size sheets, from 3 to 6 inches long, and from 1 to 6 inches wide.

Wire is sold by the foot in many shapes; the gauges range from 4 to 24. Prices are quoted by the foot, with silver and gold the most expensive. Gold, of course, is always the most expensive of metals.

HOW TO SAW METAL

Sawing metal is actually easier than sawing wood. The jeweler's saw frame is lightweight metal in the form of a squared C, with a round wooden handle. It comes in many sizes, but the 8-inch size is the most versatile. As you can see from the photograph on page 138, the depth of the frame is adjustable, with two screw clamps top and bottom to hold the thin blades.

Jeweler's saw blades are 5¼ inches long and are made in a variety of tooth sizes for different thicknesses of metal. Numbers 1/0, 1, or 2 are best for 18- or 20-gauge metal. As you work, you will develop a preference for a particular number, as much depends on the pressure exerted, the type of metal, and the design being cut. Blades come in packets, bound together with fine wire. It is best to keep each number separate, and we would suggest keeping them in individual envelopes. You can mark the number on the outside, along with any notations as to preference, or to type of metal and gauge they are used on.

The blades are thin, and when you first start to saw they will snap easily under tension. Don't worry—everyone snaps blades, even the most experienced crafts person, and that is why blades are sold in bundles. So expect your fair share of broken blades!

Inserting the blade is easy. Move the adjusting slide up so that the front opening is about 4⅜ inches. Turn the top screw just enough to insert about ¼ inch of the flat side of the blade—teeth facing out and downward—into the clasp; tighten. Next open the bottom screw. Gripping the handle in one hand, press the top of the frame against the edge of the table to contract the opening a little. Keeping up the pressure, insert the saw blade in the lower clamp and tighten the screw. Now release the pressure, and you will find that your blade is taut and straight. If this pressure is not applied to the blade, it will be too limp to cut the metal.

Metal sawing is done over the V-board, which is screwed onto the edge of a table with a C-clamp, and can be removed when you have finished working. It has an open end with a keyhole cutout. This means that you can follow scribed line on the metal by centering the cut over the opening, while the rest of the metal lies flat on the board, held in place by one hand.

Put the piece of flat metal on the V-board, with the edge

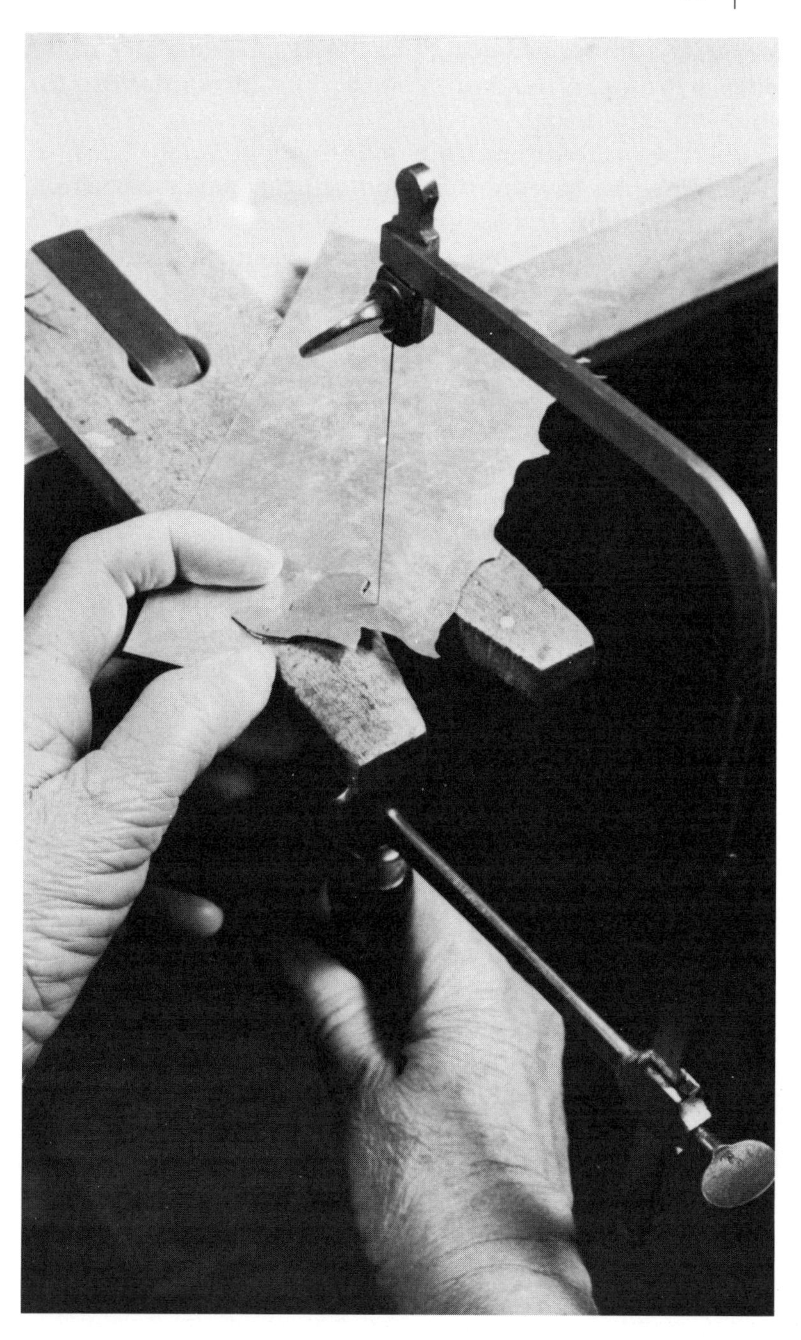

Sawing metal on the V-board. Note proper position of both hands for easy control of metal and saw.

nearest to the scribed design facing you. Make a nick in the edge with a file; this will hold the saw in position for the first few cuts.

Pull the blade through a piece of wax before beginning.

Holding the saw by the handle in an upright position, draw downward the length of the blade, letting the teeth bite into the metal, but not forcing them too hard. Push blade up, lightly, barely pulling the blade away from the metal, then down again, biting into the metal. This is the rhythm of all your sawing—cutting on the downpull, coasting on the upthrust.

Try to cut just outside the scribed line. This gives you a filing margin when you are ready to smooth the edges (all sawing leaves a rough edge).

When you go around a curve, it is the metal that changes position in relation to the saw. The saw moves up and down, facing away from you, aiming down the length of the V-board, while you turn the metal with your other hand, slowly feeding the curved line toward the saw blade.

Sit directly in front of the board, feet squarely on the floor. If you sit to one side at an angle, you will have trouble controlling the blade, which will move away from the scribed line. If you try to force it back, the tension is liable to snap the blade.

Some people like to saw with the blade slightly thrust forward at the bottom. There is less tendency for the blade to bind in the cut metal.

If you want to rewax, or you have to stop sawing for some reason, back the blade out, very delicately, following all the curves of the cut. If it jams, don't force it—just jiggle the blade a few times, gently, until it is free.

Cutting a right angle is very tricky but fun. It's like doing an impossible task and feeling great when it is accomplished. When you come to a corner, start moving the blade up and down in very short strokes, like marking time. With the other hand, turn the metal *very* slowly. Gradually, without being aware of it, you will find the saw facing straight down the next scribed line—and the corner has been turned.

As you come to the end of the V-board keyhole, move metal and saw nearer to you, and continue.

At first, all of this will be awkward, but very soon both hands will start to work together as they learn a new skill, and they will seem to be sawing the metal with very little direction from you.

When you are finished, always loosen one of the screws holding the blade so that it is put aside without tension.

To remove the center section of a design without cutting the surrounding metal, it is necessary to drill a hole first at the edge of the "waste" metal, as described in the following section. Remember that all metal is precious, and drilling is done in an area that will cause the least damage. The so-called waste metal of one design becomes the basis of another piece of jewelry!

After the hole has been drilled, the upper screw on the saw frame is loosened and the saw blade strung through the hole, with the scribed side of your design facing upward. Bring the metal down to the bottom of the saw, and apply the usual pressure to the top as you insert the blade in the jaws and tighten the screw. Saw around the outline in the usual manner. When all the area has been cut away, loosen the top screw and slip the blade out of the design.

Saw blade in position when strung through a sheet of metal. The shapes have just been cut out.

If you are cutting silver, you will want to catch the silver dust from the saw. Put a piece of plastic over your lap—a plastic garment bag will do—and when you have finished, lift it up carefully, brushing the dust into a pile at the edge. Sweep it into a small pill bottle with a cover. Do the same when you are filing edges. This dust, with soldering flux added, can be melted back into a solid piece of silver.

Also, put all the leftover, odd-shaped pieces of silver into a jar. They are all valuable, and can be used to create other jewelry designs. In fact, keep several labeled jars—one for each type of metal you are cutting.

A third type of cutting involves slicing a metal tube into sections or rings. For complete directions, see page 163.

HOW TO FILE

After any sawing, the metal edge must be filed smooth, either at right angles to the surface or beveled. This is done with the needle file. Gouges, too, are often removed with the curved back of a riffle file. The triangle end of the riffle file also gets into narrow angles and awkward places, where solder always seems to lodge.

You can stroke forward and back, exerting as much or as little pressure as is needed. Mostly you will work on the V-board.

HOW TO DRILL A HOLE

One often needs to drill a hole in a design—to hang a pendant on a chain, to link pieces of metal together for a bracelet or necklace or earring, or to insert a saw blade in a center area that must be cut out.

A hand drill is the simplest and cheapest type, and operates in the same way as a hand egg beater. A round gear on the side is turned by a handle, and this operates the drill, driving the bit into the metal.

Bits are twisted pieces of steel in various sizes that bite into metal, making holes of various widths. You will most likely need only two or three sizes—very fine, medium, and

Beginning the slicing of a section of brass tubing. Saw frame is held to one side to show the placement of the blade on the tube.

Filing a beveled edge with the needle file on a piece of metal.

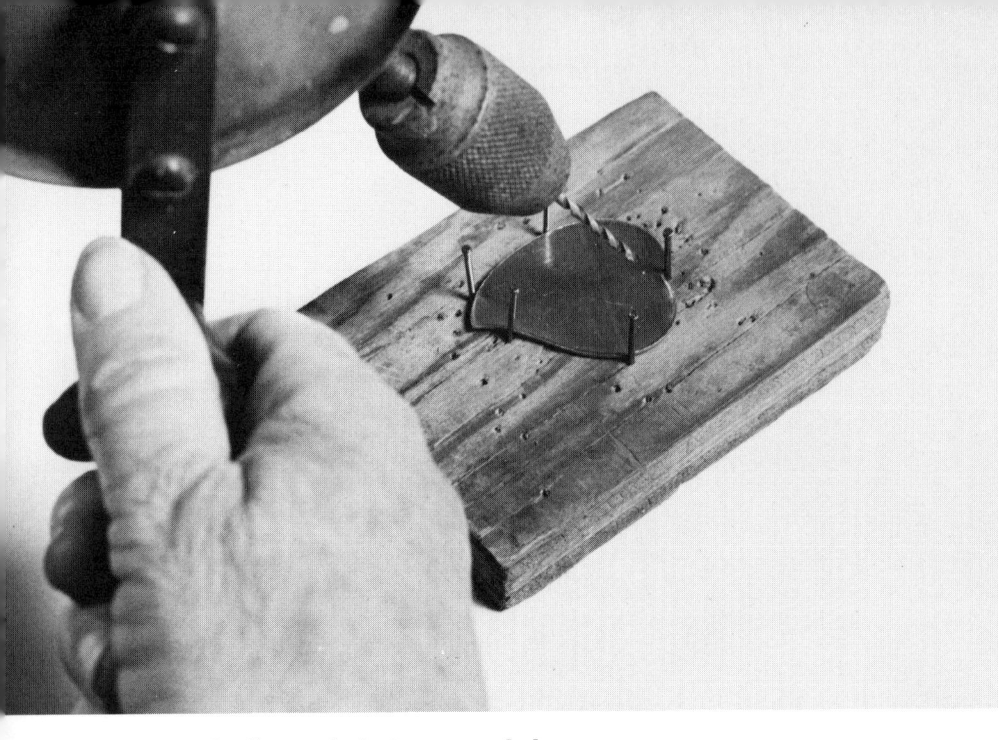

Drilling a hole in a metal shape.

large. Sizes of holes depend, too, on the thicknesses of wire jump rings that are strung through these openings.

To make a hole in metal, put your design on the asbestos tile or a square piece of wood, and hold in place with four or five small brass nails placed around the edges. These will hold things steady and free your hands to work the drill.

With a hammer and nail make a small indentation in the metal where you want the hole to be. This will steady the drill until it bites into the metal.

Place a bit in the drill and tighten. Now, holding the drill upright, place the bit in the indentation, and, turning the handle, drill away until you hit asbestos.

If there is any rough metal left around the edges of the hole, file it away.

HOW TO SOFT-SOLDER

The third most important skill in making jewelry is *soldering.* It is a method of permanently attaching one piece of metal to another by means of a melted softer metal.

All of the projects described in this chapter can be made with *soft solder,* the easiest and simplest of materials to use. There are a number of soft solders on the market, since it is a useful tool in a home-repair workshop. But for jewelry making, the *silver-color solder* bought at craft shops is best; it will not turn dark as do the lead-based soft solders. It is stronger than the other soft solders, and can also be used on pewter.

Soft solders come in round-wire form, which is flattened with a hammer as needed. A few taps with the rounded end of your hammer will thin out the wire, and small squares can be snipped off with scissors.

The next necessity is a small bottle of *soft-solder flux,* also obtainable at the craft shop where you buy your solder. This is applied with a small watercolor brush, both to the metal to be soldered and to the solder. The flux helps the solder to melt and flow along the joint of two pieces of metal when heat is applied.

Now the final step—*heat.* Soft solder does not need a tremendous amount of heat. A small *electric soldering iron* or *gun* will become hot enough to melt soft solder. Both can be bought at any hardware or craft store.

There is a basic routine that is followed in all soldering processes, and the steps are very few and simple.

The metal must be clean and free from any oil. A piece may not look oily, but in fact your fingers spread a thin film on the metal while you are working on a design, and this will prevent a good bond in soldering.

To test for oil, put a piece of metal under cold, running water, then take it away. A few drops of water will cling here and there to the metal—indicating that the *rest* of the metal surface is covered by a thin film of oil, which repels water.

To remove the grease, rub the metal first with powdered kitchen cleanser, wash off, then use a piece of absorbent cotton saturated with rubbing alcohol. You will know the metal is properly clean when a thin film of water covers the whole surface after it is held under running water. Once cleaned, the areas to be soldered must not be handled by your fingers. So, if there are any adjustments to do, use the prong tweezers to push things into position. The same care is taken in cleaning the solder.

Next make sure the pieces of metal are in perfect contact at the soldering point. If there are any gaps, your solder will not hold, and the metal will have to be cleaned and resoldered. So take the time to check carefully, and use hammer, pliers, or file to make the necessary adjustments.

Then paint the facing sides of each piece of metal with flux. Put the pieces in position on the asbestos round. If you are afraid the metal might slip or be disturbed by the soldering iron, hold things in place with tiny brass nails tapped into the asbestos as a brace, or clamp with cotter pins or paper clips.

Snip 1/16-inch-square pieces from the flattened end of the soldering wire. Pick these up with the small brush dipped in liquid flux. Make sure that each side of the joint is coated before placing the solder in position. If it is only a wire being fastened to a flat piece of metal, the chips can be placed 1/4 to 1/2 inch from each other. This is one process that cannot follow a hard and fast rule, as much depends on the size of your piece, the thickness of metal, the absorption of heat. As you work you will form your own rules and follow these. You may want to experiment with scrap pieces of metal before making a final soldering on your design. The scrap pieces can always be separated by reapplying heat and pulling the pieces apart with tweezers when the solder flows.

Heat the soldering iron or gun and bring it into contact with the metal to be soldered. Your design should be heated quickly all along the soldering area. Once the first piece of solder starts to melt at one end, stroke slowly to the next piece, and to each piece in turn as the heat is carried along. If you are soldering a narrow bar or wire onto a flat piece of metal, stroke up and down its length, keeping the heat on the side away from the line of solder. Solder always flows toward the greater source of heat, so it will flow under the wire, not over it, and complete the joining of wire to flat metal.

Let the metal cool without disturbing. If it is moved while hot the joint will break free.

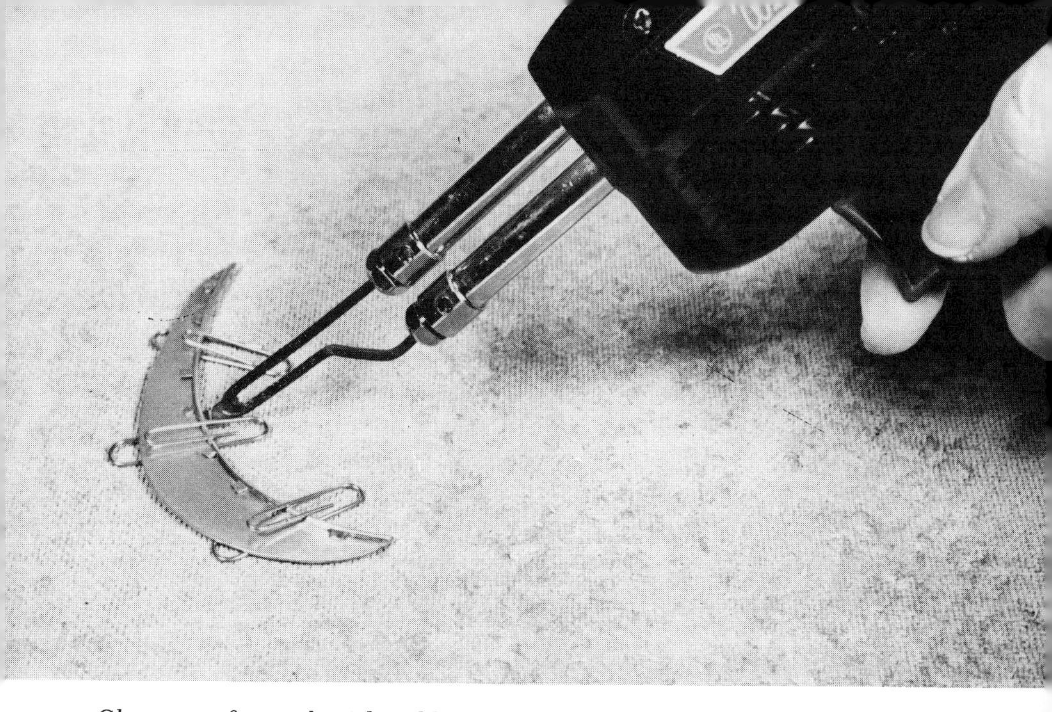

Close-up of metal with solder chips in place along the wire, which is held in place by paper clips. Note the trigger grip, which activates the heat at the tip of the soldering gun.

Another way to solder two flat pieces together is called *sweating.* After checking the fit, and cleaning both pieces, coat the underside of the top piece with flux, and apply chips of solder all over it. Heat until the solder flows. Coat the facing area of the lower metal with flux at the joining area. Put the two sides together and hold with paper clips or cotter pins. Apply heat on top until you see a fine shining line of melted solder at the crack. Let the design cool without disturbing it.

After cooling, check the edges for excess solder and file it away. Then polish with fine emery cloth.

To solder wire rings, bezels, and loops of metal, square off each end of the metal strip or wire and bring together in a circle. Push the ends into an overlapping position, which will temporarily give you a smaller circle. Then pull back to the meeting position. The tension created will hold the two ends tightly together.

Make a shallow hook of brass wire, with an upcurve at the end of the hook. Press the long end into the asbestos circle.

Hang the ring on the upcurve, seam downward. Flux the seam and place a square of solder on it. Next apply the hot soldering iron to the bottom of the ring at the outside of the seam. This will pull the solder through as it melts.

Both the electric soldering iron and gun need bright tips for the maximum flow of heat. When they get dull, clean off the copper tips lightly with emery cloth until the metal shows and the black oxide is gone. Coat the tip with flux, put a small piece of solder in the middle of a piece of tin plate (the inside of a clean can), turn on the heat, and when the iron is hot place it against the piece of solder, which will flow onto the point of the soldering iron.

HOW TO USE MEDIUM AND HARD SOLDER

The same basic techniques of cleaning and fitting used in soft soldering apply in medium and hard soldering. The heating element, though, is a hand-held propane or butane torch. The cylinder comes in two sizes and is sold with separate nozzle that is ideal for small jewelry making.

The solder is made in 1-inch-wide strips. These are cut with metal scissors into narrow, lengthwise strips of about 1/2 inch; then cut across to make tiny squares. Put a finger over the edge as you cut, so the squares won't spray all over – they are hard to find if they do!

Flux is also special. Medium flux comes in a bottle, but the hard flux is a cone of borax, which is rubbed in a little water until a milky liquid is achieved.

The rest of the process follows that of soft soldering, but heat is from a flame rather than from a hot metal tip. And after soldering, the metal is dropped while hot into a bowl of Sparex, which cools it quickly and cleans it.

File off any excess solder, and polish in the usual manner.

A PRIMITIVE NECK ORNAMENT

Materials

A flat piece of 18-gauge brass 4 1/8 by 5 5/8 inches and a length of 14-gauge brass wire 18 1/2 inches long are all you need for this stunning project.

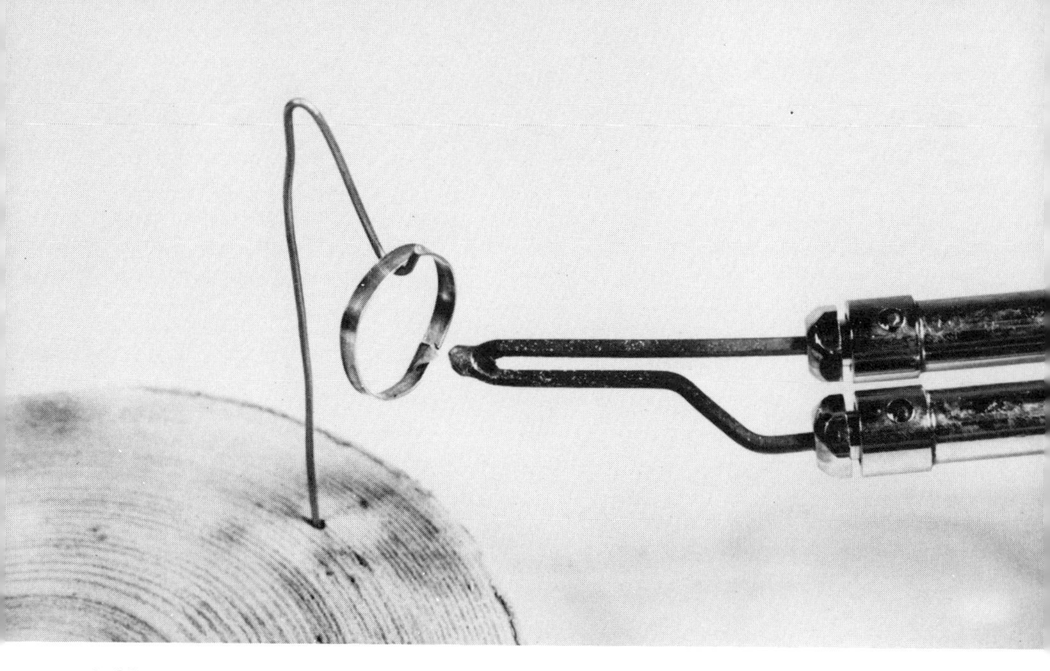

Soldering a metal loop, which is hung from a brass wire hook stuck into the asbestos circle.

Medium or hard soldering with a propane torch. Heat is being directed under *the wire mesh pad to give more even distribution and to keep the solder chips from being blown off the metal.*

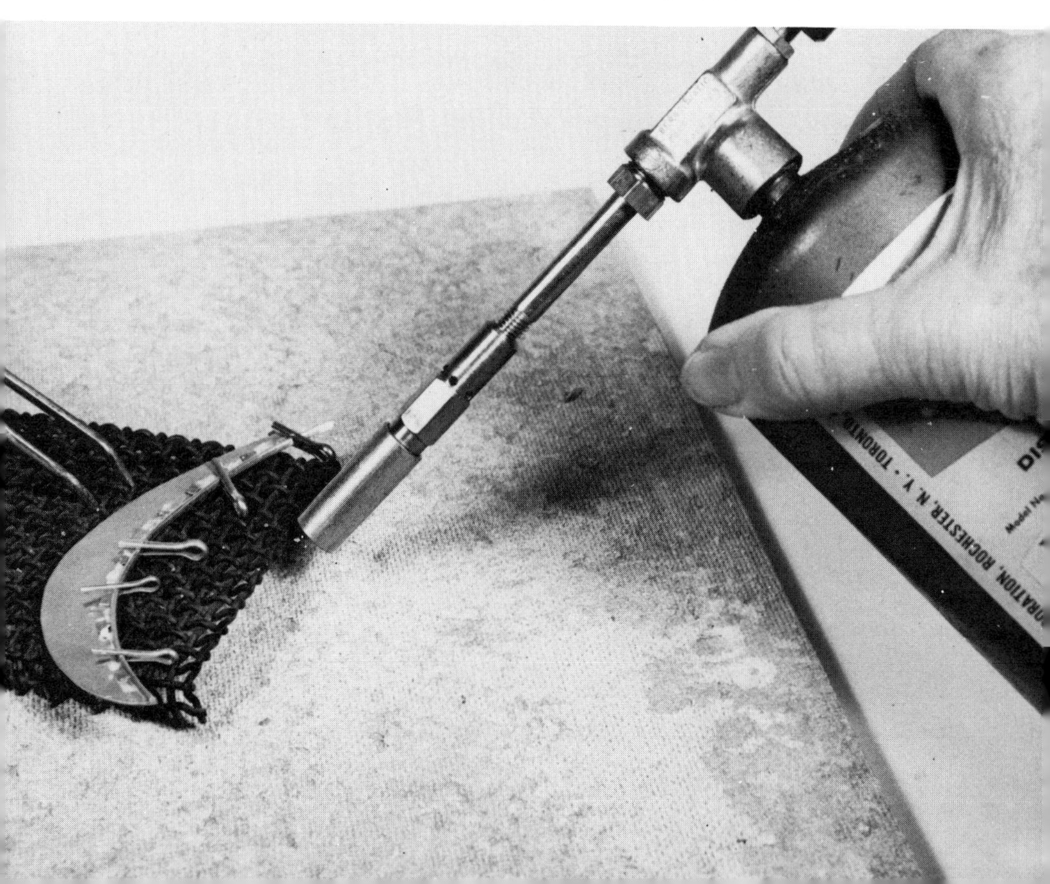

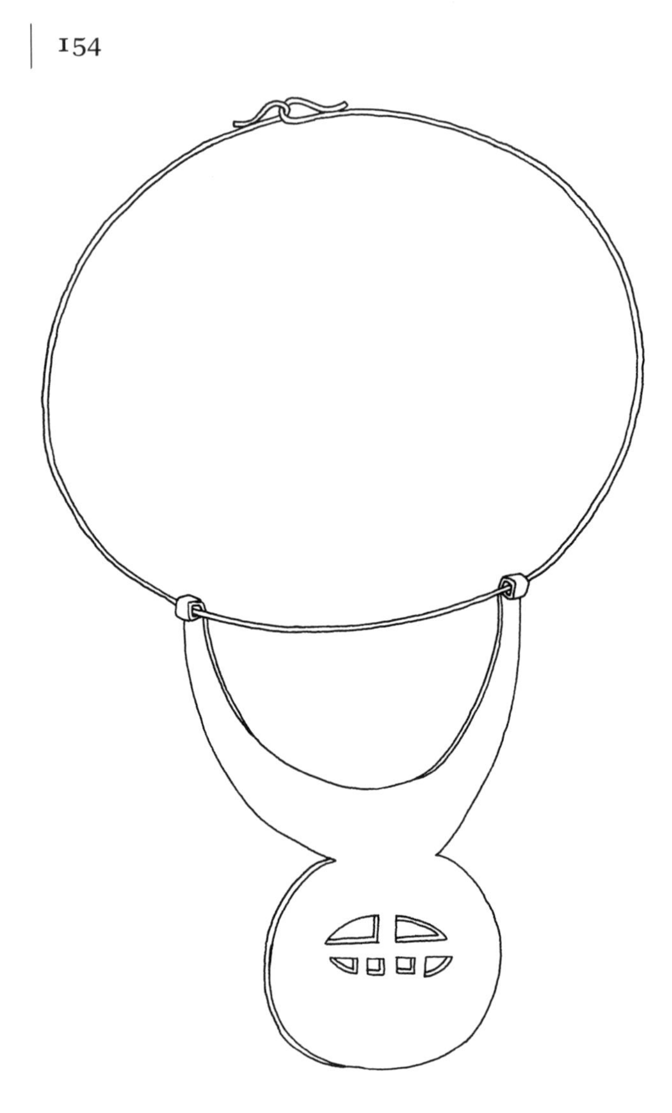

Steps

1. On a sheet of paper, mark off a 4-by-5½-inch rectangle. Enlarge the above design so that it fits into the rectangle, using a compass to make the bottom circle.
2. Using your jeweler's saw, cut a 4⅛-by-5⅝-inch rectangle from an 18-gauge, 6-by-6-inch sheet of brass (follow directions for sawing at the beginning of this chapter). This allows you an extra $1/16$ inch all around your design.
3. Put a sheet of carbon paper against the metal with the pattern on top. Trace with a hard pencil, stylus, or ball

point pen. There will be an even black outline on the brass surface. Carefully follow this black line with the metal scriber. The scratched line in the metal should be just outside the carbon lines. This gives you a margin for error in the final cutting.

4. Saw around the edge of the design, keeping a hair's breadth outside the scratched line. Be careful not to cut into your design, as later this will make extra filing for you, as you try to bring the whole outline back to the level of the nick.
5. The next step is to cut out the center design. Make a small hole with the drill in the center of one of the areas of metal which will be cut away. Poke the end of the saw blade through the hole in the metal, tighten the blade, and saw out the design. This sawing can be done a bit crudely, as it should contrast to the smooth edges of the outside cut.
6. Now, with the flat-edge file held at right angles to the outside edge of the pendant, file all around the outside, removing all irregularities left by the saw. Where the round design joins the half-moon, use the triangular end of your riffle file. File until you have achieved a smooth, straight edge all around.
7. This final filing will create a beveled edge all around the outside face of the pendant.

   Holding the flat-edge file at a 45-degree angle, and at a downward and outward slant, file an angled edge all around the design. This makes an edge that catches the light in a soft gleam, giving the effect of a thicker metal. This stroking with a file may seem to go slowly (you can do it while listening to the stereo), but there is a joy in seeing your design suddenly become jewelry instead of a piece of metal.
8. Smooth the edges of the center design by right-angled filing only. Do not bevel edges.
9. Tear off a 3-by-2-inch piece of emery cloth, and one of crocus cloth, and give the outside beveled edge a final polish, removing all traces of file marks.

   Now go over the whole piece with the crocus cloth until it is bright and shining. At first work lightly on the back, until you develop a technique that polishes without leaving streaks or gouges. Final polishing will be in circular sweeps from left to right around the circle of brass, and from left to right following the shape of the half moon. Now that you have the right feel, polish the front of the design.

10. Curl the pointed top ends of the pendant forward with the chain-nose pliers. The front of the pendant should be facing you as you do this. The points at the top should form almost complete circles of metal around the pliers.

    You now have finished the pendant; the next step will be making the neck wire.

11. The making of a neck wire is an important part of modern jewelry craft. It can be worn alone, or as a basic support for interchangeable pendants.

    First, drape a piece of string around the base of your neck, holding the pendant in place with one hand. When you are satisfied with its position, cut the string where it joins at the back of the neck. Cut a length of brass wire to match the string, but add 3/4 of an inch at each end for the two self-hooks you will make as a catch.

    Start forming and bending the wire with your fingers, with a little gentle encouragement from the chain-nose pliers. Put a piece of folded paper towel between the jaws of the pliers to prevent gouging the wire. You can also lightly hammer the wire, using a large can as a form. If the wire seems stiff, anneal it over the stove, following directions at the beginning of Chapter 5.

    Check wire against your neck often to be sure you are getting the right shape. As each person's neck is different, there can be no specific directions for length and shape.

12. Run the wire through the two loops you have made at the top of your pendant. Check against your neck to see if the length is right.

13. The next step is to make the hook closing. To form the two hooks, pound each end of wire with even strokes of your hammer, using the round-ball end. This will make two gradually sloping, tear-shaped 1/2-inch ends to the

wire circle. Shape each end into a long oval with the file.

This process of pounding will lengthen the wire a bit, so check length against the neck again, allowing 3/4 inch for the hooks. Cut away any excess with scissors if necessary, but be sure that the ends slope down to thinner metal in an oval shape. You may have to tap lightly with the hammer and refile the edges.

Place the chain-nose pliers 1/2 to 3/4 inch from the end of the wire. Curl the end over gradually, so that the wire turns over toward the outside of the neck band, with the end touching the band and forming a long loop or narrow U. With the pliers, pull the tip of the hook up slightly. Repeat with the other end of the wire.

Take out any plier marks with file and crocus cloth.

14. File and smooth the whole length of the wire circle, removing any nicks or gouges.
15. The final step is to lacquer the pendant and neck band with clear nail polish to prevent tarnishing of the metal. First cover the back, working swiftly and with sweeping strokes. Let the pendant lie on a flat surface while it dries, so that no ripples will form in the polish. Also be sure that no polish slips over the edges onto the front. When dry, turn over and do the front. Let dry. Cover the wire with polish, and dry.

    The necklace is ready for you to wear—and collect the compliments!

THE METAL-HAND PENDANT

Materials

An oblong of 18-gauge pewter, silver, or brass, 2 1/2 by 3 1/2 inches; a 4-inch length of wire.

Steps

1. Measure an oblong of metal 2 1/2 by 3 1/2 inches. Cut out with the jeweler's saw, and file edges smooth with the flat-sided file. Then angle-file the edges to give the metal a thicker effect.

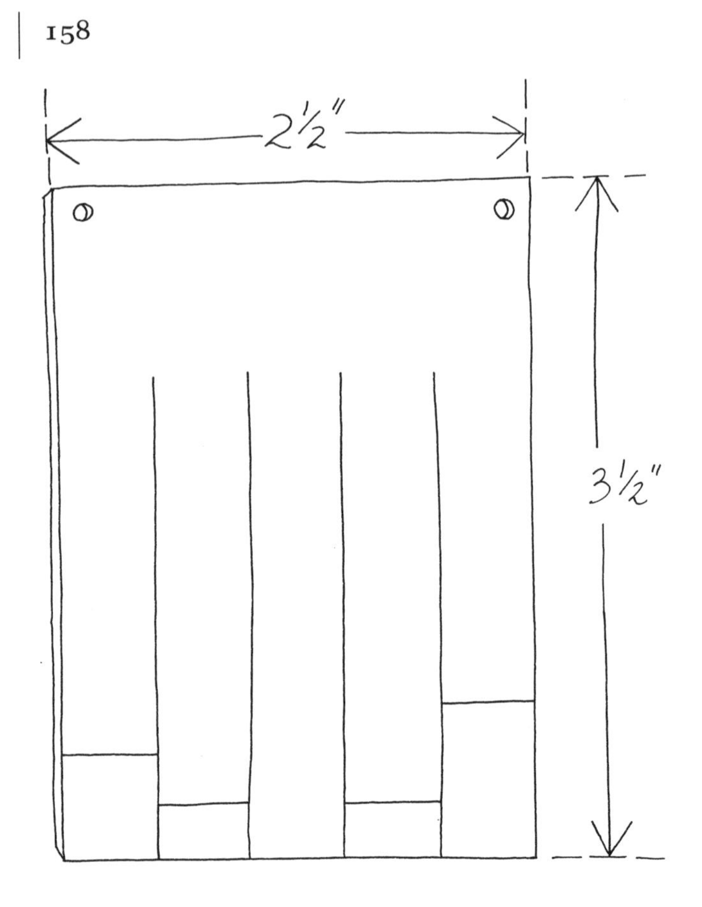

2. With the ruler and scriber, mark off the narrower 2½-inch width into five sections, each one ½ inch wide. *But* only draw the lines to within 1 inch of what will be the top edge of the pendant.
3. With your saw, cut along the four scribed lines, starting at the bottom and cutting up to the 1-inch mark. Follow directions for sawing given at the beginning of this chapter.
4. Starting at the left side of the metal—the little finger side—draw a horizontal line across one finger with the ruler and scriber, ½ inch from the bottom edge. Cut off this piece of metal with the saw.

   Next finger, measure off ¼ inch from the bottom edge, and saw off this piece.

   The middle finger is left the full length.

   The index finger has ¼ inch cut from the bottom edge.

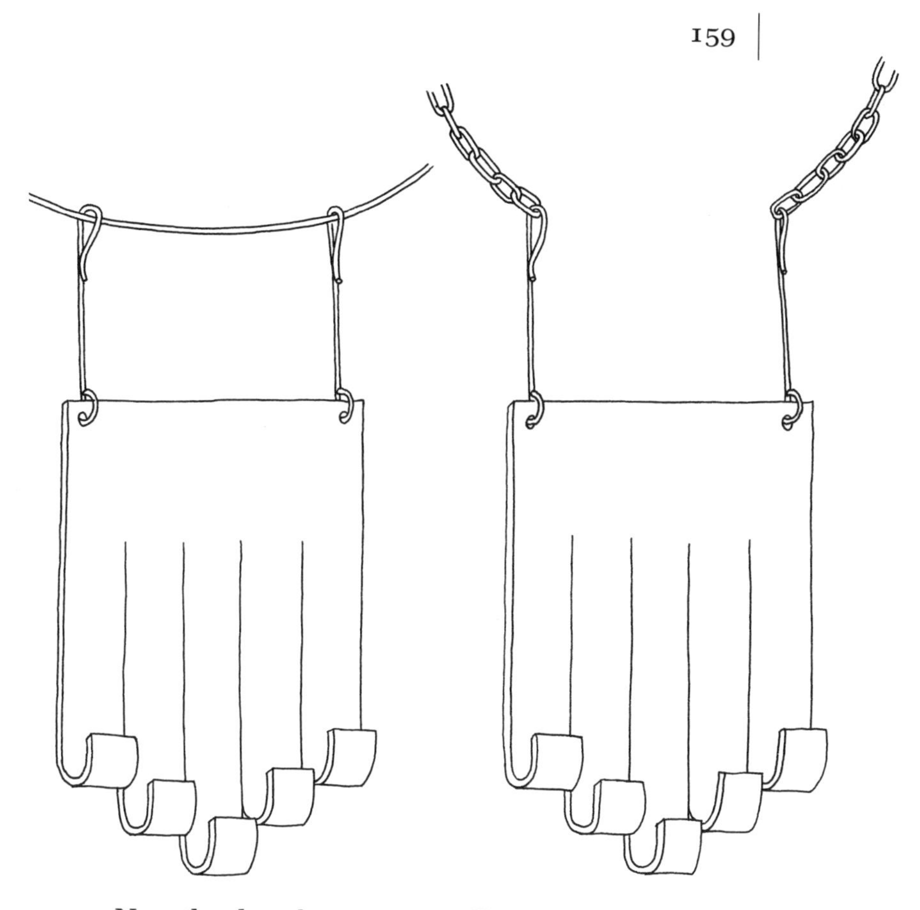

Now the thumb—measure off 3/4 inch from the bottom edge, and cut away.

5. Now smooth all the edges with the file, taking out the saw cutting marks. Angle-file the edges. Go over the flat surfaces with crocus cloth.
6. Using the chain-nose pliers, curve the ends of each finger forward in a shallow curve, like an open half circle.
7. To hang the pendant from a chain or neck wire, drill two holes, one in each upper corner.

   Make two hooks of 2-inch-long wire in the shape of a figure 8, the reverse circles at each end formed by the chain-nose pliers. Or make a hook at one end, so pendant can be removed.

   Loop one end of each figure 8 into the top holes. The other end will be fastened into the last link of a chain of the length most comfortable for you to wear, or slipped over a neck wire.

8. Before putting the pendant on the chain, cover all surfaces with clear nail polish. Let each side dry in a flat position.

Variation

Two miniature hands, strung up with two pieces of wire that come together in a triangle and then are twisted together, are hung by jump rings from earring backs to form dangling earrings.

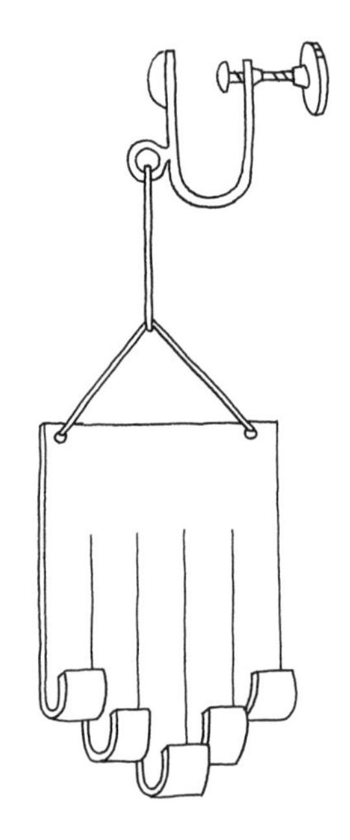

OPEN-ENDED BRACELET

Materials

A strip of 18-gauge pewter or silver, 3/4 inch wide and up to 7 3/8 inches long. Length depends on the thickness of your arm, and the position on the forearm where you like to wear a bracelet.

6 3/4"

Steps

1. Cut a strip of paper 3/4 inches wide and 8 inches long. Wrap it around one arm to measure, holding one end on your skin with tape so it will not slip. The ends should be 3/8 inch apart. Cut paper to proper length. Finish each end in a half circle.

   There are six rectangular cutouts in the pattern. For a bracelet 6 3/4 inches long, the first rectangle begins 11/16 in from the end. It is 11/16 inches long and 1/4 inch wide. The spaces between each cutout are 1/4 inch wide. For other lengths, allow for 1/2 inch between cutouts and space cutouts evenly across bracelet.
2. Place a piece of carbon paper between the bracelet pattern and the strip of metal. Trace the outlines of the rectangles on the metal. Use the ruler as a straight edge, so that the shapes will be even in outline.
3. Remove carbon paper and pattern. Go over the lines with the metal scriber, again using the ruler as a straight edge. Wash off black marks with rubbing alcohol.
4. With the saw, cut out the bracelet shape, following just outside the outline to allow for the final filing (see directions for sawing at the beginning of this chapter).
5. Take the hand drill, and make a hole in the corner of each rectangle, far enough in from the scribed outline so as not to make a nick in it.

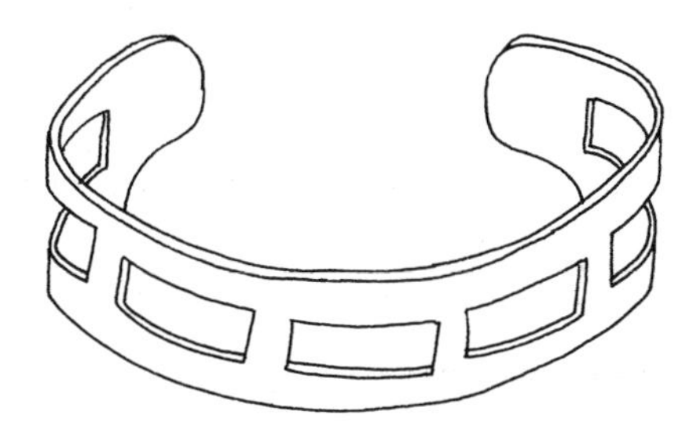

6. Thread the saw blade through the first hole and tighten screw. Saw around the rectangle, keeping inside the scribed line to allow for filing edges smooth. Keep the "waste" rectangles as they will be used in other pieces of jewelry.
7. File all edges smooth, so that no saw marks are seen. Smooth the surface of the bracelet with fine crocus cloth.

Variations

1. This design can be adapted to a finger ring, which is about ½ inch wide, and the length depends on your fingers. Both ends should just touch. The size and number of the rectangles is a choice you will make, as this depends on the length of the metal. Form the ring around a tapered-stone knife sharpener that can be bought in variety or houseware stores. Mark off the area that is the same size as your finger, and tap the metal lightly into a circle, using the hammer.
2. This type of wrap-around bracelet can be used as the base for enamel work, or stone setting.
3. Another design, also an open-ended bracelet, can be made with the opening in the front, and the ends curved around so one end swirls up the arm, the other down.

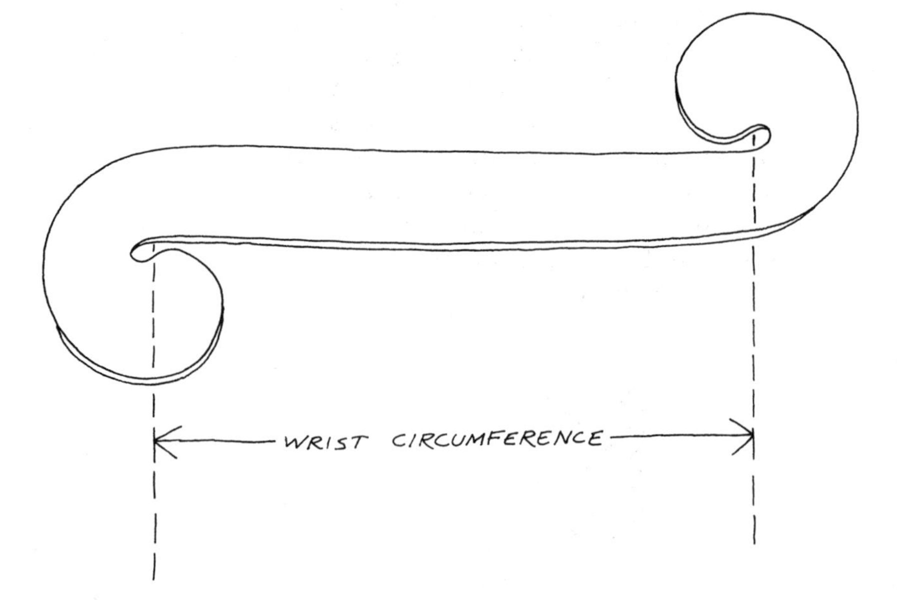

You will need a piece of pewter approximately 7 by 4¾ inches. Make a paper pattern first and try it around your arm, holding it in place with sticky tape. If it fits, transfer the outline to metal. If not, make the necessary adjustments, and then trace.

Cut out the design with the saw. File and bevel all edges, and polish metal with crocus cloth. Bend and finish following directions at the beginning of this project.

A BRASS-RING NECKLACE

Materials

For this necklace you will buy a 6-inch remnant of brass tubing, 1½ inches in diameter, at a hardware store or a plumbers' supply shop. This is the tubing used in water lines in homes, and this length will be enough to make the necklace. This tubing is also used for other designs that use brass rings. You'll also need a piece of 14- or 16-gauge brass wire, 18 inches long.

Steps

1. Clean the 6-inch section of brass tubing with a powdered household cleanser. Dry, and rub lightly with fine crocus cloth until all surface marks and discolorations are gone and the metal shines like gold. Reach as far inside the tube as you can with the cleanser and the crocus cloth. You may have to continue to clean the inside as you cut the slices of metal.
2. This is your first experimental cut, to get the feel of sawing a slice from a round metal tube. If it turns out well, it is your first ring for the necklace.

   Be sure the outside edge is even with no jagged cuts. If necessary, file the edge smooth with the flat file.

   Now, with the scriber, make a mark ⅛ inch in from the edge. All around the circle make about ten such marks, as guides for this first cut.
3. Hold the tube steady, with one hand over the top. You may find that a pot holder under the tube will keep it from rolling. The end to be cut should project about ½ inch over the edge of the V-board. Watching the scribed

marks carefully, turn the tube slowly toward you as you saw off a 1/8-inch slice of metal.

Try to keep the width even, but if there is a variation, don't worry—a change in width will give the necklace its handcrafted look. It is only machine-stamped objects that are even—piece after piece after piece.

4. Check the cut ring and decide whether you want the rest to be thinner or thicker. Mark the tube accordingly and proceed to cut the metal rings. You will probably need thirteen or fifteen circles for a long necklace. The uneven number means that one circle will be in the center front.
5. When all rings are cut, file the rough edges with either the curved or flat side of the file, whichever is easiest for you. Finish with crocus cloth for a smooth surface. Put aside until you make the wire links.
6. You will first need to anneal the wire for easier bending, by heating about 6 inches at a time to a dull red over the gas flame. Hold with the heat-proof tweezers. Immediately plunge the hot end into a deep pot of cold water. (For annealing process, see the beginning of Chapter 5.)
7. To make the links between the circles, measure off 1 inch of wire at the softened end. Also make a center mark at 1/2 inch.

   Take the chain-nose pliers and gently curve the end of the wire into a circle with the end not quite touching the 1/2-inch mark. Now cut the wire at your 1-inch marker, using clippers or saw. File the cut edge smooth.

   Holding the curved end firmly between thumb and index finger, repeat the curved-end process on the other end. But curve this end in the opposite direction, forming a figure 8. Make thirteen or fifteen figure 8s. You will have to anneal the end of the wire again after you make the first six cuts.

   File away the marks left by the pliers. Polish wire with crocus cloth.
8. The next step is to make the hook catch.

   Again, anneal 2 inches at the end of the wire. Lay this end on the metal strip (top of the C-clamp) of your V-board. Tap the very end with the rounded end of the hammer. Do this lightly at first, then harder, thinning out and lengthening about 1/2 inch of metal. It should be broad at the end and taper back into the round wire.

With a file smooth the metal a bit, but do not remove all the hammer marks—you will want to keep this crafted look.

Smooth the edges into a gradual rounded curve. Measure off 1/2 inch, and place the nose of your pliers there. Slowly curve the metal over into a long hook, until it almost touches the round wire. Then, with the pliers, curve the end up a bit. From the tip of the hook, measure 1/2 inch back on the straight shank of your length of wire and cut. File cut end, and bend into a circle that matches the circle of the figure-8 links.

9. Now put it all together. Slip the center ring into a circle at the end of a figure 8. You may need to open the circle a bit with the pliers. After the ring is in place, close the circle, so that the end of the wire is touching the 1/2-inch mark. Attach another figure 8 to the other side of the center ring.

   Now alternate rings and figure 8s until your necklace is the length you want it. End up with a figure 8 on one side, the hook catch on the other, fastened to that side's last figure 8.

   Check all parts for any areas that need touching up with file or crocus cloth.

10. Suspend necklace by its hook from a thin wire or thread

in some free-standing area. Go over *all* the metal with clear nail polish, starting at the top. Let dry well—4 to 6 hours. This clear covering prevents the metal from tarnishing.

Variations

1. The links can be longer lengths of wire, 2 inches, with small loops on each end, so that the effect of the necklace is one of rings and straight wires. In this case make fewer rings and wires.
2. Make two figure 8s and two rings to hang as earrings.
3. Make four or five rings and figure 8s and link together as a bracelet, using a spring ring and jump ring for a closing.

A RING PENDANT

Materials

For this pendant you will also need brass tubing, and about 2 inches of 18-gauge brass wire.

Steps

1. To begin this design, follow steps 1 through 5 of the preceding project, cutting five rings from the brass tube.
2. Make a solution of Sparex, to have ready for an "after-soldering" bath for the pendant.
3. Now that you have cut the five rings from the brass tube, you can assemble them.

   First file a flat spot on opposite sides of four rings. These will be their joining areas, and the filing makes for better soldering.

   Next wipe off the rings with powdered kitchen cleanser. Rinse in clear water to check for grease. If the metal is completely covered with a thin film of water and no "dry" (i.e., greasy) spots remain, the metal is clean. Dry and wipe with rubbing alcohol. Try not to touch the soldering areas with your fingers from now on.

   Put all four circles in position on the asbestos ring.

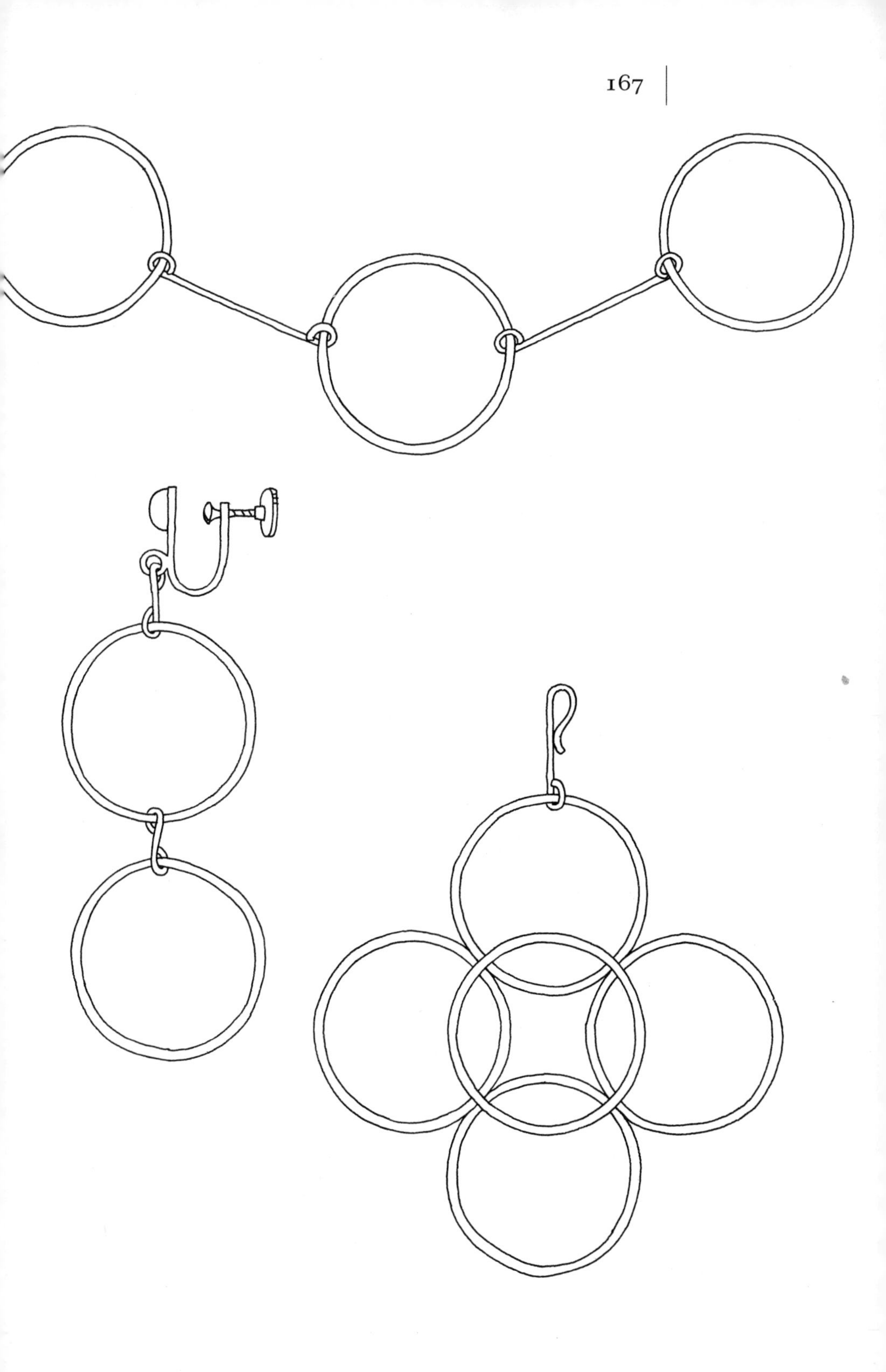

Two by two, they form a square. Reserve the fifth ring, which will lie in the center on top of the other rings, for the second soldering process.

4. With the tweezers, move the rings apart slightly, and paint the soldering areas with liquid flux. Push them back together. Brace the circles in position with small brass nails, using eight nails around the outside. Tap or push these lightly into the asbestos circle.
5. Wipe the solder with rubbing alcohol. With the scissors cut small pieces of solder, 1/16-inch square, and put one piece on top of the four joining areas of the rings.

   Place the hot soldering iron or gun on the inside of the first metal ring, near the solder but not touching it. Hold in place until the solder melts and runs down between the rings. Repeat this process on each of the other three circles. Let them cool in place.
6. Slip the piece out of the restraining nails and check all joints for the effectiveness of the soldering. If there is a weak joint, repeat the soldering process at this point.

   If all is well, check both sides and file off any excess solder. Also decide which side is the front and which the back of the pendant, choosing for the front the side that shows the least solder.
7. Wipe off the pendant with alcohol, and put back within the restraining nails, front side up, being careful not to touch the top. Place the fifth ring on top in the center, and mark the contact areas on the other four rings. Remove, and apply flux at these four points.

   Now rub off the fifth circle with powdered cleanser, wash, dry, and wipe with alcohol. Holding it with the tweezers, put flux around the bottom edge, and place this edge over the four circles, touching their fluxed areas. Hold together with fine wire or paper clips.
8. Now cut four pieces of solder. Balance these inside the top ring at the four joining areas. Place the hot point of the iron or gun on the joining area *outside the circle.* This will pull the solder between the two metal areas. Repeat until all four contacts are secure. Let cool. Pick up and check if any spot is not solid, and if necessary repeat the cleaning and soldering process.

9. If all areas are tightly held, put the pendant in the bowl of Sparex to soak until clean. File off any excess solder, and go over the whole piece with fine crocus cloth. Cover with clear nail polish.
10. To make the hanging loop, make a mark on the brass wire 1/2 inch from one end. Curl over using the chain-nose pliers as you did in making the figure-8 necklace links in the preceding project. Cut wire even at the 2-inch mark, file and smooth, and curl over in a circle in the *same* direction as the loop at the other end. You can also make a hook at this end. File away any marks from the pliers, and polish with crocus cloth.

Slip one of the pendant rings through a loop, and attach the other loop to the center ring of the brass-ring necklace, or to a chain or neck wire.

You now have a diamond-shaped pendant of five brass rings.

A GILDED-LILY NECKLACE

Materials

A strip of 16- or 18-gauge brass 1 1/4 by 5 3/4 inches; a piece of chain long enough to go around the base of your neck; nine oval jump rings in yellow-gold color; a piece of brass wire, 3/4 inch long.

Steps

1. First, measure the length of chain. It should rest around the base of your neck, so that the hanging lilies will form a bib-like decoration.
2. Make two tracings of the design—one to cut up as a mock-up to plan the number of lilies you will need, the other to use as a tracing pattern for the metal. You should always have an uneven number so that a single form hangs in the middle.

   One of the charms of this design is its economical use of metal, which also means simplified cutting—and a slight irregularity in the size of each lily.
3. Using carbon paper, transfer the design to the strip of

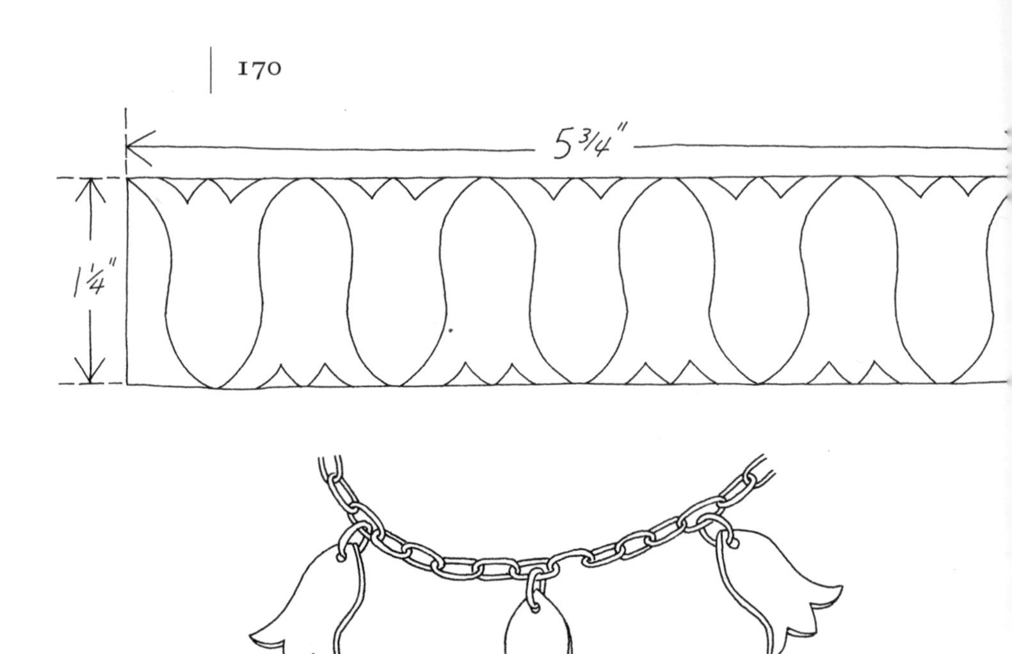

brass. Then follow the carbon line on the metal with the scriber. Clean off the line with rubbing alcohol.

4. Starting at one end, saw around the scribed outline, following directions at the beginning of this chapter. You will finish up with nine lily designs. File all edges smooth and polish with crocus cloth. With the hand drill, using a small bit, drill a hole at each rounded end.
5. This step is optional, as the lilies can be left flat. Otherwise, place each form in turn on the sandbag, and tap with the hammer, lightly at first, then more firmly. This will slightly dome each lily, giving it a contoured look. When these are hung on the chain, all the rounded sides can be on the outside, or they can be alternated, convex, concave, convex, and so on.

   The points of the lilies can also be curved out and up slightly with the chain-nose pliers.
6. Open up the nine jump rings by pulling the wire apart, sideways. Slip through the holes on the top of each lily. Hook into a loop of the chain, 1 1/4 inches apart, beginning with the center pendant. Now bring the ends of the rings together and tighten.

7. Make a hook from the 3/4-inch piece of wire (for directions see page 31). Slip the circle end through the last link of the chain. Use the last link of the other end of the chain as the catch for the hook, or add a separate jump ring.
8. Lay the chain flat and cover the lilies with clear nail polish, front and back, drying well between these two applications.

Variations

1. Instead of lilies, make a design of fish. These can also be hung on a longer chain, alternating with circles. The center fish can be larger, cut from a separate piece of metal. You can use the same or a contrasting metal.
2. The lilies or fish can also be hung from a neck wire, with the individual forms separated by 3/4-inch-long brass tubes. These are bought in fishing tackle stores as *sleeves.*
3. Wire-wrapped stones can alternate with the metal forms. The forms can be set with cabochon stones, or covered with enamel. (You'll learn about these techniques in Chapters 7 and 8.)

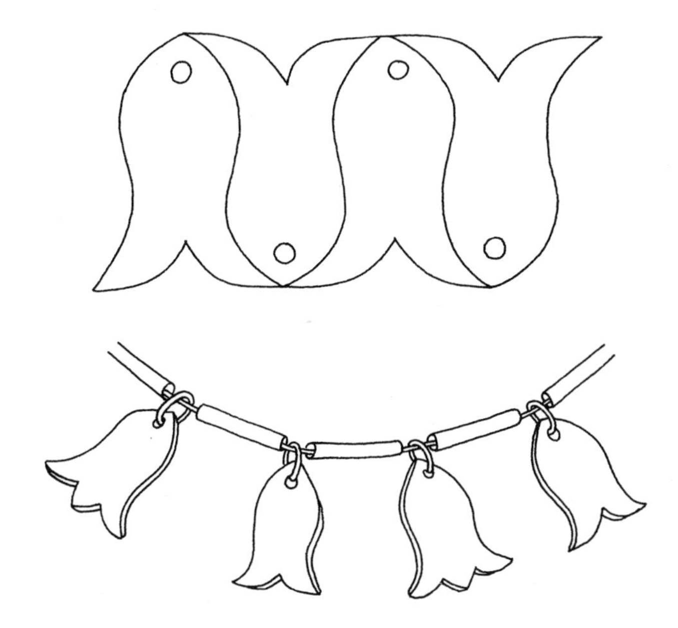

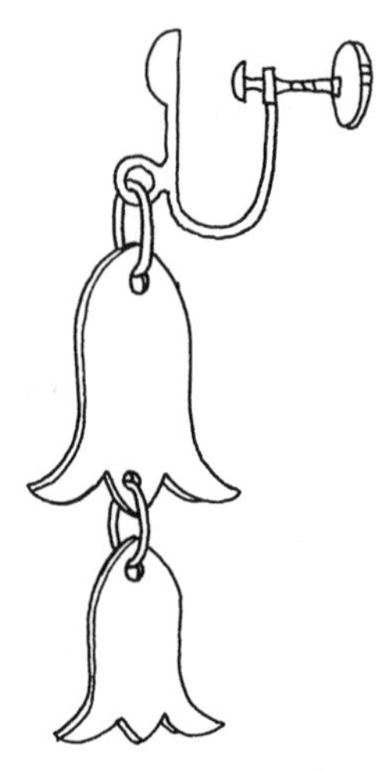

4. For earrings, cut the forms smaller than for a necklace. Cut two each of two sizes. Hang a small and a large form together—one above the other—using wire hooks and jump rings, suspended from earring backs.
5. The forms can be linked by jump rings to form a bracelet, with a spring ring and jump ring closing. Again there are many variations: head to head, and tail to tail; all forms going in the same direction; or forms side by side, linked top and bottom by jump rings.

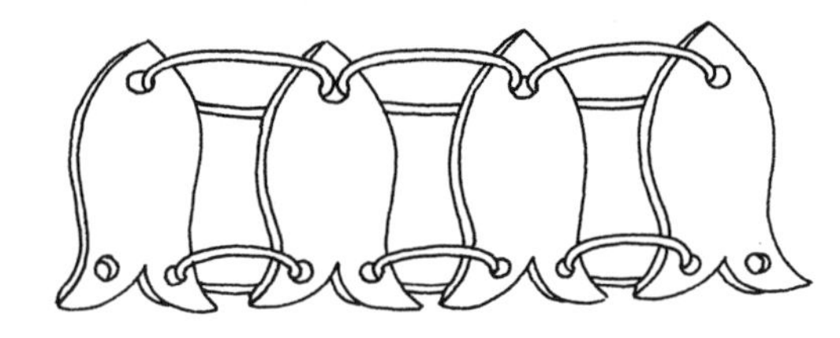

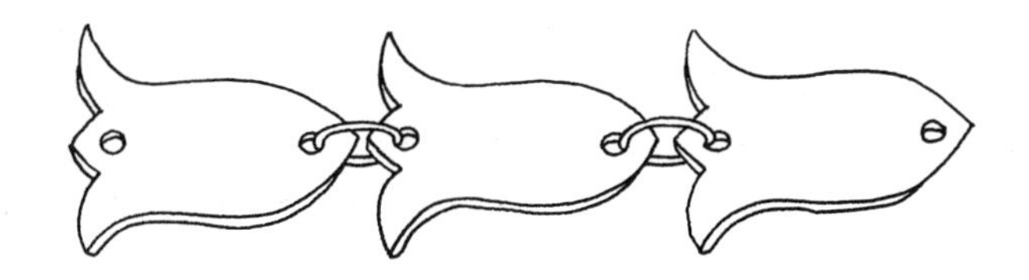

A MELON-SLICE NECKLACE

Materials

Pewter or silver wire, 16 gauge, and 21 inches long; a piece of pewter, 3¾ inches square. (You will be using either copper or silver if you are following this design for the enameling project on page 243.

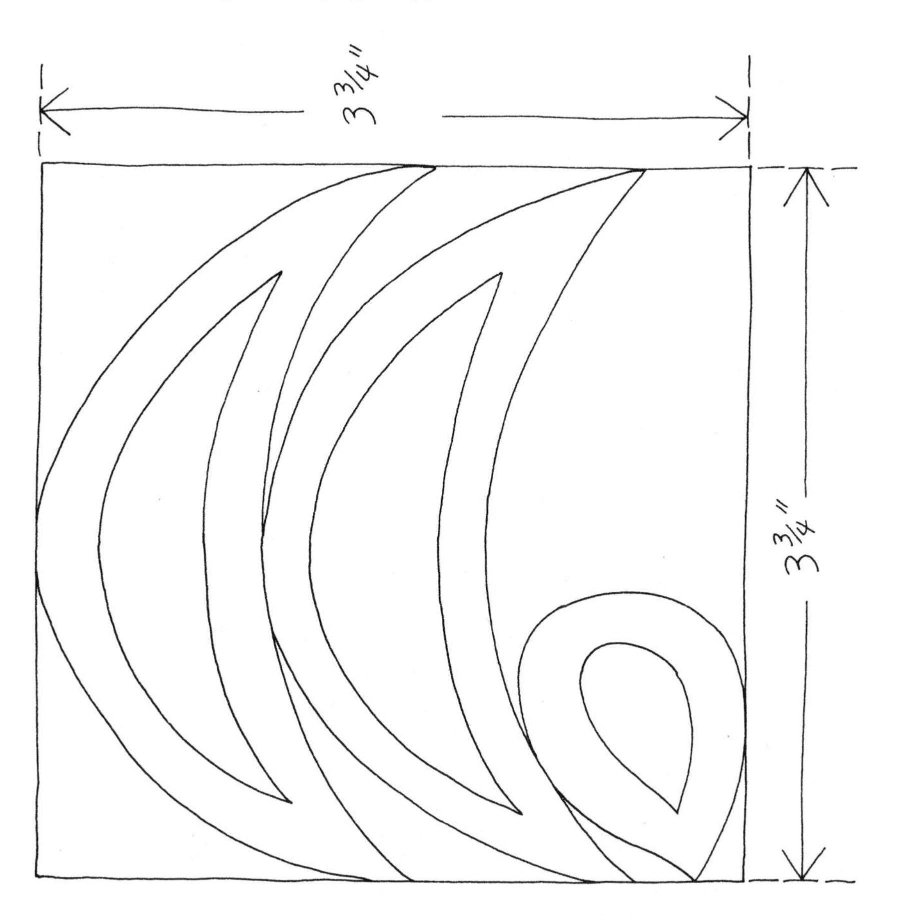

Steps

1. First cut off the two pieces of wire needed in steps 7 and 8—one piece 1 inch long, the other 1⅝ inches long. Form the rest of the wire into a U-shape, with the curved part going around the back of the neck. Alter-

nately form it with your fingers and try it around your neck. The ends will be longer than you need, but do not cut until the melon slices are finished. Put aside.

2. Make two tracings of the melon and teardrop shapes. One tracing is cut out and used as a mock-up to get the effect of the necklace before cutting the metal. If the size is right for you, use the other tracing to transfer the design to the metal. If not, adjust the pattern and make a new tracing.
3. Arrange the carbon paper and tracing over the metal, and transfer the design. After removing these papers, follow the outline on the metal with a scriber. Remove carbon line with rubbing alcohol.
4. Cut out the design with the jeweler's saw. Make a small hole with the hand drill just inside the center outline on all three shapes. Cut out this inner metal. (For instructions on sawing and drilling, see the beginning of this chapter.)
5. File all edges smooth. To give a heavier look to the metal, file the outside edges at an outward 45-degree angle, using the flat file. This gives the illusion of metal being thicker than it is, and also creates a highlight around the edge.
6. With the hand drill, cut the hanging holes at each point of the melon slices and at the top of the teardrops. Holes should be large enough for the linking wires.
7. Take the 1-inch section of wire and form it into a long narrow oval with the ends meeting in the middle of one long side. Open the ends, sideways, and slip into the holes at the center points of the melon slices. Be sure the two ends are in the back. Bring ends together and solder. Close up this link in the center by squeezing the wires together with the pliers. The link will now resemble a figure 8.
8. Next, form the 1⅝ length of wire into a hooked hanger for the teardrop. Beat ⅛ inch of one end to flatten. File into a round end, and curl up ½ inch to form a hook that curves back to the straight wire and out again.

   Grip the other end of the wire with the chain-nose pliers, and curl over into a ⅜-inch circle in the same direction as the hook. Open it up enough to slip over the center of the figure 8 holding the two melon slices. Close up. The hook should be facing outward. Now hang the teardrop on the hook.

9. For the final assembly you will feel that you really need three hands! But with patience two will do. Hold the melon slices in front at the base of your neck. Hang the wire around your neck, and measure off the spot at which the wire is to be cut on each side. Allow an additional 1/2 inch on each side for the two hooks.

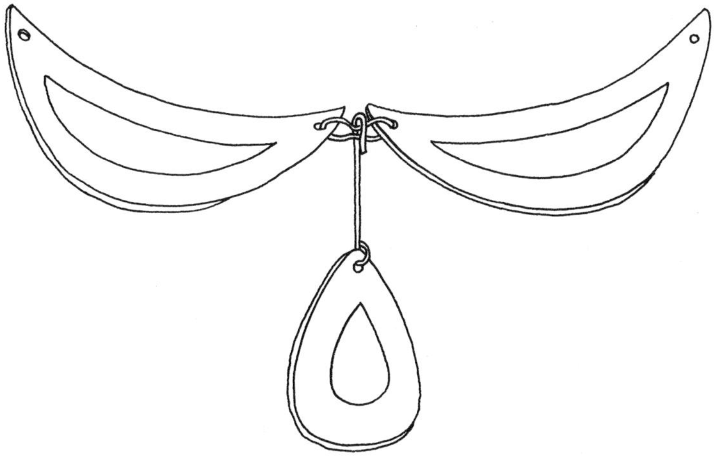

Follow instructions in step 8 for making the hooks.

Slip one hook into the upper hole of one melon slice and put necklace on. Hook other side. If the length is right, unhook one side and take off.

10. Put melon slices flat and cover the back with clear nail polish. Let dry for several hours undisturbed. Turn over and do the front. Hang neck wire by a fine wire, and cover with clear polish. When everything is dry and hard, put back together and wear.

Variations

1. You can make other pendant shapes to hang on the hook. These can be plain metal, metal covered with an enameled design, or set with stones.

2. Instead of melon shapes, use rectangles, curved top and bottom. For a further variation, cut the center waste pieces into four pieces each, and use thin wire to hang them from holes along the bottom edges of the rectangles. The center pendant can be a long, narrow rectangle.
3. In this variation, the neckpieces are long, pointed ovals. Use the same pendant pattern as for the melon-slice version, but hang the center cut from the pendant to get a double-pendant effect. And take the cuts from the neckpiece to make dangling earrings.

The variations are infinite—it's all up to you.

THREE-FISH PENDANT

Materials

A flat piece of 18-gauge metal, brass, pewter, or silver, 1 inch by 3⅛ inches.

Steps

1. This design is unusual in its very economical use of metal, and might be one to try in silver. Make a paper pattern by tracing over the one shown, which is to exact scale. As you see, the three fish fit into one another on the metal.
2. Stick a piece of tape across the top edge of the pattern, with half the tape strip lying above the edge. Attach a second strip of tape to the back top edge of the metal in the same manner. Put the piece of tracing paper over the metal, sticking the two pieces of tape together. Slip the carbon paper between the metal and the tracing paper. Transfer the design to the metal, then remove carbon paper and pattern. Go over the lines with the scriber. Wipe off black so that just the metal scratch line shows.
3. With the saw, cut out the three fish and the straight bar. (For directions on sawing, see the beginning of this chapter.)

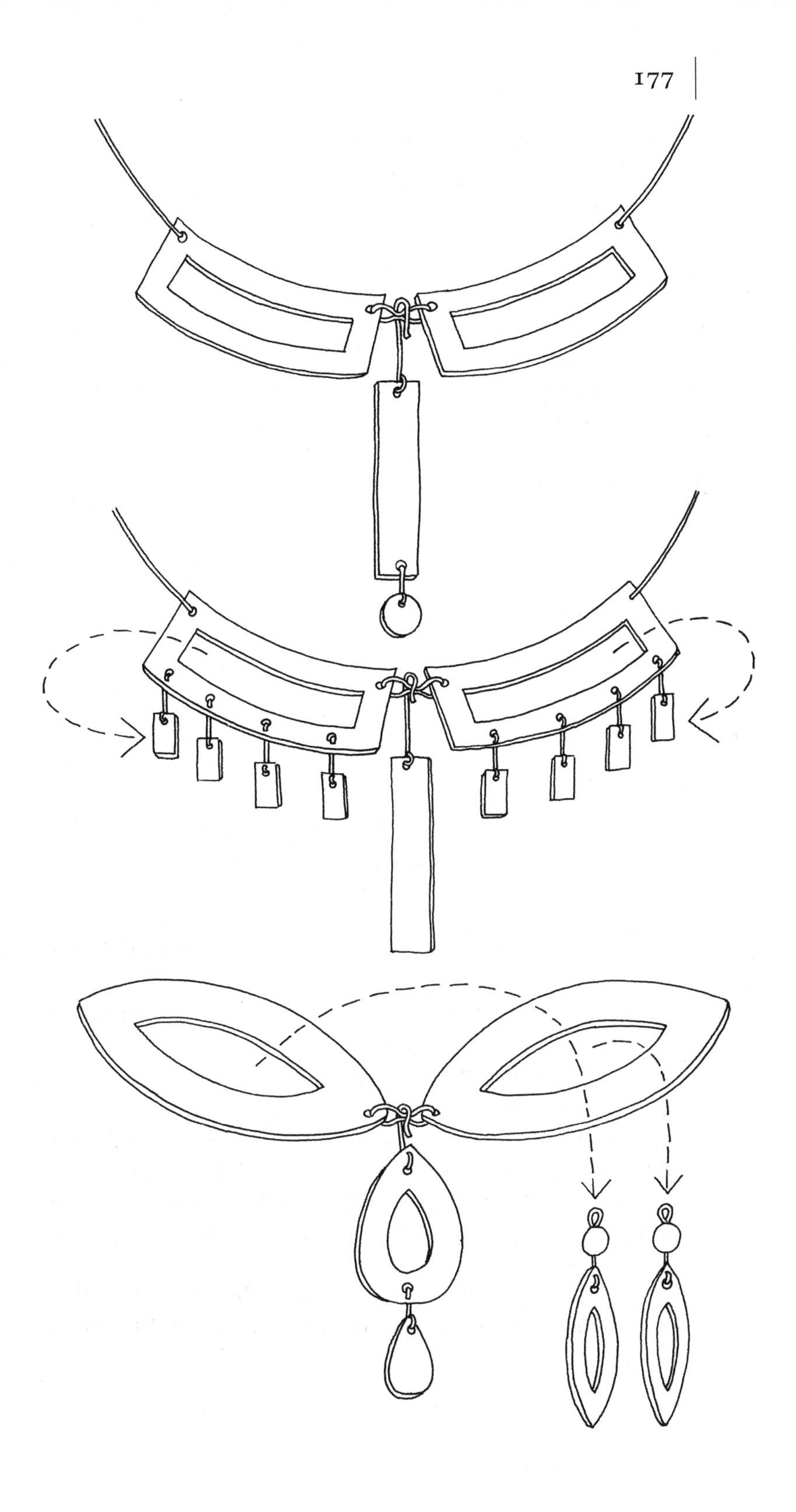

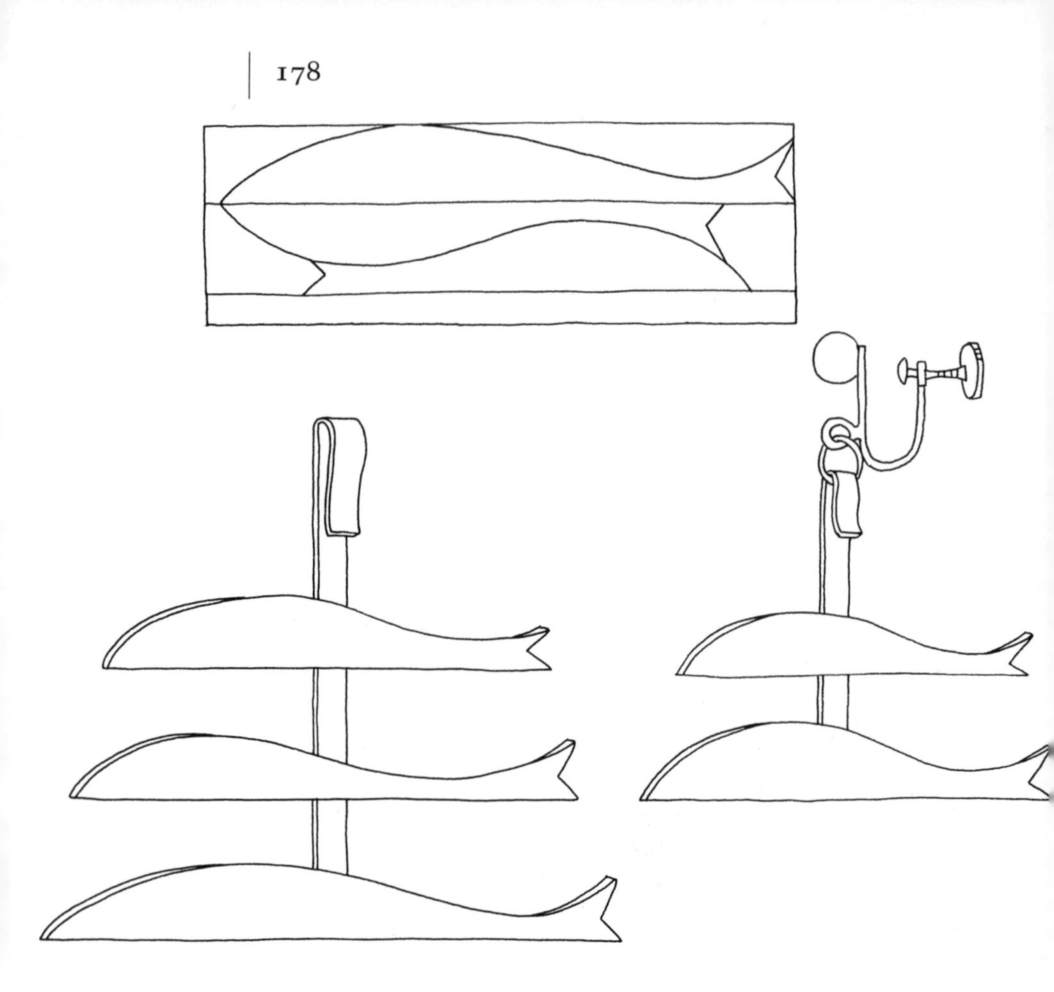

4. File all the edges smooth, and polish the flat surfaces with crocus cloth.
5. Put in the eyes with the hand drill, using the smallest bit. Or you can just make an indentation with a small nail, hitting a sharp blow with the hammer.
6. To make the hanging hook for the pendant, place the end of the chain-nose pliers on the narrow strip at a point 1/2 inch from the end. Slowly curl down the metal until the 1/2 inch is parallel with the rest of the strip and the bend is rounded. Curve up the end a bit, close to the bar.

   With the file, round the corners of the hook, and also remove any marks left by the pliers. Polish with crocus cloth.

7. Measure off the middle of each fish. At this point make a fine vertical line on the back of the fish.

   Clean off the fish and the hook with kitchen cleanser, and test under running water.
8. Put the hooked strip on the asbestos tile, flat end nearest to you. Paint 3/8 inch of this end with flux. Also paint a matching strip over the center line on the back of the largest fish.

   Lay the fish across the bar in a horizontal position, fluxed strips together, the head on the left, the tail on the right. The end of the strip should align with the bottom of the fish.

   Two 1/16-inch squares of solder are placed on the strip at the curved edge of the fish. Apply heat to the fish over the center line. When the solder melts and runs between the fish and the strip, remove heat and let fish cool.

   You can hold the strip and the fish together with a paper clip while soldering.
9. Now place the middle-size fish across the strip, and add the small fish above it. Move the two fish up and down a bit until the distance between them looks right to you. They will be approximately 1/2 inch apart.

   Put a small guide mark with the scriber on the narrow strip at the bottom of each fish. Remove the fish and clean soldering areas.
10. Solder on the medium-size fish, following the directions in step 8 for the large fish. Then solder on the small fish.

    When cool, check your soldering; if all is well, file off any excess and polish your piece with crocus cloth.
11. Cover back and front of pendant with clear nail polish, allowing time for drying before turning the design over. Keep pendant in a flat position so that polish will stay smooth. If you hang it up the polish will dry in irregular scallops.

Variations

1. By adding a pin back vertically, the pendant becomes a pin.
2. Reduce the whole design proportionately, and use for

earrings, attaching the strip to earring backs by jump ring or solder.

3. A variation with a totally different look is achieved by using cross-strips rather than fish shapes. Wrap small tumbled stones with fine 24-gauge wire (see page 198). Hang by jump rings from holes drilled in the bars. Center strip should project below the bottom cross piece about 1/4 inch, and a middle stone is hung from it. This means five stones along the bottom, four on the middle bar, and two on the top bar. Stones can be all the same color or each row a different color.

GO-FLY-A-KITE PIN

Materials

A length of 14-gauge square wire, 10 3/4 inches long, plus 2 inches of round 18-gauge wire; seven or eight colored beads, approximately 3/16 inch in diameter.

Steps

1. The square wire is cut into seven pieces to form the kite shape. As a fraction of metal is lost each time you saw, it is best to measure each section *after* sawing off a piece.

   Saw the wire for the first four pieces—that is, the

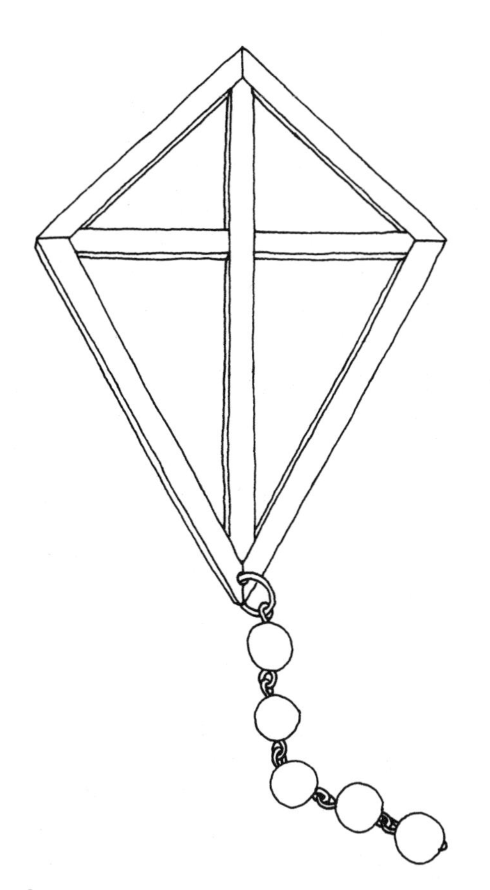

outline of your kite. For the upper half of the diamond, cut two $1\frac{1}{4}$-inch lengths; for the lower half of the diamond, cut two 2-inch lengths.

The center spine is $2\frac{3}{8}$ inches long, and the two horizontal crosspieces are $\frac{7}{8}$ inch each. However, do *not* cut the crosspieces or center spine until after the outline sections have been soldered together.

2. Make an exact, measured drawing of your kite on a small, soft asbestos tile. This will make the fitting and soldering of your design much easier.
3. Put one of the upper $1\frac{1}{4}$-inch pieces on the asbestos tile pattern. With the scriber mark a vertical line, starting at the top center edge; make a horizontal line across the face of the lower edge. Saw or file the metal to these lines. Repeat with the other $1\frac{1}{4}$-inch strip, so that the top edges of the two strips meet evenly in a vertical line at the top of the upper triangle.

Go through this same process with the lower 2-inch pieces. All four meeting areas are now *mitered*, coming together in straight lines.

4. Check all four pieces over your pattern, making sure they fit snugly at the four corners. File away any irregularities until each piece fits tightly against the next one. Otherwise the solder will not bind the two pieces of metal together.

   Once the fitting has been accomplished, wipe off each facing area, first with powdered cleanser, then with rubbing alcohol. Put back in position on the asbestos tile, the front side facing downward. Paint each touching edge with flux, and push the kite shape together, so all the edges are tight. Hold in position with small brass nails driven into the asbestos.

   Cut 1/6-inch squares of solder, and pick up each piece with a brush soaked with flux. Place one chip of solder over each joint. Apply heat to the metal wire near each joint, using an electric soldering iron or gun. It is better to hold the heat point at the side and bottom of the wire near the joint, as this will draw the solder downward. As soon as the solder melts, remove the heat source.

   Let the piece cool. Check to make sure that all the joints are secure, and resolder any that are not. This often happens!
5. To form the center spine, hold the kite in position over the remaining piece of uncut wire. Make a triangular mark with the scriber at the top and at the bottom of the wire, following the *inner* outline of each end of the kite shape. Cut the wire well outside this line with a saw, because your scribed mark is well inside the actual measurement. It is better to file away extra metal, as you cannot add to it!
6. Solder on the center section, following directions in step 4.
7. The two horizontal crosspieces are next. Again mark the triangular points and file to fit. The inside ends are straight, since they are against the center spine. Mark, cut with a saw, and file even. Solder the pieces onto the frame and the center spine.

8. To make the tail of the kite, flatten with the hammer a little bit more than 1/16 inch at one end of the 2-inch piece of round wire.

   Clean and paint with flux. Clean and paint the underside of the bottom point of the kite with flux, and put the flattened end of the round wire in position. You can hold the two pieces together with a paper clip. Support the free end of the round wire with a scrap piece of square wire to keep it level.

   Add a 1/16-inch square of solder beside the flattened wire. Apply heat to the side opposite the solder so as to pull the solder through the joining. Let cool before removing the paper clip.
9. Put on the pin back, placing the catch and the pin holder on the crossbar, 1 3/8 inches apart (follow soldering directions at the beginning of this chapter).
10. Go over the whole design with file and crocus cloth, taking off any excess solder, nicks, or other imperfections. Polish all over with the cloth.
11. Slip colored beads on the round wire, leaving enough at the end to curl into a circle and flatten against the last bead. Curve wire and beads into a gently curving figure S.
12. Cover all metal parts with clear nail polish and let dry.

Variations

1. Small kites can be made for earrings.
2. Instead of a pin back, a hooked wire can be soldered to the top of the kite, and the design hung as a pendant from a chain or neck wire.

A TULIP PENDANT

This is made from "waste" metal left from cutting out the three-chopper necklace in Chapter 8, page 252.

Materials

The metal left from the three choppers—or make a tracing of that part of the design and cut from a fresh piece of copper, silver, or pewter 2 by 2 1/2 inches; a length of wire

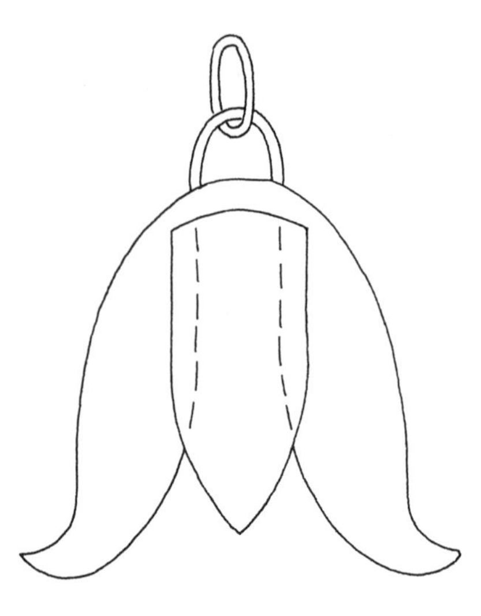

$1^3/_8$ inches long for the hanging upper loop; an oval jump ring.

Steps

1. Separate the two-petal bell shape from the original metal. Cut the third petal from one of the side pieces. File all edges smooth and bevel. Then do a final polishing with crocus cloth.
2. Clean off metal for soldering. Solder on the middle petal. (For soldering procedure, see the beginning of this chapter.)
3. Flatten ends of round wire, and form into a $^3/_8$-inch-wide U. Solder ends on top back of tulip.
4. The three points can be left flat or curled forward. Clean off all excess solder, polish with crocus cloth, and cover with clear nail polish.

A PEWTER BELT BUCKLE

This is a basic shape, and can be worn plain or embellished with semiprecious stones, enamel or copper, added metal decorations, cutout designs. As with all basic shapes, it's what you do with it that counts. And suggestions can be found in other chapters on pages 224 and 225.

Materials

In this case, pewter—but copper and brass can also be used. You will need a 3½-by-2⅛ piece of 16-gauge metal.

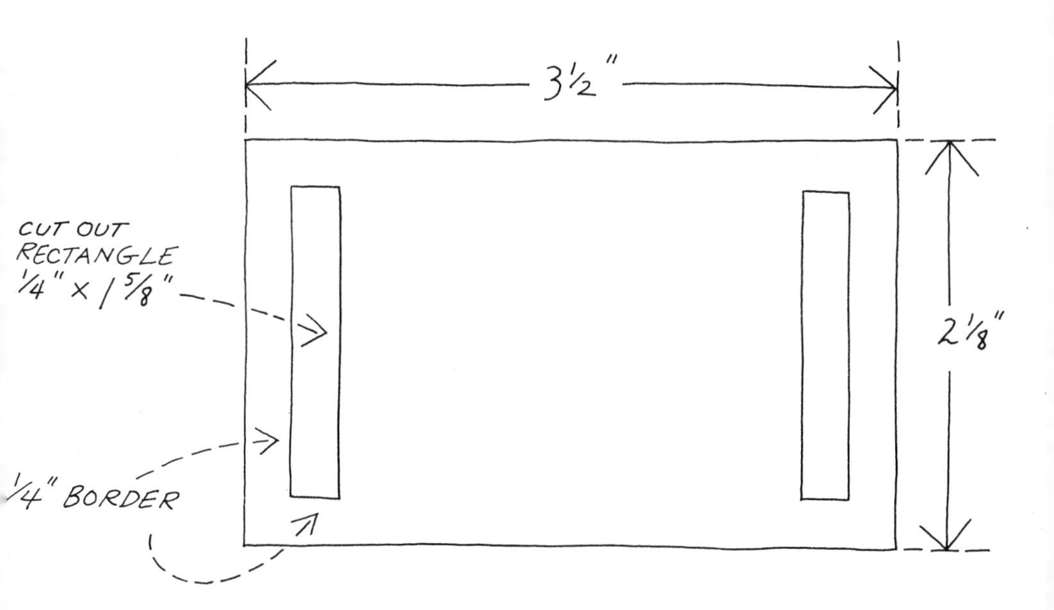

Steps

1. Trace the pattern and transfer to the metal with carbon paper. Then remove the paper, scribe the line, and wipe off the carbon with rubbing alcohol.
2. Saw out a rectangle at each end, ¼-by-1⅝-inch. Leave a ¼-inch border of metal along the outside edge. File off saw marks, and bevel edges. Polish with crocus cloth. Cover with clear nail polish.
3. Attach belt material by looping it through one end slot and sewing one side down permanently. Add hooks and eyes to the other end as a closing, also looping this end through the slot.

Variations

1. An open design can be cut in the center. Saw out four triangles to make an interior design of a metal X. This X can be left plain or decorated with four brass lilies or fish soldered onto the crosspieces.
2. The design can be varied by using 14-gauge metal—brass is best.

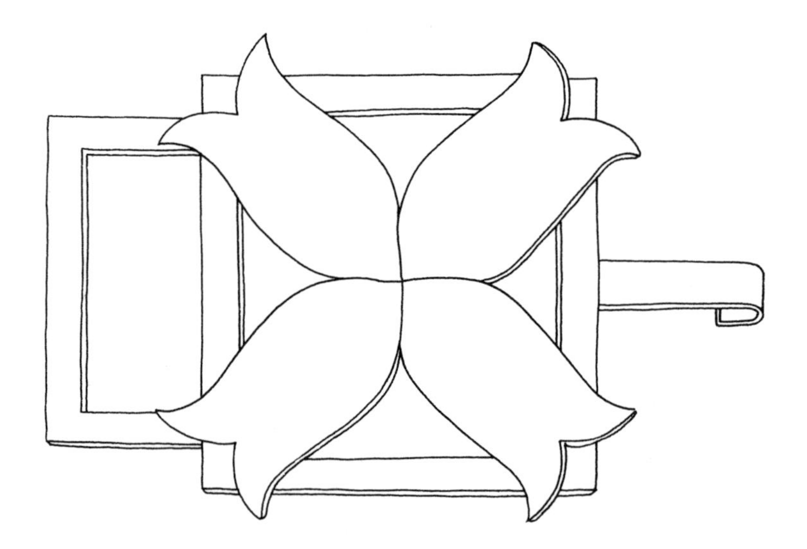

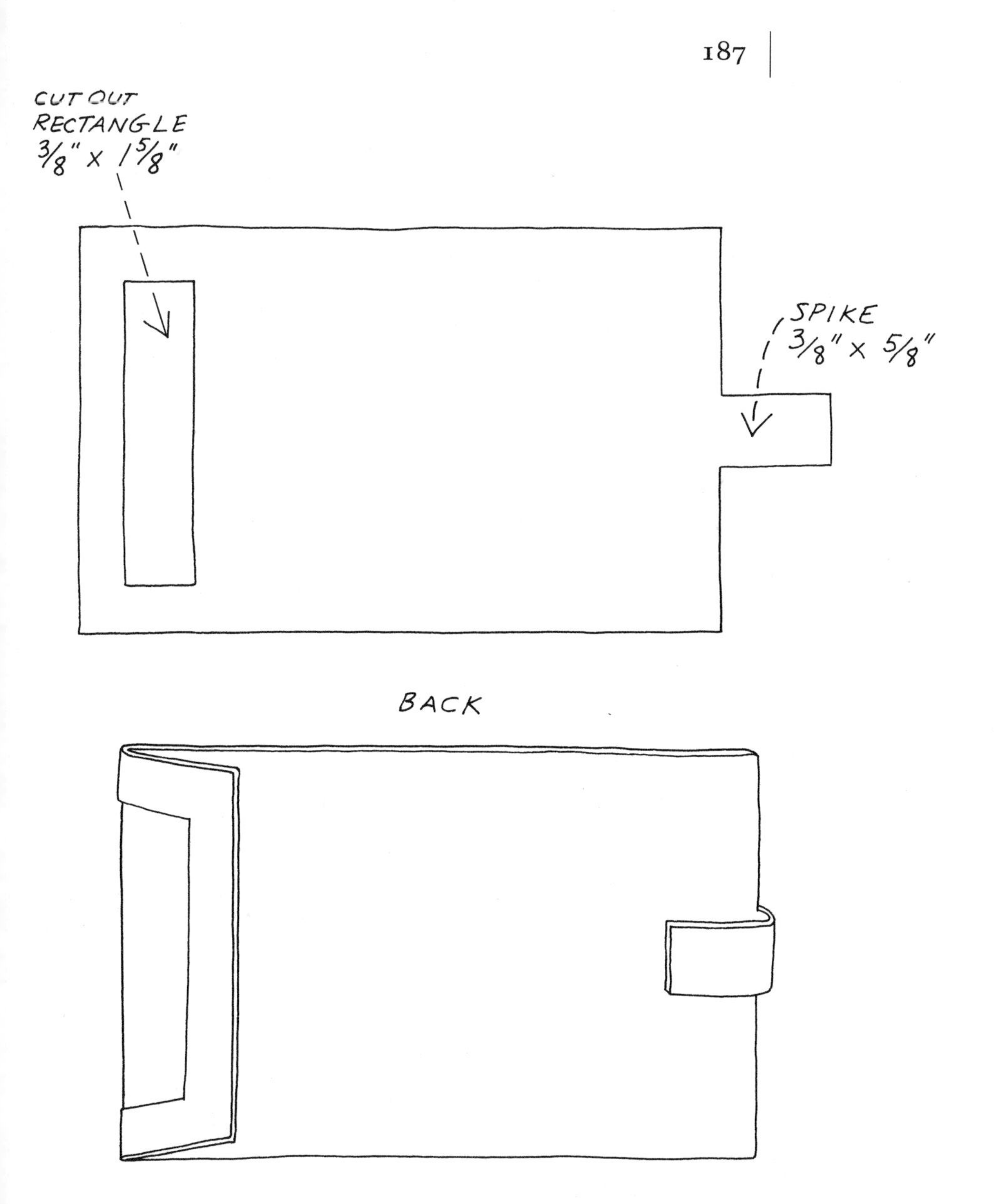

3. Cut a wider rectangular opening 3/8 inch wide on the left-hand side. The center section is 2 3/8 inches long, but instead of another rectangular opening on the right, cut a narrow spike 3/8 inches wide and 5/8 inches long, projecting out horizontally from the middle of the center section.

File edges and bevel. Then bend over the rectangle slowly until it is at right angles to the front. File a rounded end to the spike. Now turn back the spike in a slow U-curve until it parallels the back of the buckle.

A leather belt is snapped over the turned-down rectangle. The spike is slipped into an oblong hole in your leather belt. The free end of the belt is also strung through the rectangular opening.

A BRASS WATERFALL

This pendant design is a combination of brass wire and silver or pewter rectangles left over from the open-ended bracelet on page 160.

Materials

You will need: 17 inches of 16-gauge brass wire; a 2¼-inch strip of 20-gauge brass, ¼ inch wide; the cutout "waste" rectangles (or rectangles cut especially for this project).

Steps

1. For the waterfall part, cut the wire into three pieces—4½ inches, 6 inches, and 6½ inches. Make three U-shapes, each one with even ends. Use spools, wooden handles of kitchen spoons, or rolling pin—whatever will make an even curve of the proper width.

   You can also make a tracing of the pattern, and put it over the soft asbestos tile or a wood block, and drive small nails into the curve, bending the wire around these guides.

   The 6½-inch length is the outside piece and is the widest curve; the next piece is the 4½-inch length; and the narrowest inside curve is the 6-inch length.
2. Flatten ⅛ inch of each end with the hammer as a soldering surface for the rectangles.
3. Cut off 3/16 inch from the ends of the two rectangles that will hang from the middle wire. File and bevel all edges smooth.

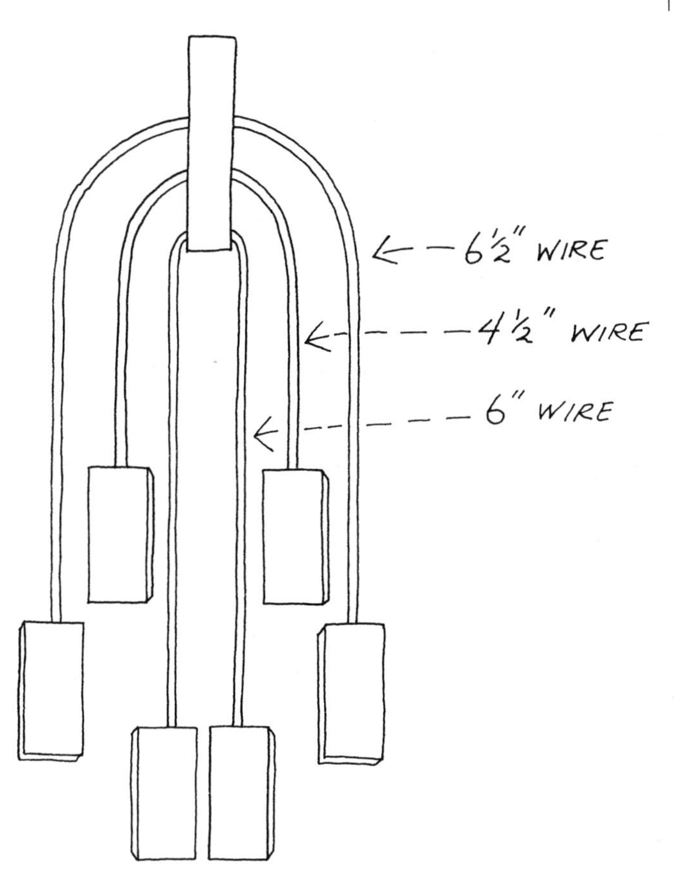

If you do not have the leftover metal, you can cut six pieces for this project. Four pieces are 1/4 by 3/4 inch, and two pieces are 1/4 by 1/2 inch.

Check the rectangles and the wires in a mock-up to be sure that when the three pieces of wire are in their final position, the rectangles will not overlap. Adjust the curve of the wires if necessary. Clean both wires and rectangles.

4. Apply flux to the wire ends and to the center of the top of each rectangle. Hold the two pieces of metal together with paper clips. Put a small square of solder beside each wire, apply heat on the opposite side of the wire until the solder melts. Solder all six pieces and let cool.
5. The strip of brass will wrap around the middle line of the

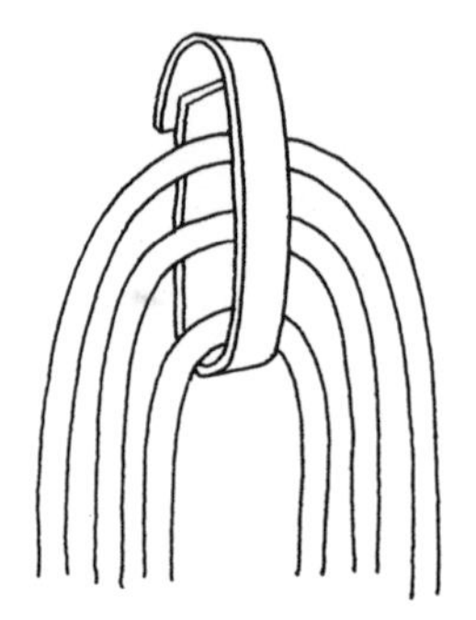

three U-shapes, back and front, holding them in position and forming the hanging loop. The wires will be soldered to the back half of the strip; the rest of the strip will be brought forward to form the front.

Put the strip flat on the working surface. Measure down 1 inch from the top end, and put the top of the innermost loop on this point and solder.

Lay the next-in-line U above the first one, being sure there is clearance between its rectangles and the wire of the center loop. There should probably be a 3/16-inch space between the top curve of the two U-wires. Solder.

Now place the last and outermost U in position, again about 3/16 inch above the middle wire, checking the clearance between the top of its rectangles and the bottom of the middle-U rectangles. Solder.

6. Curve the top of this back brass strip forward in a shallow curve. Bend the bottom of the strip up and over the wires. Before bringing it completely over, measure the length of the back strip. Transfer this measurement to your front strip, then put pliers just above this point and bend into a curve that will curl over the top of the back strip, and carry down in an overlapping effect.

   The front-facing metal should fit tightly against the wires. Cover this with a thin piece of wood or heavy cardboard, and tap lightly with the flat face of the hammer, so the blows are evenly distributed and do not mark the metal.

   Adjust the top curve so both pieces of metal fit tightly together.

Turn piece over and solder the overlapping seam.

7. Clean and polish the whole piece, finishing up with crocus cloth. Cover with clear nail polish, and let dry. Slip pendant over a neck wire or hang by two jump rings to the center of a chain.

Variation

Cut wires for a plain brass pendant, with no rectangles, in the following lengths; outside 8 inches, middle 7 inches, inside 6½ inches.

Follow the above directions for cutting and soldering. But the wires should be even at the bottom, and may need a final sawing or filing to achieve this effect after the soldering has been completed.

7. Adding Stone to Metal

THE setting of semiprecious stones into metal is just an extension of the skills you have already learned—sawing, bending, soldering, and filing. Many of the designs in the previous chapters can be decorated with a jewel set into a metal bezel or prongs.

Stones come in all colors, and are opaque and transparent, cloudy and chatoyant. They can add a quiet elegance, or color, or a touch of the barbaric to a metal design.

There is an excitement in looking through trays of stones, picking out colors or shapes, and visualizing a finished design that will grow out of the jewels you have collected.

TOOLS

All of the tools you have used to make jewelry in the previous chapters will be used in the new designs described in this chapter. Only two new tools are added for setting stones. These are:

A *burnisher*—a highly polished, curved, thick piece of steel, 2 inches long, with a wooden handle about 3½ inches long; it is used to smooth and polish the edges of the silver band, called a bezel, that surrounds a stone and holds it in place on a piece of jewelry.

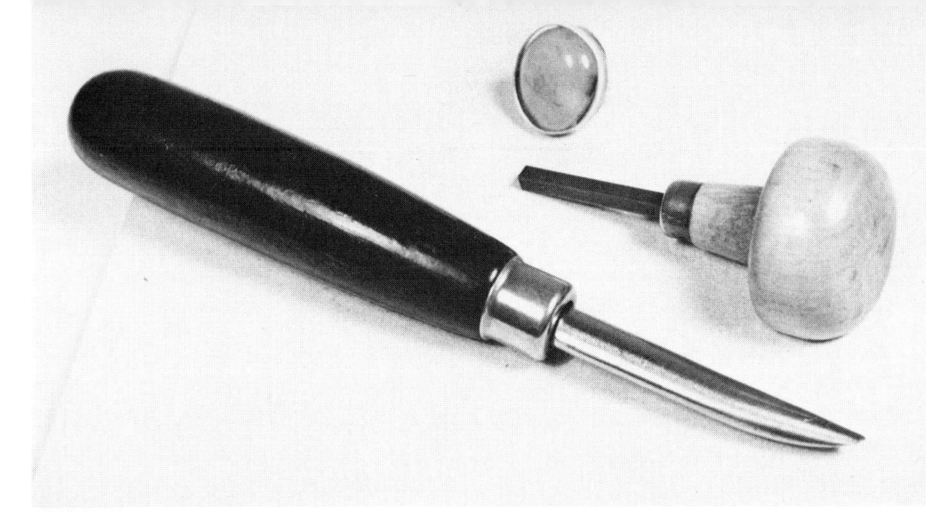

Burnisher (below), stone setter (above), and stone set inside a bezel.

A *stone setter*—a 1 1/8-inch-long, four-sided piece of steel set into a mushroom-shaped wooden handle, which is 1 1/2 inches long, with a top 1 1/4 inches in diameter; this is sometimes used as the first tool to push the supporting metal against the stone.

MATERIALS

Minerals and semiprecious stones are sold in several shapes and many varieties. The most useful and easiest to obtain are discussed in the following section.

Bezel wire and gallery wire for holding stones in position is 1/8 inch wide and 26 gauge in thickness. It is usually of fine silver rather than sterling, because fine silver is softer and can be smoothed and bent around a stone with less pressure. The wire is available plain, beaded, or patterned. Gallery wire has an added shelf in the middle to support a shallow stone. Plain 14- or 16-gauge half-round wire, which you have used in other projects, is best for prongs.

The same flat metals described in Chapter 6 are basic for the jewelry designs in this chapter. You might want to buy small pieces of 26-gauge copper, brass, or pewter to cut out your own bezel wire for setting stones when these metals are the background of your design.

Depending on which design you are following you will

need various findings—chains, catches, jump rings, bell caps, pin backs, earring backs, cuff-link backs.

VARIETIES OF SEMIPRECIOUS STONES

Polished semiprecious stones suitable for jewelry making can be bought in craft or hobby rock shops, or by mail order from many suppliers around the country. A few of these places are listed in the Supplies section at the back of this book. At hobby rock stores you can also find small mineral specimens that need no polishing and have intriguing shapes.

The most easily obtained of the clear or semiclear stones are:

Aquamarine—a clear, clear stone that ranges from almost colorless to medium blue-green—the color of a tropical sea.

Amethyst—sometimes clear, sometimes slightly cloudy, ranging from light lavender to a deep, almost black, purple.

Quartz—this mineral is found in a multitude of colors, and the descriptive names are obvious. *Clear* is just that. *Smoky* is a grayish or brownish clear color. *Rose* is a pink, slightly clear or cloudy stone. *Rutilated* is slightly yellowish clear, with fine needles of another mineral suspended in the stone.

Topaz—a warm yellow to tawny clear color.

Tourmaline—you can get a green tourmaline, or a pink tourmaline, or a combination of both, depending on what part of the crystal was cut. The colors are beautiful together.

The opaque colored stones most commonly used are:

Agate—actually a variety of quartz, there are many colors and patterns, though the spectrum remains within the browns, tans, and whites. It is a fascinating group, with wonderful names like fortification agate, moss agate, picture agate. They are worth reading about in a mineral book or a book on agates. The stones are found in many parts of the country, and if you are near one of the areas, you might go looking for them. You may find yourself into a whole new thing—rock hunting.

Bloodstone—a dark-green stone with specks of red scattered through it and showing on the polished surface. Hence the name.

Carnelian—dark red-brown, and very popular in the Victorian and Roman days when it was carved into designs for seals and signet rings.

Jade—many shades of green, some dark, some bright, some translucent, some mottled with dull white or black. Wyoming jade is inexpensive, readily available, and beautiful.

Lapis lazuli—not too easy to come by, but its deep, dark blue is worth the search. The blue is sometimes flecked with the gold of pyrite—fool's gold.

Obsidian—a glossy, black, hard material from the Southwest.

Sodalite—a lighter blue than lapis lazuli, and often mottled with off-white.

Tiger-eye—tawny colors in browns and yellow-browns in stripes of various widths. Its effect is chatoyant—the colors catch the light and glow as the stone is moved around. Even the lines seem to move. Also available in shades of blue.

Turquoise—a blue-green stone from the Southwest that is sometimes a solid color, sometimes has black lines through it. Used in Indian jewelry.

Rhodochrosite—a vivid pink of varying shades with circular lines like tree rings when the material is sliced. Tumbled stones have random patterns.

These stones are sold as separate pieces, priced according to size and variety. Prices range from twenty-five cents to three dollars or more, depending on the quality and the shape. You can also buy packets of assorted stones. This can be fun, like a grab bag—you never know what you have until you go through it.

SHAPES OF STONES

Stones used by craft jewelers are usually of two types:

Cabochon is a round or oval shape, domed on top, with a flat bottom. Cut from a flat slab of material, it is polished by holding it against a flat disk covered with a polishing compound.

Tumbled baroque (often shortened to tumbled) are random-shaped stones chipped off larger rocks, broken fragments of crystals, agates found in stream beds or on lake shores. They are put into a container with a polishing agent and water, and tumbled mechanically until all rough edges have been smoothed and the stones gleam.

In addition to these basic shapes, *assorted shapes* are also made from slabs and polished—leaves, hearts, squares, stars, masks, arrowheads, and many others.

Slices of geodes, agate, sections of rhodocrosite, petrified wood, many crystals, all with irregular outlines, are polished and ready for setting into jewelry.

Mineral specimens bought at rock shops have to be carefully chosen for size and weight, as well as suitability for a project. Many of these, such as pyrites, azurite with malachite, zoisite with ruby crystals, and many others, make exciting, chunky pendants and pins.

Faceted stones are not included in any designs in this book, as they require more intricate settings. However, the skills you have learned can be used to design and make settings for faceted stones.

SETTING A STONE WITHOUT SOLDER

Bell Caps

The simplest method of incorporating a stone into jewelry as a pendant is to use a commercially manufactured bell cap. This is just what its name implies, a bell-shaped piece of metal that fits over the pointed end of a tumbled stone like a can. The caps come in many designs and the edges are split into petals so that they can be adjusted to any size of baroque tumbled stone. Made of sterling silver, silver plate, filled gold and gold plate, the prices vary according to size, design, and metal—going from twenty cents to $2.75 a dozen.

Tumbled stones are usually irregularly long and narrow. To set them in bell caps, follow this procedure:

Fit the cap over one end of the stone with a slight pressure from a chain-nose pliers. Once it has been fitted prop-

Various shapes of stones used in jewelry making. Clockwise, starting top right and going around the outside: a mineral specimen of a combination of azurite and malachite, a tumbled quartz, a thin irregular piece of jade from Taiwan, a narrow cut of jade, three cabochons, a tumbled aquamarine and a tumbled amethyst, three other tumbled stones, and another mineral specimen of azurite. In the center, left to right: a tumbled piece of tiger-eye, a slice of rhodochrosite, tumbled rhodochrosite, tumbled Wyoming jade.

A commercial bell cap; behind it, a bell cap in position on a baroque stone.

erly, take the cap off and apply epoxy cement to the inside, as well as to the top of the stone. Let dry undisturbed for 24 hours.

An added tool that assures a perfect cementing is a *bell-cap clamp.* You can buy eight in a package for less than two dollars, and they hold cap and stone firmly together until the epoxy dries.

Wire Wrapping

An irregularly shaped tumbled stone can be wrapped with wire in a spiral or crisscross design.

For the spiral design, the wire goes around and around a stone, ending with a single wire at the top. This is formed into a hook to hang on a chain or ear wire.

A tumbled amethyst, wrapped with 24 gauge silver wire, which is twisted into a hook at the end.

In the crisscross design, two wires are wrapped in a crossing-over pattern, ending at the top. Here they are twisted together to form the hook.

Also, one end of a single wire can be carried up the back of a stone, while the other end is wrapped in a spiral pattern around both the stone and the back wire. The two ends join at the top, ending in the hanging hook.

The length of wire used depends on the size of the stone and the design of the spiral or crisscross. It is best to start with a 1-foot length of wire and anneal it over the gas flame. Then, starting with one end, wrap the stone, and cut off any excess. In twisting the wire use fingers and chain-nose pliers. Carefully remove any plier marks with file and emery or crocus cloth.

Self-prong Setting

Stones can be held firmly on a design by metal prongs that are part of a design's own metal, rather than by soldered-on bezel or wire prongs. This method is excellent for holding a cabochon on a flat metal design where there is a flat margin of metal around the edge. Sometimes a tumbled stone can also be set this way.

After cutting out your metal design and polishing the surface, put the cabochon in position. Lightly draw around the outline with the scriber.

If you find it difficult to hold the stone and make a neat line, press a strip of colored tape on the bottom of the stone, and cut out a pattern with a nail scissors. Remove the pattern from the stone, being careful not to stretch the tape, and press onto the metal. Make a mark around the edge with the scriber and remove pattern. This enclosed area will be larger than your stone.

The next step is to mark the guide lines for the four triangular prongs. The width at the base of the inward-pointing triangles depends on the size of the stone to be set, as well as personal taste. In any case, the width should not be less than 1/16 inch. At the middle of each end and side, mark off 1/16 inch or more; using a ruler, scribe along triangle toward the center. The points should not meet. When cut out, these triangles will be bent up to form the prongs that hold the

Cutting out a self-prong setting from a brass pendant shape.

stone in place. If you have a very large oval stone you will want to put two triangles on each long side.

A second line must now be marked on the metal, inside the stone line; this allows for the shoulder to support the stone. This should be 1/16 to 1/8 inch in from that first line—and do not cross over the triangle areas.

Cut out all the interior metal with the saw, following the inside line, and going up and around the triangles. When all the center metal has been removed, saw a thin line down the sides of each triangle almost to that first outline of the stone. After you bend up the prongs, you may have to make one or two strokes with the saw, but it is better not to cut too far at first.

With the chain-nose pliers, very gently bend the prongs to an almost upright position. Metal is always bent slowly, to allow it to stretch and adjust to its new position. File the edges of the prongs, and blunt the points a bit. The shoulder edges are smoothed with the file. The first scribed mark on the flat metal is removed by rubbing with emery cloth.

Anneal the points by heating them and dropping the piece while still hot into cold Sparex solution. Do this before the findings are put on.

The triangle prongs are a basic design, but they can be filed into other shapes. The prongs can also take a rectangular shape. Small nicks alternating on each side make a wavy

design. Or file the triangle into a half moon, or split the rectangle into two curved ends. These are suggestions, and you will find many more as you look in jewelry store windows.

Try out the stone in the setting, and make any necessary adjustments. Take it out, and bring the prongs forward as far as you can, curving the tips forward—but leave enough room to put the stone back without forcing it.

Solder any findings on the back before putting the stone in its permanent position.

Self-prongs, cut out and pulled upright, with jade cabochon ready to be put into position.

Self-pronged pendant, with the stone set in, and a hole drilled at the top.

Now put the stone into its setting. Grip the stone-setting tool in the palm of your hand, forefinger and thumb braced on the metal shank, and press against the prongs, first at one end, then at the opposite end, then at each side in turn. Continue *in this same order*, pressing harder each time until the prongs lie flat against the stone. Sometimes you will need to tap the head of the tool lightly with a hammer to bring the metal closer to the stone. The burnisher is another tool used to stroke the metal around a stem.

This is a skill not learned at once, but once learned it is always with you.

SETTING A STONE WITH SOLDER

Bezel Setting

A bezel is a strip of thin metal that holds a cabochon stone in place on a design. It is soldered directly onto the metal design. Often a pin or pendant is nothing more than a cabochon backed by metal and surrounded by a bezel.

There are several ways of measuring the length of bezel wire needed, including a mathematical one involving *pi.* It is best, though, to get used to a manual method, as one often has to construct a bezel around an irregular stone, where mathematics without a computer back-up would break down completely.

So—take a short length of thin, soft wire and fit it around the bottom circumference of the stone to be set. Twist the ends of the wire to tighten. Slip it off the stone, cut at the base of the twist, and straighten out the wire.

Another method for measuring is this modern one. Place the stone on the sticky side of a piece of tape, and cut around the edge with a pair of small scissors. Peel off the tape and place it on a piece of paper. Measure the circumference of the tape pattern with a piece of string, cutting it at the joining point. The string now serves as the pattern for the bezel.

Cut bezel (or gallery) wire with saw or snippers just a little longer than the pattern to allow for filing the cut edges smooth.

Make a final check to be sure that the bezel fits the stone snugly. If it is too tight, the stone will crack; too loose, the edges will crimp. Correct the length if necessary, making sure that the two facing ends meet evenly—solder will not jump the gaps. Remove the stone. Bend the ends of the strip just beyond each other, then back to touching. This creates a tension in the metal that will hold the ends together while soldering. For an oval stone, the joining is in the middle of one long side of the stone.

Next, make a wire hook on which to hang the bezel while soldering. Take a 4½-inch piece of stiff brass wire. At the 3¼-inch mark, bend the wire over and down in a broad loop, so the bent-down section is about ⅜ to ½ inch away from the upright wire. Then form a shallow outward hook with the last ¼-inch piece of wire. The bezel will hang from this hook. Poke the lower end of the wire into the asbestos ring so it stands upright.

After cleaning off the bezel with kitchen cleanser and wiping with rubbing alcohol, paint the joint with flux. Hang the bezel on the hook, seam downward. Place a small square of solder over the seam, and apply the hot soldering iron or gun to the underside of the seam. As soon as the solder melts take away the heat source. Let bezel hang until cool. File off any extra solder. The joint should be practically invisible.

With the fingers and pliers make adjustments in the shape of the bezel so that it fits the stone perfectly.

You are now ready to solder the bezel to the flat surface of your design. Put your cleaned design on the asbestos tile and place the bezel in position. It should lie flat, touching the metal all around. If not, file until it does. Put a line of flux around the inside joining of bezel and flat metal. Add 1/16-inch pieces of solder in this area. Apply heat from the outside, and proceed with the soldering and cleaning.

If the bezeled stone is to be the total design, then a flat piece of metal cut to the size of the bottom of the stone is dropped inside the bezel. The fitting should be close. Follow the procedures above on fluxing and soldering.

Now come two variations.

If the stone is opaque, the solid metal backing is left

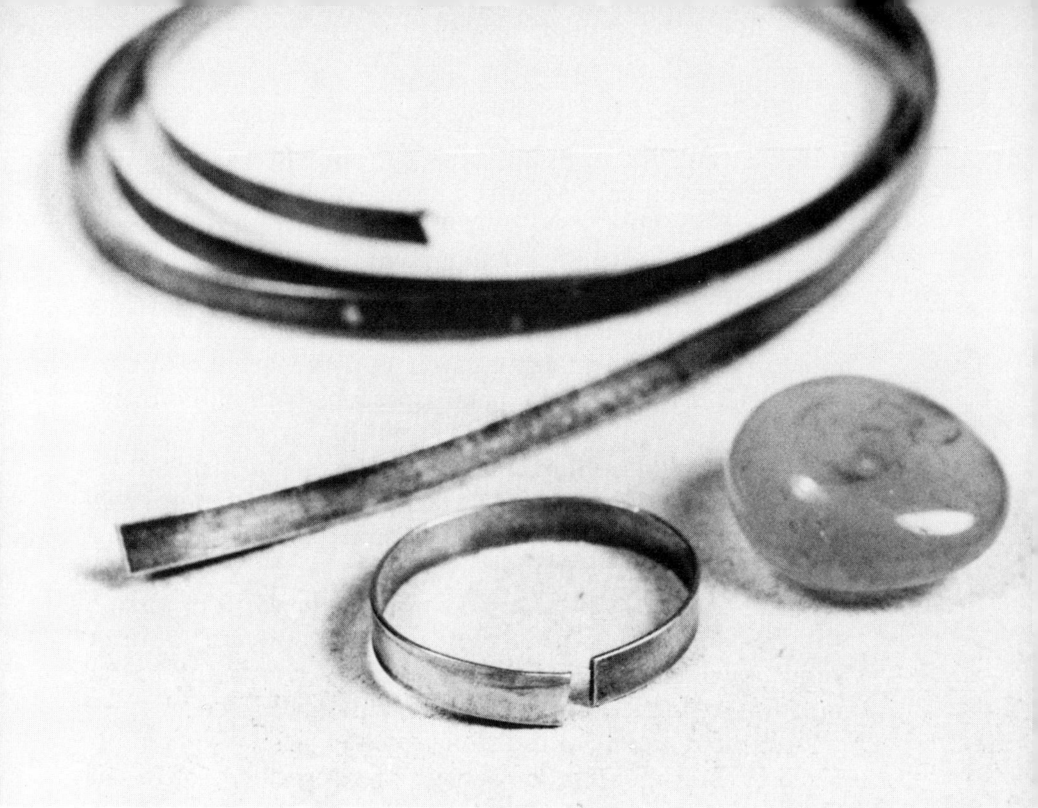

Bezel wire and formed bezel with its slightly irregular beach quartz stone.

Bezel ready for soldering, hanging on a hook stuck into an asbestos coil. The fluxed piece of solder is in place.

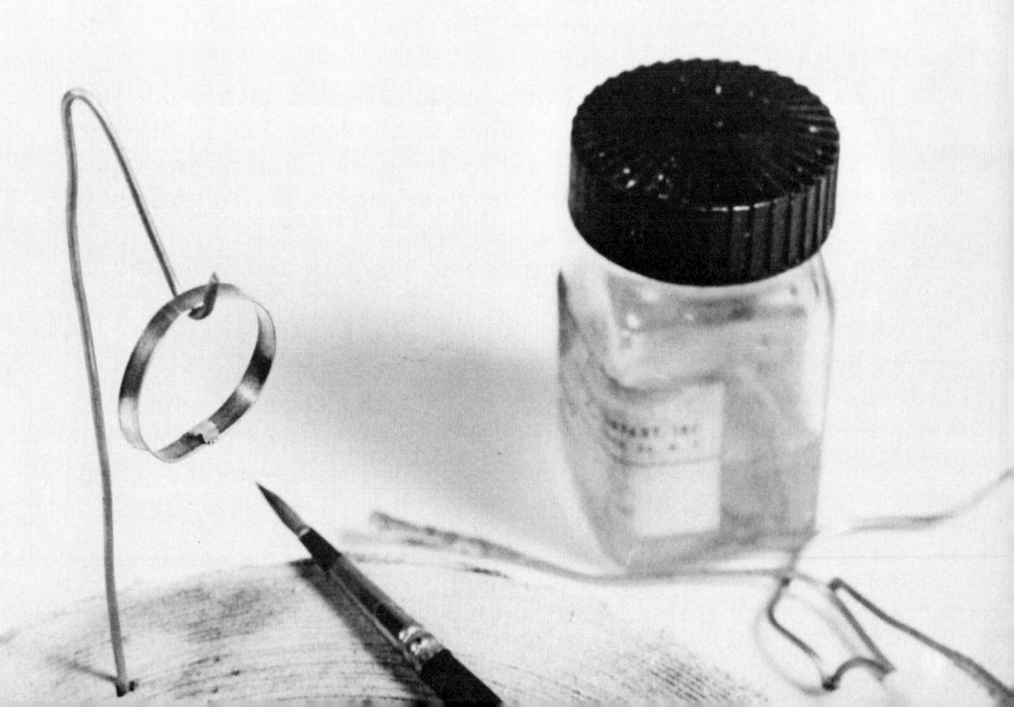

under it. But for a transparent stone, you will want to let in all the light you can. After the bezel is soldered on, draw a line on the backing at least a full 1/8 inch in from the edge—more if the stone is large. Cut out the center section of the metal with the jeweler's saw in the usual way.

The bezel edge can be left plain, or a design can be filed into it. The decision depends on the effect you want to achieve. File the edges into points, scooped-out half circles, or scallops.

A bezel should be high enough on the stone to grip it firmly, but not so high as to hide it. Too wide a strip of metal will be hard to smooth down over the stone without crimping the edge.

If the bezeled stone is to be worn as a pendant or pin, or several combined in a bracelet, any findings such as jump rings, catches, pin backs, earring backs, or cuff-link backs must be soldered on before the stone is finally set.

The actual setting of the stone into the bezel is very similar to the self-metal prong setting just described—only you have more metal to work with.

Put the stone inside the bezel area. With the index finger pressing on the top end of the stone, and the middle finger acting as a brace outside, apply pressure with the stone setter. Now change the setter to the opposite end, and exert pressure. Give the setting a quarter turn and press against the bezel; then press the opposite side. In other words, always press against opposite sides; *never* press around the stone point by point.

Fill in the untouched areas, always working first one side, then the other. Remember your succession of pressure points, as you should follow the same series as you repeat around the bezel. Rock the stone setter a bit. You may have to tap it lightly with a hammer.

Finish with the burnisher, scraping and polishing all around.

Bezel-and-Prong Setting

This type of setting shows off a stone to its full advantage. The stone, resting on *top* of the bezel, is seen right down to the bottom, being held in place by wire forming the prongs.

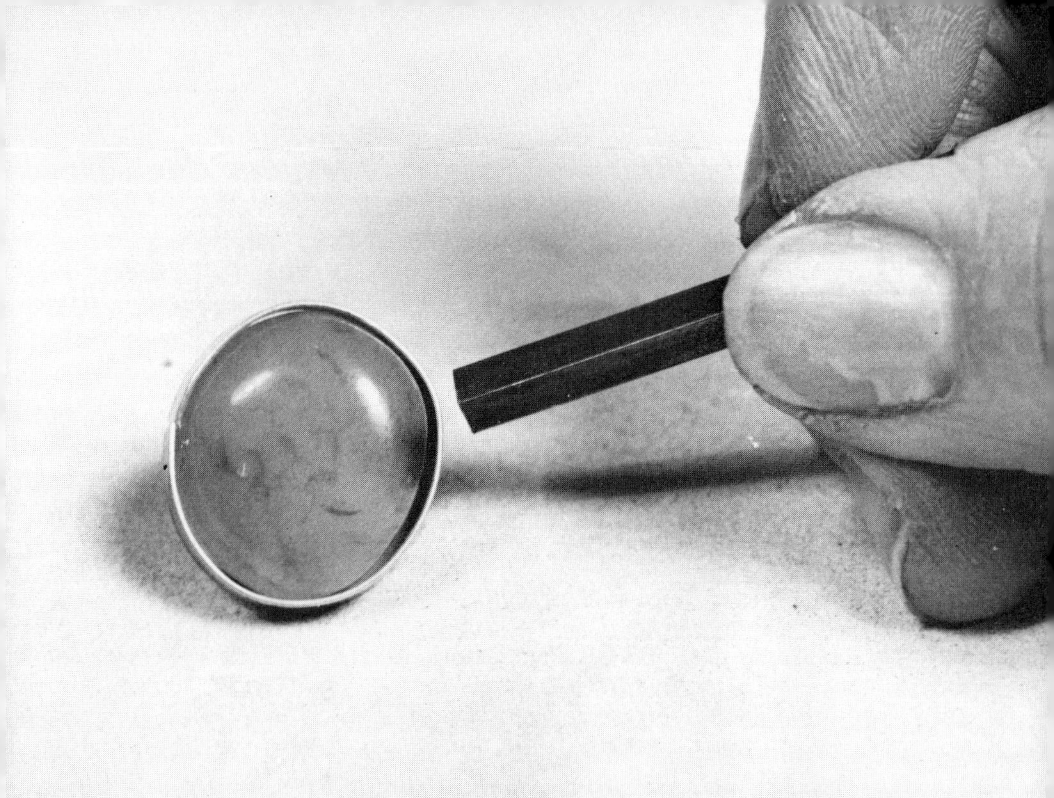

The working angle of the stone setter. Metal backing and pin back (not visible) have been soldered onto the bezel.

The working angle of the burnisher as it smooths the metal over the stone.

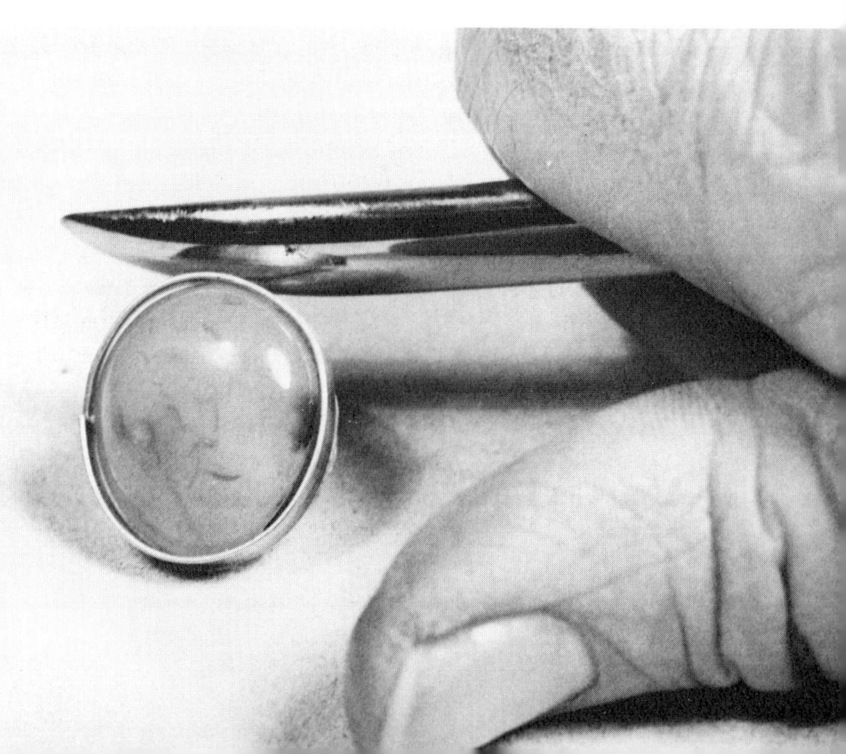

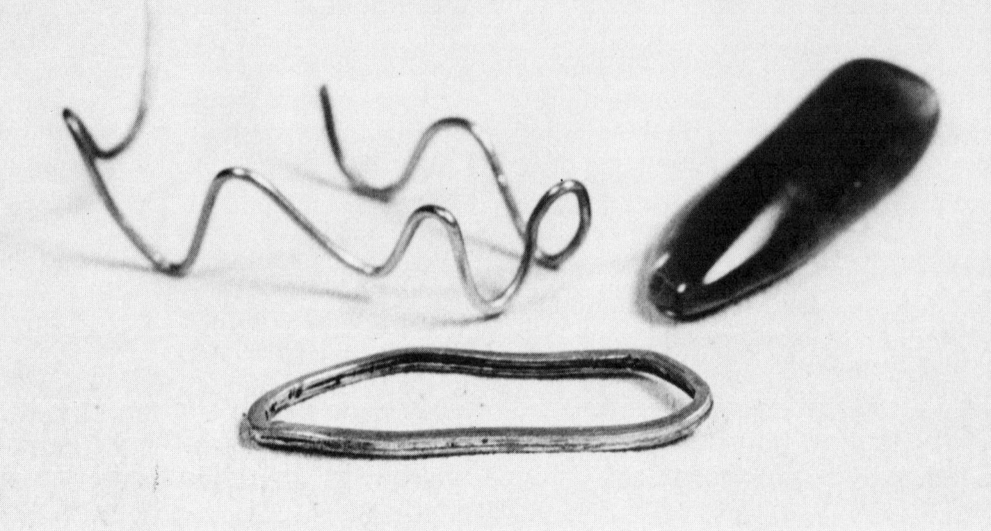

Square-wire supporting bezel with continuous curved-wire prongs, shown with tumbled amethyst.

This supporting bezel can take several shapes, and is measured to fit the stone's *bottom*, right at the edge.

The first type of supporting bezel has the same depth as the bezel described in the previous section, 1/8 inch, but it is made of heavier metal, 18 or 20 gauge, which gives more support. The deep bezel has an advantage in ring making, as there is enough metal from which to file a curve to fit the curve of the finger ring. This bezel can be made from rectangular wire or cut from a metal sheet. Scraps from other designs are often long enough.

The second type of supporting bezel is made from square wire, 14 or 16 gauge, bent into the bottom shape of the stone. This wire will have to be annealed before bending. Prongs are similar to previous prong-and-bezel settings. Or you can use a continuous, curved-wire prong (see photo), which is soldered to the outside of the supporting bezel.

This is a particularly good bezel for irregular tumbled stones or mineral specimens, because the wire makes it easier to follow the outline of the stone. Stick a piece of colored tape to the bottom of the stone—the flattest area—and cut it out along the upright edges of the stone; peel off. Stick the tape onto a piece of white paper, and follow this pattern in bending the wire, using fingers and pliers. This is an easier method than trying to hold a slippery stone and bend stiff wire at the same time. Excellent for cabochons, too. It's a modern method, taking advantage of sticky tape, which the ancient jewelers didn't have.

A third decorative bezel is made from twisted wire. Take a length of 18- or 20-gauge annealed wire, and loop it so the ends meet. Hold the ends in the chain-nose pliers. Insert a pencil in the other end of the loop, and start twisting the two wires together. When you have made the rope as tight as you want, slip out the pencil and form the bezel in the usual way. File a flat area wherever a prong is to be set. This will make for a better soldering bond.

After the bezel has been soldered, you will add the prongs. The half-round wire is used, as it has a flat surface to solder against the bezel, and to press against the stone. Cut four or six lengths of wire long enough to reach from the bottom edge to the top edge of the bezel and to overlap the top edge enough to hold the stone in place.

On the bezel, measure and mark with the scriber the four or six equally spaced points for the prongs. Clean bezel and prongs. Add flux for the first prong, and clip the wire in place on the outside with a paper clip. Add solder and hang bezel on the hook, prong upward. Solder from inside, cool, and repeat process with the other prongs.

Clean away excess solder and polish with crocus cloth. Thin out the points of the prongs with the file. Prongs can be patterned at the ends if you wish.

Add findings, if they are used, at this point.

Set the stone following directions in the preceding section.

Crossed-wire Prong Setting

There are several ways of using wire alone for setting both cabochons and baroque tumbled stones; crossed wires and a straight wire with two curved wires attached at each side are two of the simplest.

Crossed wires form the simplest prong setting of all, and will fit a round stone.

With a piece of soft base-metal wire or heavy thread,

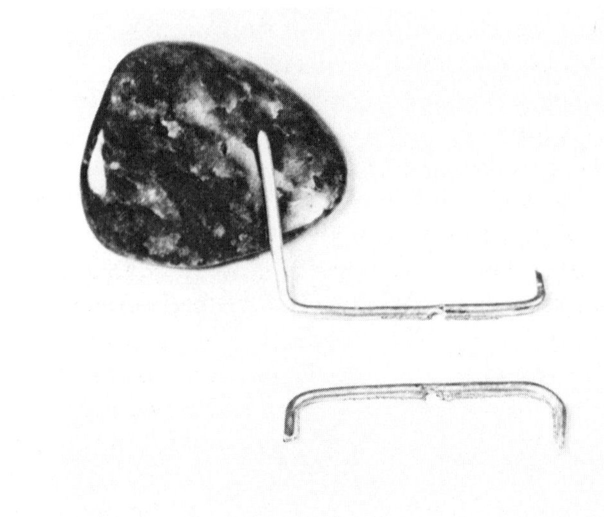

Crossed wire prongs, showing matching rectangles filed into the wire. Tumbled piece of jade in the background.

measure the length of prong wire you will need. Beginning at the point where the prong will end, measure down and across the bottom of your stone up to the opposite side, again to the prong ending; cut off. If the stone is round or square, measure two equal lengths of wire. If it is oval or rectangular, you will have to take a second measurement, and cut one prong wire of each size.

For this type of setting, use round wire, 16 or 18 gauge, depending on the size of the stone and the effect you want.

The only soldering point will be at the back where the two wires cross. In order to achieve a flat surface for soldering, and an even surface for the stone to rest on, you will file two shallow rectangles out of each wire, so that they fit into each other at the center crossing point.

In the wire nearest the stone, you will file a rectangle on the surface facing away from the stone halfway through the wire. In the outer wire, the matching rectangle will be filed on the upper edge, halfway through the wire. When the wires are put together, the crossing area will be the thickness of only one wire.

Next, with the round end of the hammer, very lightly tap an area about 1/16 inch at the end of each wire. This will thin out the end that presses against the stone. File into even ovals. You may have to file away a bit more after the wires are bent around the stone, as the tapping will lengthen the wire.

Clean the metal, and flux each hollow rectangle. Put together and hold with a paper clip. Place the crossed wires on the asbestos circle, and add a 1/16-inch square of solder at the joining area right beside the top crossing wire. Apply heat on the opposite side, to pull the solder through. Remove heat as soon as the solder gleams and runs. Let cool.

File away excess solder before centering the stone on the crossed wires. With the scriber, mark the edge of the stone on each wire. You will be turning the wires up at these points. Now file a shallow triangle at each mark. The prongs, when bent up at these spots, will form a sharper angle with this bit of metal removed.

With the pliers, gently bend up the wires. This has to be done slowly, giving the metal a chance to stretch and adjust; otherwise the wires will snap off.

Check the height of the prongs against the sides of the stone. If too high, file away some of the metal, and reflatten the ends if necessary.

Take out all marks from the wires, and polish with the crocus cloth.

Before doing any stone setting, complete any other soldering processes.

Put the stone back between the wires. Now, press one prong against the stone, then press the opposite prong, using the stone setter or burnisher, rocking it a bit as you exert pressure. Now press the other two wires. Keep alternating in the same pattern, finishing up with the burnisher.

Curved-wire Prong Setting

This prong arrangement creates six prongs. It is made of three wires: a straight wire down the center of the stone; and two wires, one on each side, that curve into long ellipses. They are attached to the straight wire in the middle with solder.

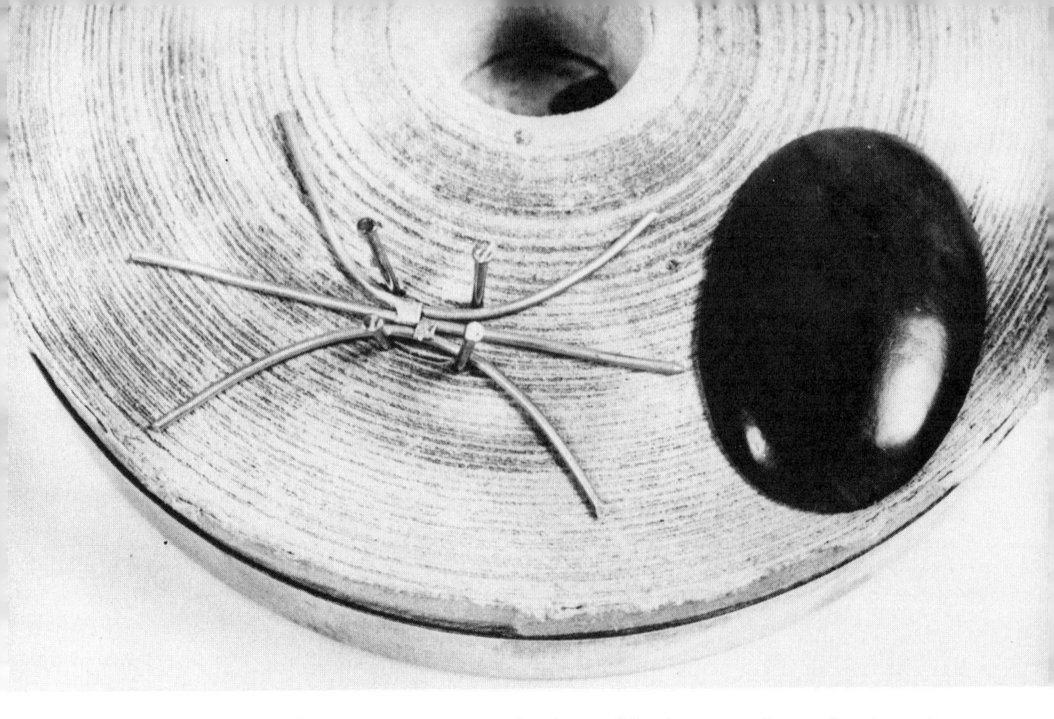

Curved wire prongs ready for soldering on the asbestos ring. Jade cabochon is to the right.

Cut a length of round or square wire long enough to reach across the center of the bottom of the stone, and up each side as far as the prongs need to go in order to hold the stone firm. Next measure the amount needed for the ellipses using thread or expendable soft wire. These ellipses should touch the straight wire in the middle, then curve out to the edge of the stone, each end reaching over the edge to form a prong. Cut two pieces the same length—*unless* you are setting an irregularly shaped mineral specimen, in which case you will have to measure the two curved wires separately.

If you are using round wire, file a flat place on all three wires at the middle meeting point. Form them so that they fit the stone.

Clean and put the wires on the asbestos circle, holding the joining area together with brass brads. Flux and solder according to standard procedures, then solder on any findings.

Place the stone in the center of the wire arrangement, and mark its edges on the prongs. File and bend the prongs as described in the preceding section. Clean up the wires and polish. Set the stone in the usual way.

DANGLING JEWELS

This project turns two basic techniques into several styles of necklaces, bracelets, and earrings. The *bell-cap* method is one technique. The other is the *wire-wrapped* style. Here are the variations, subvariations, and subsubvariations—as many different combinations as there are stones and colors.

Variations

1. For a bib necklace, measure a chain around your neck, then attach a back fastening—either with a commercial spring ring or your own hook closing.

   Now space out the stones across the front of the necklace. Crowd them together or space them out, depending on your design and the number of stones available.

You can use opaque stones or transparent stones, in a single color or a mixture of colors. Or you can use a combination of clear and opaque stones, within the same color range or in contrasting colors. You can choose stones all of one approximate length, or have two lengths and alternate the long and the short. Or you might want long stones in front, short at the sides. As you can see, the changes are endless, and no two necklaces will be alike.

2. In this long-chain version, the stones are hung along the length of a chain singly or in clusters. This, too, has all

the variations that can develop from the choice of stones and color. You can add plain rounds of metal as a contrast to the stones. This is a fun project, and the field is wide open.

3. Both bell-cap and wire-wrapped settings can be adapted for bracelets, as matches for necklaces or as independent designs.
4. For earrings, attach small lengths of fine chain to the front loop of an earring back, and hang small stones from the end of the chain. Or hang a stone directly on the loop.

OPEN-ENDED BRACELET WITH STONE

This project follows the basic design for an open-ended bracelet given in Chapter 6. In this version, however, a stone is set in the center.

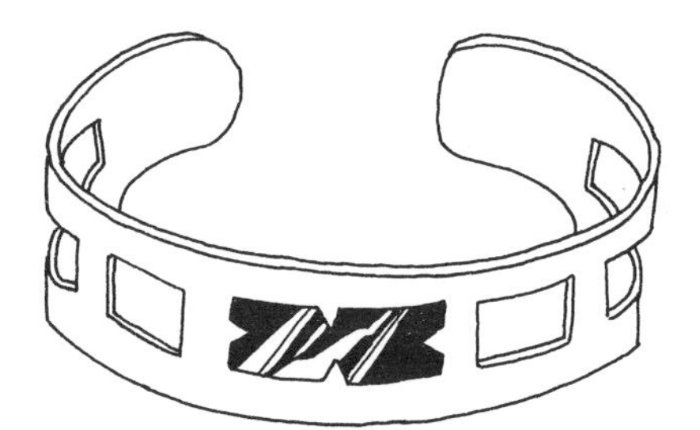

Steps

1. Buy a rectangular stone, choosing one that approximates in size the cutout openings you are planning for the design.
2. Prepare open-ended bracelet, following steps 1 through 9 on pages 161-162. But adjust the pattern to allow for the stone in the center, and space out the rectangular cutouts accordingly. You will want two or three rectangles on each side of the stone, depending on the size of the stone and your own design preference.
3. This will be a self-prong setting, so measure the center area and cut out, following instructions on pages 199-203.
4. Before pulling up the triangles, curve the bracelet into its final form, leaving the center area flat where the stone will be. Follow directions for setting the stone on page 203.

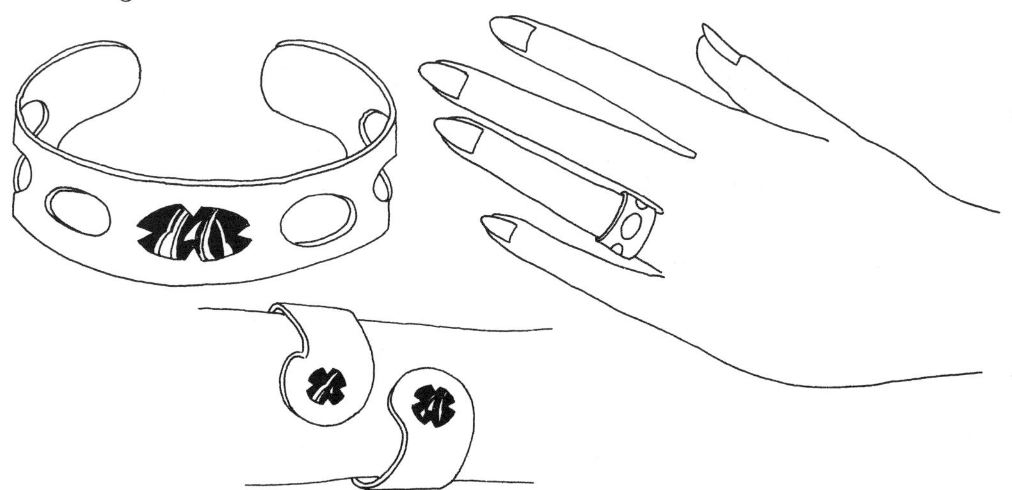

Variations

1. The openings and stone can be round or oval.
2. Instead of prongs, make a bezel setting, soldering it on after the bracelet has been formed into an arm shape.
3. Add stones, either pronged or bezeled, to the swirl-ended bracelet variation after it has been shaped to fit the arm (for basic design, see page 162).
4. Make a small shape to wear as a finger ring, setting a stone by bezel in the center.

HANGING FISH

Follow the directions for making the gilded-lily necklace, substituting the fish shape (see pages 169-171). Use pewter or silver as the metal, and make an *even* number of forms. You'll also need an oval-shaped cabochon.

Steps

1. After cutting out and polishing the fish put them aside. Now cut out a *larger* fish for the center. The size will depend on the cabochon you have bought. Make the fish large enough to hold the stone, with an edging of 1/8 to 1/4 inch of metal showing around the edges.
2. Follow the directions on pages 199-203, marking the stone area and cutting out the self-prongs. Since this is a fish design, you might want to make wavy edges on the

prongs by filing alternate nicks on both sides of the triangles and smoothing these areas into semicircles.

3. Drill hole at top for the jump ring.
4. Set stone, according to the procedure given on page 199.
5. Add jump rings and hang all the fish on the chain.

A JEWELED COLLAR

Materials

A flat piece of pewter—or silver, if your budget allows—3¼ by 6¼ inches; thin silver wire, 6 feet long, 24 gauge (you will use approximately 7½ inches per stone); 2 inches of 18-gauge wire for the hooks; a length of chain 10 to 11 inches long.

The choice of stones is up to you, but they should be no longer than an inch, and approximately ⅜ inch at the widest point. You will need nine stones.

Steps

1. Before you buy your supplies, make a paper pattern of the metal collar. Hold it in position with paper tape at the front of your neck. Measure with limp package string the length of chain needed.
2. Transfer the pattern to the metal, using carbon paper and a hard pencil.
3. Cut out the metal with a jeweler's saw. File and bevel the edges.
4. Drill nine holes across the front to hold the hanging jewels. Also drill a hole in each point of the collar, where the chain hooks will be attached.
5. Wrap the nine stones with the wire, following the directions on page 198.
6. Make the wire hooks and attach these to the end of the chain (for basic hook technique, see page 122).
7. Lacquer the collar with clear nail polish one side at a time back and front, and let dry in a flat position after each application.
8. Hook jewels through the holes at the bottom edge of the collar. Tighten the hooks with the pliers so they are close to the metal but still swing freely.
9. Slip a hook into one point of the collar and tighten. Use the second hook as a catch, to take the necklace off and on.

THE GOLDEN FROG

Materials

The gold, in this case, is brass—softly polished until it looks like gold. You will need a piece of 18-gauge brass, 1 7/8 by 2 5/8 inches; pin back or jump ring; an oval, shallow-domed cabochon, 1 1/4 by 3/4 inches. To carry out the total golden look, a tiger's eye or a golden smoky quartz would be a good choice of stone. On the green side, try a piece of Wyoming jade or bloodstone.

Steps

1. Make a tracing of the frog outline. Transfer to your

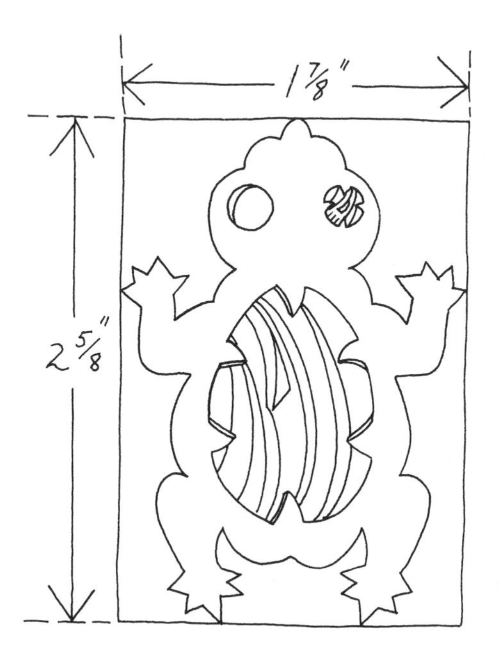

piece of metal, using carbon paper and a hard pencil. Follow the carbon line with the scriber, then wipe off the black with rubbing alcohol.

2. Cut out the frog with the jeweler's saw, following directions for sawing at the beginning of Chapter 6. File and bevel edges, and polish metal with crocus cloth.
3. Now, using the stone as a guide, mark off the center area to be cut out. You will need six self-prongs for this stone (for directions, see pages 199-203).
4. Cut out center section. Lift up prongs. File all edges smooth.
5. Drill a hole in the center of each eye section, and cut out the small piece of metal. These can just be open holes, or you can make self-prongs and set two small circular stones.
6. Solder on pin back just above the center of pin, so that it will not hang forward. For a horizontal pin, put catch just below the spot where the arm joins the head in the neck area. The hinge is placed just below the area where the leg joins the body.
7. Set the large cabochon, using stone setter and burnisher (for directions, see page 203).

8. Put pin in hinge. Lacquer frog with clear nail polish, being careful to keep it out of the catch.

Variations

1. Set cabochon in a bezel, rather than prongs.
2. Cut a rectangle of brass 2 by 2⅝ inches. Saw out the center into self-prongs to fit a jade cabochon 1³⁄₁₆ by 1¹³⁄₁₆ inches (see page 202). Hang the pendant by a hook from a neck wire.

A SILVER STARFISH

Materials

A piece of 18-gauge flat metal, silver or pewter, 2⅛ by 2½ inches; a round cabochon stone, clear or opaque; pin back, if design is to be worn as a pin. If a pendant, buy a jump ring, or make a hanger of 2 inches of wire.

Steps

1. Trace the pattern and transfer it to the rectangle of metal with carbon paper and a hard pencil.
2. Cut out with the jeweler's saw. File edges smooth, and bevel.

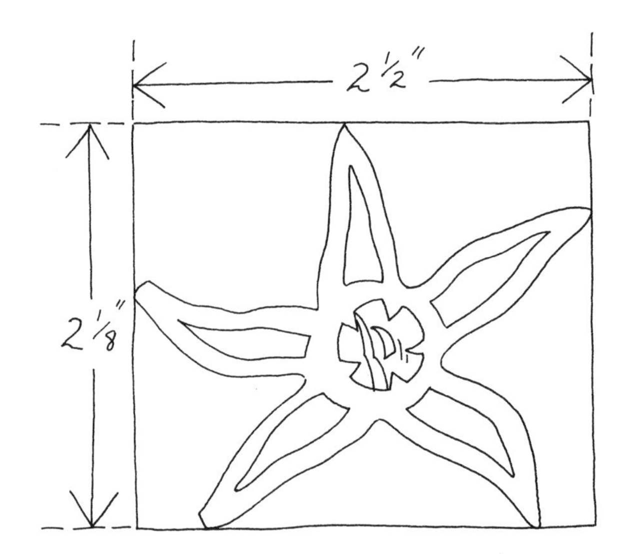

3. Next make a small hole with the drill in a corner of the cutaway area of one of the arms, and saw out metal. File edges, and bevel.
4. To make the center circle, trace around the stone with the scriber. Also measure off the triangular prongs to hold the stone. Prong triangles are opposite the base of each arm. Follow directions for cutting self-prongs on pages 199-203.
5. Solder on the pin back. Or, if the design is to be a pendant, drill a hole at the end of one of the arms. In either case, turn the pin around first and decide which arm is up—the starfish develops a different personality depending on which way you turn it.
6. Go over the whole starfish, front and back, with file and crocus cloth, taking out any nicks and giving it a final polish.
7. Set the stone using stone setter and burnisher. Follow directions on page 203.
8. Put the pin in the hinge. Cover first the back, then the front, with clear nail polish.

Variations

1. Set the stone in a bezel instead of self-prongs.
2. Cut two 1¼-inch starfish and hang from a ¾-inch hooked hanger inserted into the loop of earring backs.
3. Make a solid starfish from very thick silver, 8 gauge, with

six curling arms. Small snippets of wire are soldered down the center, and the stone is set into a bezel. The result looks like a cross between a starfish and an octopus. But you might need a torch to solder on the little bumps, as this very thick metal will absorb heat.

CABOCHON BRACELET

In this classic bracelet, bezeled cabochon stones are linked together with oval jump rings, with a spring ring as a catch. The choice of stones is up to you—all alike or each one different. The number of stones depends on their size and the size of your arm. So buy your stones first.

Materials

The opaque or clear cabochons are supplied in standard sizes. The best size for this bracelet is designated as 14/10, which means it is approximately 9/16 inch long and 3/8 inch wide. Buy the number that you will need. (The instructions given here are based on using seven stones of this size.)

In addition you will need: a piece of flat silver or pewter, 1 by 2 1/4 inches, for the flat backs of the stones; two round jump rings for each stone; one oval jump ring to place between each setting; a spring ring and two extra rings; bezel wire. Allow 1 5/8 inches of wire for each bezel, and multiply this by the number of stones you plan to use. Always buy an extra bezel length, plus 1/2 inch to allow for sawing space or spoilage.

Steps

1. With thick thread or string, measure the length of bracelet you will want on your arm. The length of the bezeled stone with a jump ring soldered at each end will be ap-

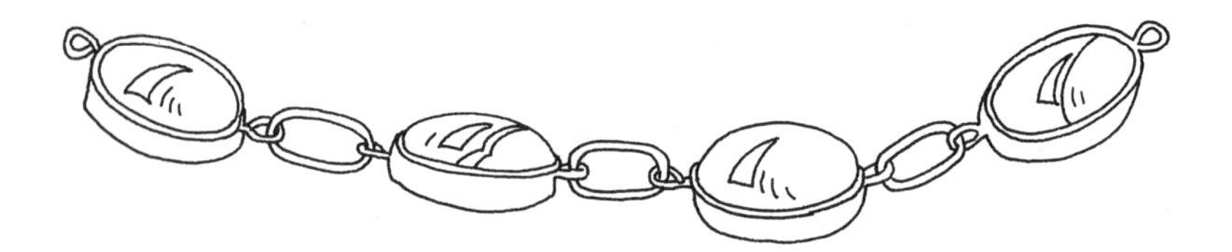

proximately 13/16 inch. The oval links between the stones are 1/4 inch. Using these measurements and including the catch and ring at each end, a bracelet 7 3/4 inches long will need 7 stones.

You can always adjust the fit of the bracelet and the number of stones by using larger jump rings, and longer or shorter oval links.

2. Transfer pattern for seven ovals to the flat piece of silver or pewter. Leave a little space between ovals to allow for saw thickness. Also, cut ovals just slightly larger than

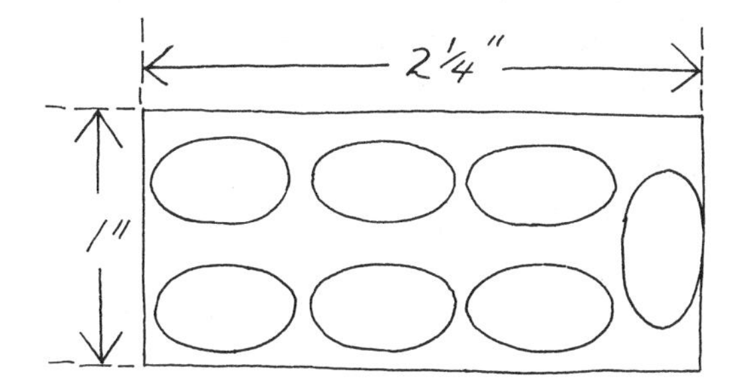

the stones, then file edges back to exact fit. These will end up being slightly smaller than the stone, as the bezel will be on the outside.

3. Measure, cut, and fit the bezel (for directions, see pages 203-206). Cut each bezel separately for each stone, in case there is a slight variation in size.
4. If metal is discolored from soldering, put into Sparex solution until clean. Rinse off in running water.
5. Put each bezeled oval on the asbestos ring, oval side flat. Place a jump ring at each end. Hold everything in position with small brass nails. Apply flux and solder. Apply heat until solder melts, then cool.
6. If the bezel is too high for your stone, file it down. The edge may be left plain, or filed into a pattern – or you may use a commercially patterned bezel wire.
7. Link the jump rings together with the oval jump rings, and solder the joinings, being sure that they are at the back of the bracelet so the soldering does not show. Slip one of the two end ovals into a jump ring (for the catch) and the other into the spring ring.

8. Set stones in bezels, following usual directions. Give bracelet final polishing with file and crocus cloth.
9. Finish with clear nail polish, and let dry for several hours, until no tackiness remains.

Variations

1. Using the same design, make a necklace of cabochons, with the stones going all around the neck.
2. Hang five or six wrapped stones from the center links in the front of the necklace.
3. Add a large center cabochon pendant to the cabochon necklace. Use the curved-prong setting.
4. Hang one or two linked cabochons from the loop of ear-ring backs.
5. Make a bezeled pair of matching cabochons, and solder to cuff-link backs. You can solder a single bezeled stone to a tie tack or clasp.
6. Solder a large bezeled cabochon to the pewter belt buckle (page 184).
7. A total change in the oval base shape opens up a whole new set of variations. Cut bases in a seed shape, larger than the stone by 3/16 inches, going to a point at each end. Set the bezel on top of the base, and solder on. Drill a hole at each point and attach oval links, or round jump rings to which oval links are attached.

With this new shape, you can run through the whole set of variations just described.

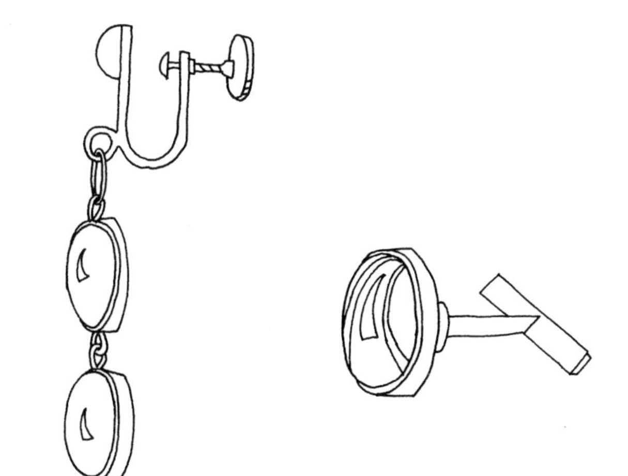

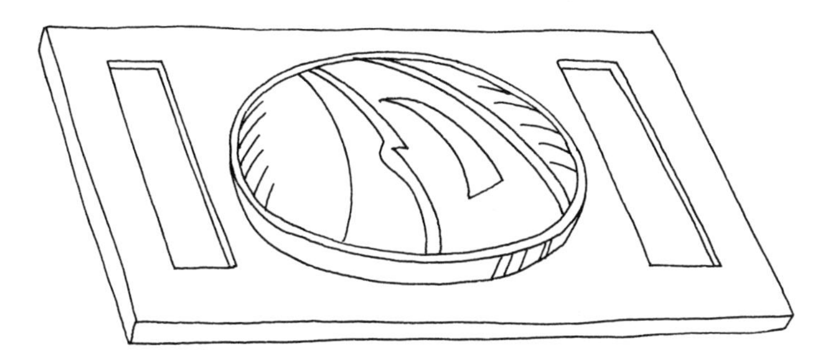

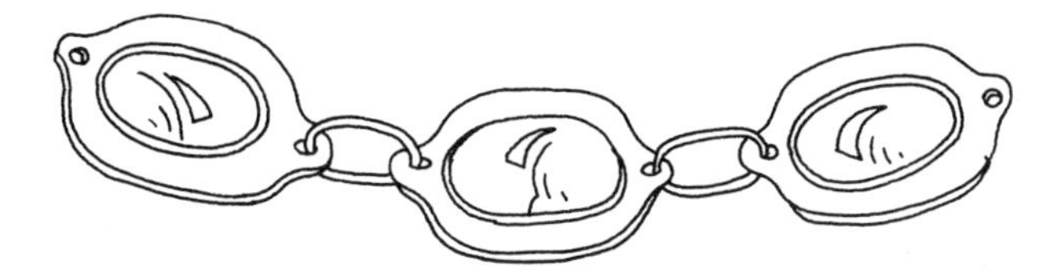

8. The Sparkle of Enamel

A JEWEL-LIKE effect is created by enamel. As a material it is easy to apply, the heating element (a kiln) is small, and the melting time is only a few minutes.

Melting a special kind of glassy powder onto metal surfaces is an ancient process for decorating jewelry and church ornaments. In museums one can see Byzantine plaques from the eleventh century with enamels filling the areas between outlines of metal, and reliquaries from the twelfth century ornamented with intricate designs. In China and Japan, in Germany and France, and in Russia, the art of enameling was a part of a jeweler's practice. Coming down to more modern times, the enameled jewelry of Fabergé, the court jeweler of Russia, is legendary.

So, from as far back as the Celts, who were making decorations for their shields in the third century, to the present day, the craft of enamel has been practiced with very little change in materials or methods.

Vitreous enamel is a silica mixture—a form of glass with mineral colors added. It is melted and cooled. The lumps are ground to a measured fineness and sold in this form. This granular powder is applied to metal, then put into a kiln, and heated until the material is once again molten. The heat is turned off, and the enamel slowly cooled. In the high temperature of 1,500 degrees, the enamel has been fused or bonded to the metal—and will stay this way for centuries. But ordinary windowpane or bottle glass will *not* hold on metal.

TOOLS

To *melt* enamel, the main tool required is a *kiln*. Because all jewelry projects are small in size, you will not need a large kiln, as you would if you were making tiles, ashtrays, or bowls. The small 5- to 7-inch-diameter kilns are sufficient, and achieve the right amount of heat. These are, essentially, electric hot plates with covers—either metal, with an open-shut viewing area, or special heat-proof glass, domed. Approximately 1,500 degrees of heat is needed to melt enamel, but this is not hot enough to melt the metal used for the jewelry base.

The special small tools used for enameling include the following:

- A small square of 4-mesh Nichrome or stainless-steel *mesh* on which the metal design covered with enamel powder is put into the kiln. A 4-by-4-inch size is large enough for most pieces. If you can get a piece of expanded metal (it has tiny holes in it), it's even better.
- A 4-inch square of mica, used in the *plique-à-jour* process described on page 256.
- *Tongs* to hold the metal mesh while putting it into and taking it out of the kiln. These can be the same tongs with a heat-proof handle that you use in soldering.
- A special *enameling spatula*, about 1 inch wide and 2 inches long, with a handle approximately 7 inches long. This is used to slip small pieces on and off the mesh. Or you can use a putty knife, bought in a hardware store.
- Stainless-steel *stilts* for supporting some types of enameled metal, and placed on the floor of the kiln or on the mesh square. These are particularly useful if you are counter-enameling your design, that is, applying enamel to both sides of the metal. The small points support the piece and will not stick to the metal. This is also true of

the star stilts, which are made of an already fired ceramic with small steel pins imbedded in each of the four points.

To *wash* enamel: small china, plastic, or glass *dishes*, approximately 2 inches in diameter and 1 inch deep, are large enough to hold both water and enamel.

To *apply* enamel, you will need the following:

- Two or three empty *shaker jars* or *shaker tops* for applying dry enamel to large areas.
- A *spatula* 6 inches long with a small curved blade, which looks like a miniature golf stick. (Your dentist's small, discarded spatulas are very useful).
- Three camel-hair *brushes*, in small, medium, and large sizes, used in adding water to enamel powder if it dries while applying, as well as in picking up enamel grains that have strayed into the wrong area. Brushes are also the applicators of other liquids used in the enameling processes.
- Paper *toweling* to absorb excess moisture after the enamel has been applied.

To *smooth* enamel, you will need a *carborundum file* or stick for grinding down the irregular surface of fired enamels. This process is known as *stoning* the enamel. You will also need a *nail brush* for scrubbing off the enamel surface after using the carborundum file.

For forming and preparing the metal bases of your designs, you will need the tools used in the previous chapters.

MATERIALS

Enamels

Enamels are sold as finely granulated powder, usually designated as 80 mesh. (This means that the fine grains will shake through an 80-mesh wire screen). Packaged in bottles of various sizes, the 2-ounce size is sufficient for a number of jewelry projects. It is better to buy a small quantity, as you are then assured of freshly ground material. Enamel tends to break down if kept too long, and more "dust" has to be washed out of the transparent enamel powders.

There are two types of enamels—opaque and transparent.

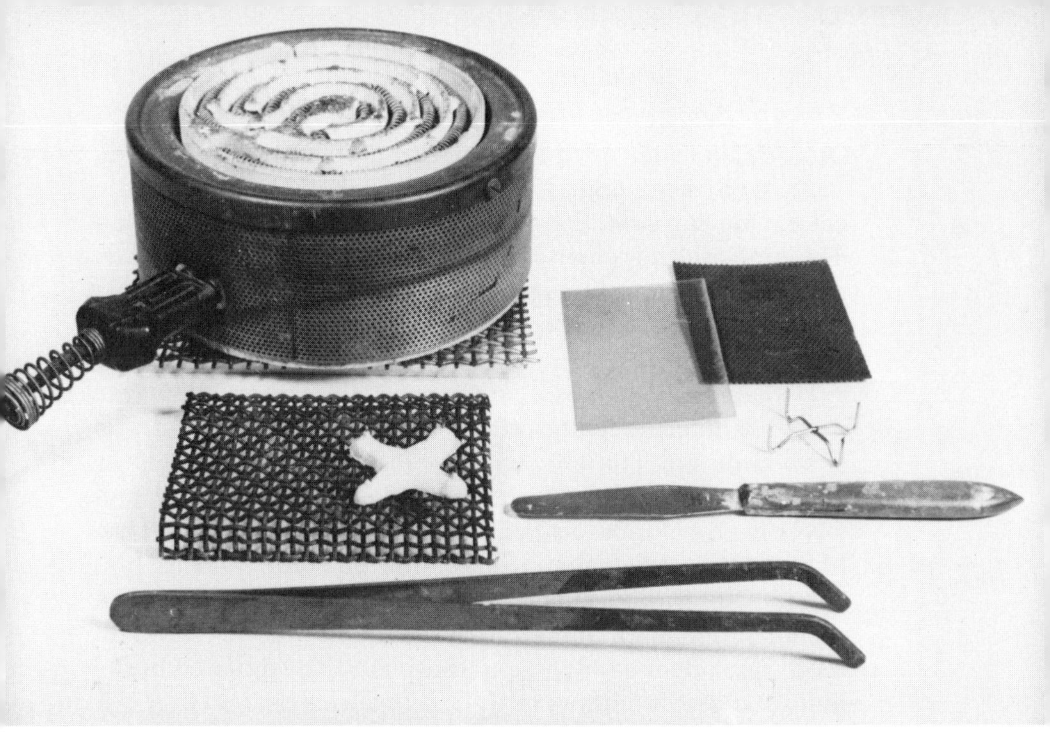

Tools for enameling. Top left, the bottom half of the small kiln, showing the heating element (a metal cover goes over the top). To the right, clockwise: a piece of mica and a piece of expanded metal wire stilt, palette knife, copper tongs, wire mesh support, and ceramic star stilt.

Enameling materials. Left to right: ceramic dish used in washing enamels, shaker-top container, several sizes of enamel jars, two other types of containers for washing enamel. Foreground: carborundum file, brushes, and spatula for applying enamel.

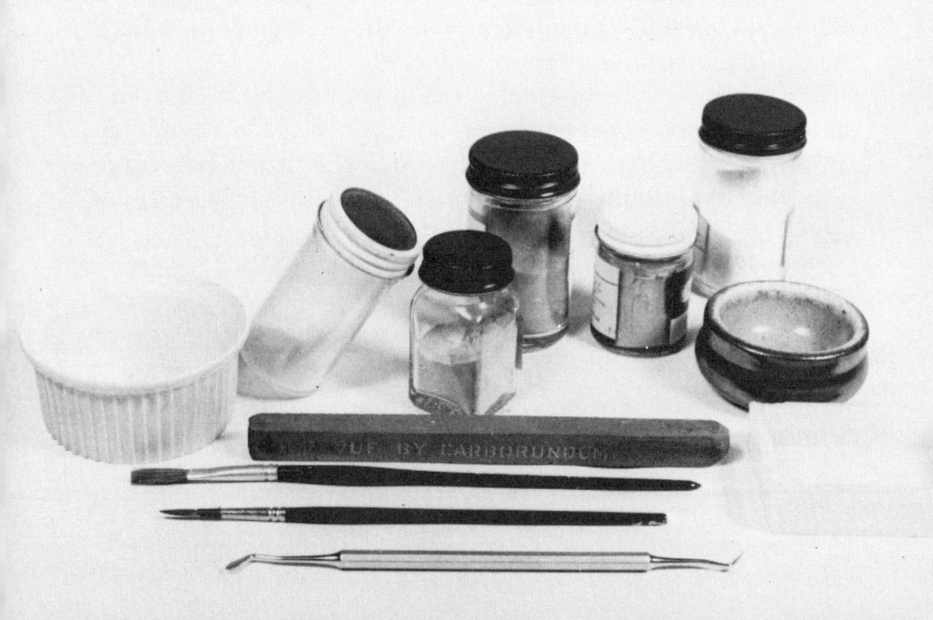

Opaque enamels are just that—solid colors, light or dark, that cover the metal surface totally, so that all you see is the color. One can partially cover a fired opaque enamel with a design in another color—and the second color will fire true, masking the color underneath. As a rule of thumb, opaque colors can be fired on copper without using a first coat of transparent flux.

Transparent enamels are clear colors that allow the metal or another color, either transparent or opaque, to show through. The effect is like looking through clear or colored water. Transparent enamels on both copper and silver need an undercoat of *transparent flux*, a clear glass-like surface. The colored enamel is put on over this first layer. The flux prevents chemical interaction between metal and enamel. Some transparent colors can be fired directly on copper or silver, and these are so designated in the manufacturer's catalog or the craft store's list.

Both opaque and transparent enamels are made in all colors, each with ten or more shades, lights and darks and subtle changes, so that you can achieve a number of tones with the enamels. These powders cannot be mixed with each other to form another color, but must be used just as they come from the bottle.

Novelty enamels give a decorative effect in certain designs. There are transparent lumps that are placed on a smooth surface and, when fired, melt into irregular shapes like brilliant jewels. Opaque enamel threads can be bought in 8-ounce boxes of assorted colors, or individual colors. These, too, are placed on an already fired surface, then fired again to give a line effect to a design.

When you see the enamels in their containers, they have a faint powdery approximation of each color. It is only in melting under high temperatures that the true colors come out. However, many craft shops selling enamels have small discs of copper showing the final results.

Aids in Applying Enamel

A 2-ounce bottle of liquid *gum tragacanth*—Klyr-Fire or another trade-name product—is needed. This material holds the dry enamel powder in place on metal before firing.

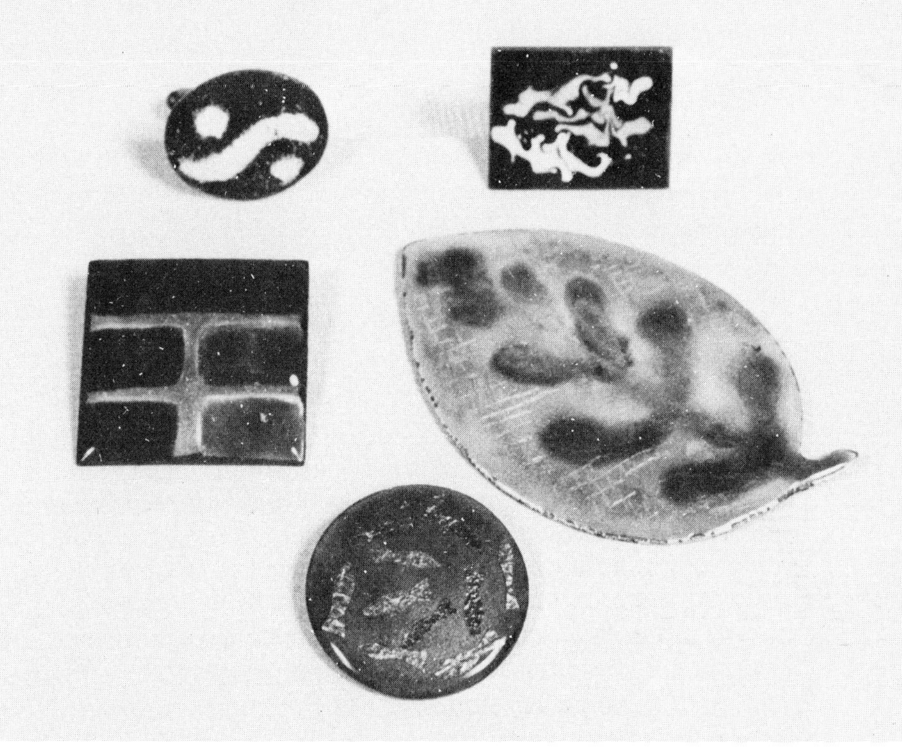

Types of enamels. Clockwise, starting top right: a square of black enamel whose surface threads have been pulled into a design while hot; two colors of transparent enamel on a leaf shape; a circle of transparent enamel with silver and gold foil fishes suspended between two layers; square with rectangles of transparent colored enamel built up over a clear enamel base; dark opaque enamel circle with a stenciled white opaque design.

Scalex and *Amacote* are two trade names for a preventive of black fire scale, which forms on the exposed back of a metal shape when enamel is fired.

Metals

The metals used in enameling are *copper, silver,* and *gold.* Copper is the best for a beginner as it withstands the heat of repeated firings and is not as expensive as silver. The other metals, such as brass, steel, aluminum, and pewter, are unsuitable, because of chemical reactions or a too low melting point of the metal.

HOW TO APPLY ENAMEL TO METAL

The secret of all enameling is perfectly clean metal. No oil must come between the enamel powder and the metal to spoil the bond created by the heat in the kiln. Oil cannot be seen as such—but it comes from the fingers as one handles metal, or from polishing with steel wool, and is just unavoidable. Therefore, just as in soldering, you must clean the metal surface thoroughly before you proceed with the enameling. (For the water test for grease and oil, see page 149.)

So, after finishing your metal design, and giving it a final polish with very fine crocus paper or fine steel wool, scrub it under running water with a nail brush to remove any particles of the polishing materials. Be sure not to touch the top surface. This is true throughout the cleaning process!

Next, using a clean cloth, wipe the surface with powdered kitchen cleanser. Hold under running water. If the water clings all over when you take the metal away from the faucet then it is clean. If not, repeat the cleaning process. One small spot of grease can cause trouble, spoiling a whole surface.

Sometimes a detergent is suggested, but some detergents seem to have their own form of soapy substance that is deposited on the surface and is hard to remove. Gradually each craft person develops a favorite method of cleaning metal for enameling.

Once the metal is clean, set it aside to dry, or drop it in a glass of water so it will stay clean until you are ready to enamel.

The first step in enameling is to cover the back of the dried metal design with Scalex or a similar product so that fire scale will not develop during the firing. It is hard to remove later on. And scale can blow off and settle on the front enameled surface during a firing. Most small pieces of jewelry do not need to be counter-enameled on the back—it is a tricky process, and best left until you are more proficient in applying enamel. The Scalex method is the easiest. Remember, do *not* touch the front surface during the application.

Fine screen on the shaker bottle.

Opaque enamel being shaken on a copper shape.

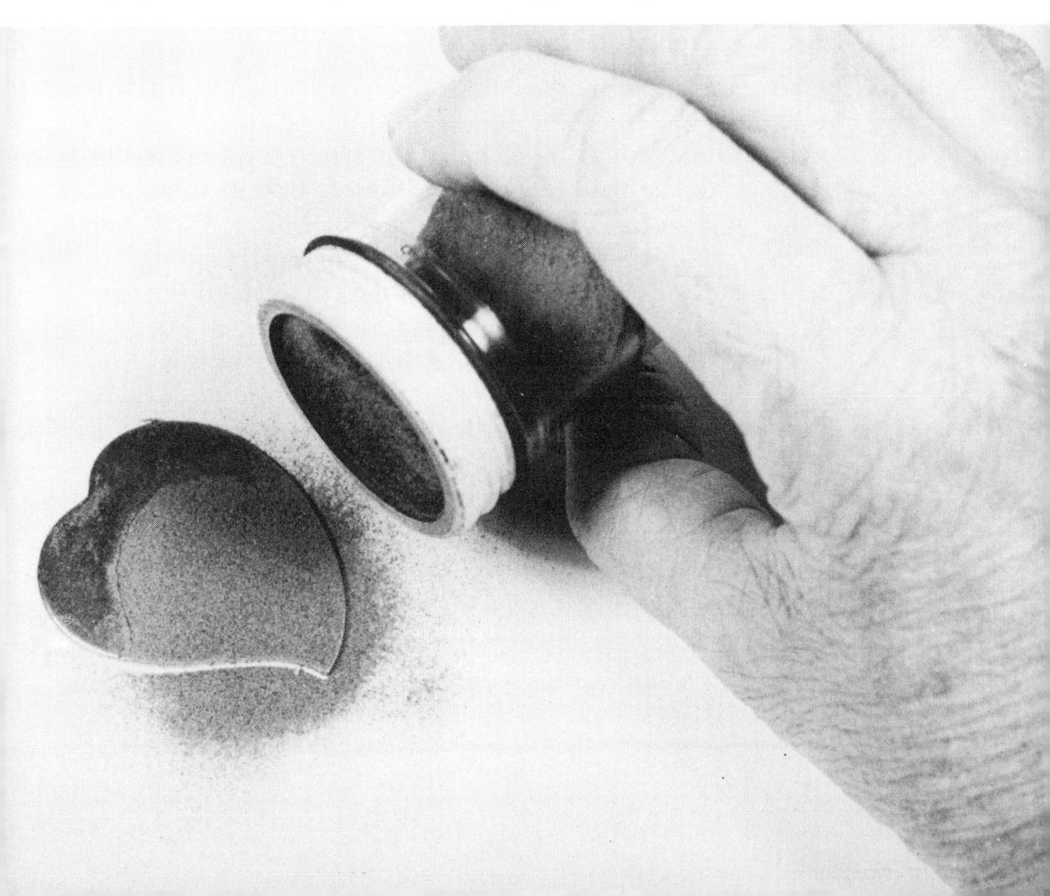

Opaque Enameling

Opaque enamel is easy to apply as it can be used in its dry form directly from the jar. Cover the metal with a thin coat of liquid gum tragacanth or other "stick-um" product. Place metal shape on a piece of clean typewriter paper. Put a teaspoon of opaque enamel into an empty shaker bottle – or, if you have a shaker top on your supply jar of enamel, use the powder directly from this jar.

Now shake a thin layer of opaque enamel over the gummed metal, being sure that all the metal is covered and that you cannot see any gleams anywhere. Metal must be covered completely, or else fire scale will develop on the exposed surface. Even if the spots are as small as pin points, the fired enamel will be pitted with little black dots, or bubbles.

But the enamel should not be put on too thickly, as several thin coats are better than one thick one. The quicker the firing time, the better the final effect will be. A thick enamel means a longer firing, and some essential chemicals and colors may be partially burned out.

Once the surface is well covered (and you will develop a good judgment after one or two pieces), transfer the metal to the wire-mesh square, using a small spatula or a putty knife.

After transferring the metal to the wire mesh, bring the two sides of the paper together to form a trough, and pour excess powder back into the container.

If it is wintertime, you can put the wire mesh holding the enameled piece on top of a radiator cover to hasten the drying process. The gum does not take too long to dry, but drying time does depend on the size of your piece. In any case, give it at least 15 minutes to be safe. You might cover a piece of scrap metal with a thin coat of gum at the same time that you cover your design, and use this as a check for a final dry state.

Start the kiln, heating it up according to the manufacturer's directions, as each kiln takes a different length of time to reach the maximum firing temperature of 1,500 degrees. When hot, slip the wire mesh with the enameled

Enameled shape being put on the heating element of the kiln. Kiln cover will be put over the top.

piece on it into the kiln. Close the cover, and check the melting process through the peephole. This should not take more than 2 to 4 minutes—so stand by!

First the powder will turn black and grainy. Next the surface begins to melt, but looks scummy and dull. When everything shows a shiny gloss, turn off the heat and open the kiln, leaving the piece inside so it can cool down a bit. If you bring it out right away, there is a chance that the enamel, cooling too rapidly, will crack.

Once the piece has cooled a bit, take out the mesh square with tongs and put it on a square of asbestos. Wait until the metal is well cooled before touching it with your fingers.

Pick up the piece and check the surface for any pits or fire scale. (You will have to dig out these areas, rub down the metal, and reenamel.) In any case, stone the whole surface smooth with the carborundum file while holding the piece under running water. Work very gently at first, supporting the metal with one hand.

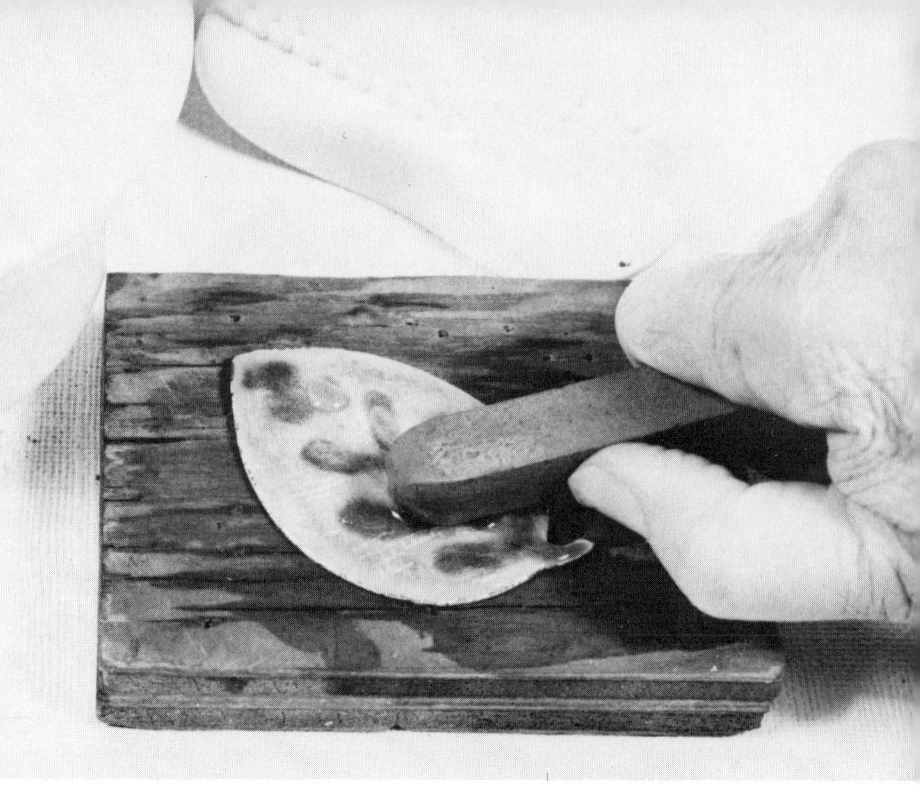

Rubbing wet enameled surface with carborundum file.

You can also put a piece of wood flat in your sink under the faucet, placing the metal flat on the surface while working over the entire enamel area with the carborundum file. Or you can put board and enameled piece on your work surface, scrubbing off the enamel frequently in a nearby bowl of water as the carborundum file smooths out the rough spots. In these last two methods the whole surface is treated equally, and there is less chance of digging too deeply into one area. When the surface is evenly dull, with no shiny spots, scrub with the nail brush. During this process, *try not to touch the surface with your fingers,* in order to avoid grease marks. Wipe with rubbing alcohol, just to be sure all is clean.

Now add a coat of gum, and dust the wet surface with a second thin layer of opaque enamel, dry, and fire in the heated kiln.

When the piece is cool, check the surface. If it is smooth enough your piece is done. If not, grind down any irregularities with the carborundum file, wash, and refire until the surface is glossy.

At this point of second stoning, you can add another color—either opaque or transparent, clear enamel lumps, or threads—as decoration. Or you may feel your design needs a third layer of the same color enamel.

Transparent Enameling

Transparent enamels are like colored jewels, with the light going through the enamel to catch the surface of the metal below. There is an effect of great depth even though the coating over the metal is so thin. Designs can be engraved on the metal to shine up through the clear enamel. Small designs in special silver or gold foil can be cut out and fired between two layers of enamel, so they seem to float in space.

These enamels require only one extra process—washing. Pour a tablespoon of enamel powder into a small, wide-top container. Add water, almost to the top. Stir lightly with a small spatula. The water will turn milky. Tip the jar to the side, letting the water run out slowly. Do not spill any of the enamel. Repeat the process for several washings until the water is clean. This assures that the enamel will be clear and sparkling. If the fine dust were left in, the enamel would be clearer than opaque enamel, but still cloudy.

The clear flux is also washed in the same way.

The first step is to apply Scalex to the back of the cleaned metal to be enameled. Dry, and turn over to the right side.

It is better to apply the clear flux and transparent enamels while they are wet, as there is less chance of dust reforming. Wet enamel, too, will stick to the metal, and there is no need to use gum or other substances as a holder. This, again, assures a clearer enamel. So put the cleaned metal on your work surface. Float a little water on it with a brush. Scoop up clear flux with the spatula, and spread it over an area of metal with a shoving and slightly chopping motion. Keep adding flux until the whole surface of metal is covered and no metal gleams through—but keep the coating as thin as possible.

The surface should be moist but not floating away. Now

Washing transparent enamel in small ceramic container.

Applying wet transparent enamel to a metal shape with the spatula.

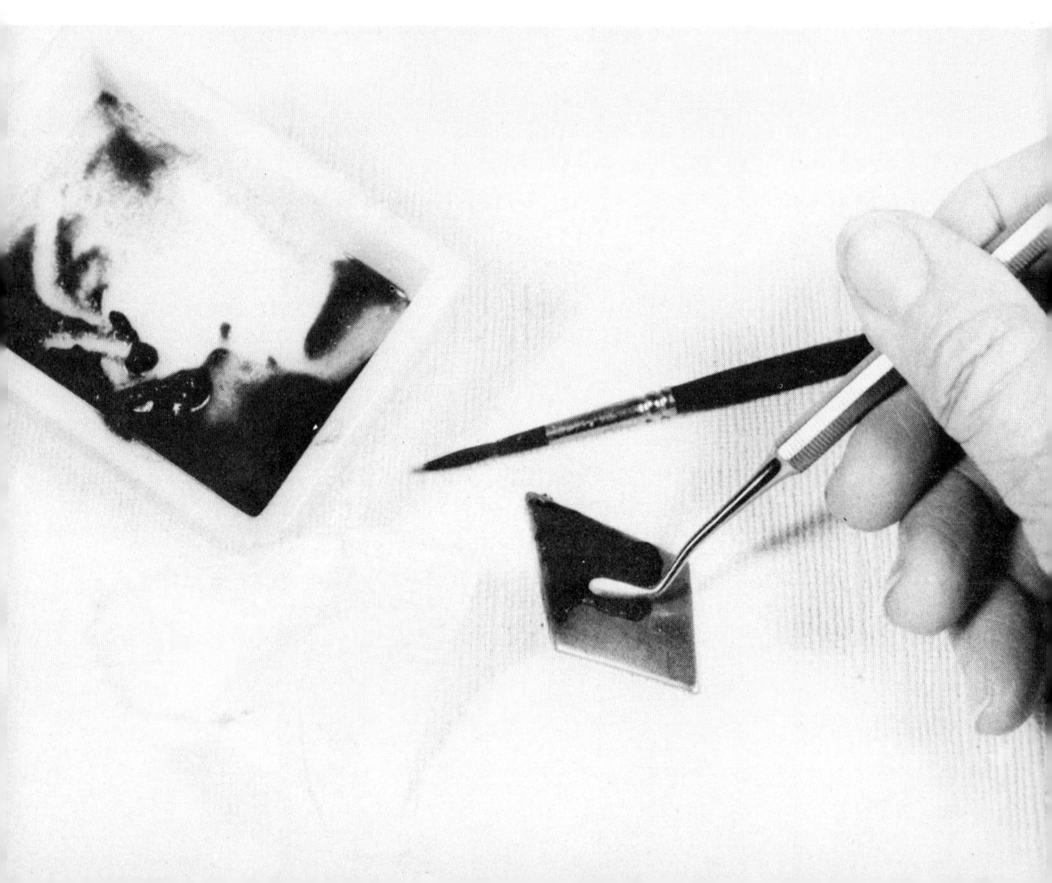

place a fingernail against the edge, in the middle of one side of the metal piece. With the spatula, lightly tap the opposite side. This little shock will settle the particles of glass grains suspended in water into a smooth surface.

Next, put the torn edge of a small piece of paper towel at the edge of your piece. The water still left in the enamel will, by capillary action, be drawn right across the whole grainy surface to the paper. Fun to watch. Repeat until the scraps are dry.

Place the metal on the wire-mesh square to dry. When ready, place in a preheated kiln and close the cover. When the piece shows a shiny surface turn off the kiln. This should be in 2 to 4 minutes. Some enamels fire faster than other—so there is no exact timing.

Proceed as you did with the opaque enamels for cooling and grinding down the surface.

Now add the color glazes over the transparent flux. With transparent enamels it is even more important than with opaque to have a succession of thin coats. Once the first coat is on and the metal covered, the succeeding layers can be extremely thin. One to three color layers are necessary, depending on the depth of color and the smoothness of application. Grinding down each layer is important for an even and sparkling surface.

The last glaze, too, should be ground down, and the enamel scrubbed. Put the piece back in the kiln when dry for the final gloss firing. Fire until the surface shines, then cool slowly.

Take out, and when completely cool, wash off the back and clean with emery cloth if necessary. File off any fire scale around the edge so that a rim of clean metal shows all around.

Decorative Processes

On both opaque and transparent enameled surfaces, small lumps of clear glaze can be placed, either at random or in a pattern. Then put the piece in the kiln on the mesh square until the lumps melt. They will spread out a bit, so be careful not to use large pieces. After cooling, these are not ground down, as you will want an irregular surface, raised above the background.

This same process can be followed with *enamel threads*, placing them on top of the final ground-down enameled surface in a crisscross or zigzag pattern, scattered at random or arranged in straight lines. The metal is fired until the enamel background is glossy. Then the piece is cooled as usual, but not ground down again.

A *stencil design* can be cut out of typewriter paper with small nail scissors or a razor blade. Smooth the design into position over the moistened ground second coat of enamel, then dust another color of enamel over the opening. Carefully lift up the stencil paper, leaving the design on the surface. Put on the mesh square and fire in a preheated kiln. You may find that you will have to apply gum tragacanth or water before dusting on the enamel.

Another method is to apply gum through the stencil design only. Lift up the paper, and dust enamel over the whole surface. Then shake off excess enamel. Enamel will stick only to the stenciled area.

After cooling, decide whether you want your design slightly raised from the background or ground down. If the latter, use the carborundum file and refire until the surface is glossy.

You can also produce see-through designs, or *sgraffiti*. After the first firing, put on a thin coat of gum or other product. Dust another color of enamel over the whole piece. Now, with a wet brush or a pointed tool—a skewer or small nail—remove some of the top layer, so that the bottom layer shows through. Follow a previously drawn design. This can be initials, a flower or fish shape, a circular line going into the center like a snail, geometric shapes, or whatever. Make the lines very clear, being sure that there are no small grains of enamel left in the scratched-away areas.

Dry, and fire on the wire mesh. Let cool. Stone the surface under running water, and refire until glossy.

There are additional design techniques that can be used only with transparent enamels. One of these utilizes small pieces of special silver and gold foil. Hold the foil between the two sheets of transparent paper, and cut out the design you want. (Design may be drawn first on the paper.) Use nail scissors to do the cutting. Since the foil is so thin, the two sheets of paper give it a stability in the cutting. They also keep your fingers—and the grease that could be transferred!—away from the foil surfaces. Prick the surface of the foil all over with a fine needle, so no moisture or air will be trapped between the enamel and the foil in firing.

Put the foil in position on the stoned flux or first color surface which has been covered with a light gum solution. Put into kiln and heat partly, then take out the piece and smooth the foil with your small spatula to eliminate any wrinkles or blisters. Cool, and add a coat of colored transparent enamel. Fire in the kiln, and stone in the usual manner. You may want to add another layer of color, or return the stoned surface to the kiln for a gloss firing.

A multilayer effect can be achieved by adding a second level of foil, covered by enamel. In this way a depth is created, since the first level of foil is covered by two coats of enamel, and the second by only one coat.

You can also produce designs on the metal before enameling that will show through layers of clear enamel. You can *scratch* or *engrave* a design in the copper or silver surface with a sharply pointed skewer or nail. Or, holding the nail at an angle, hit it with the hammer, making small angled nicks in the metal. There are tools called *punches*, made of steel, which have raised designs on the ends. When the opposite end is hit by a hammer, the design is lightly impressed into the metal. There are also tools called *engravers* that scratch the surface of metal. Round-end wooden *sticks* put into a drill can be whirled over the metal surface to make a pattern.

Findings

Findings are applied with soft solder after all the enameling and cleaning of the back metal is finished. They cannot be applied before enameling, as the heat of the kiln would melt the solder. This also applies to any design made of soldered pieces. The only solder that will survive kiln heat is hard solder, and for this it is necessary to use special fluxes and butane torch heat.

Now you know the basic and classic ways of applying enamels to metal to create a thing of beauty. Following are a number of projects that utilize all these techniques. And each one will give you additional ideas. You will find yourself looking at enamel jewelry in stores and in museums with an added interest and an understanding of how it was done. And the knowledge, too, that you have made similar pieces yourself—or will do so with the skills you have now acquired.

STAMPED SHAPES ENAMELED

Materials

Any of the stamped-shape metal pieces described in Chapter 5, plus enamels of your color choice, either opaque or transparent.

Variations

1. The stamped copper or silver shapes can be enameled following the directions given in the beginning of this chapter. They can be mixed or matched, hung on long or short chains, made into earrings, pendants, pins, or cuff links.

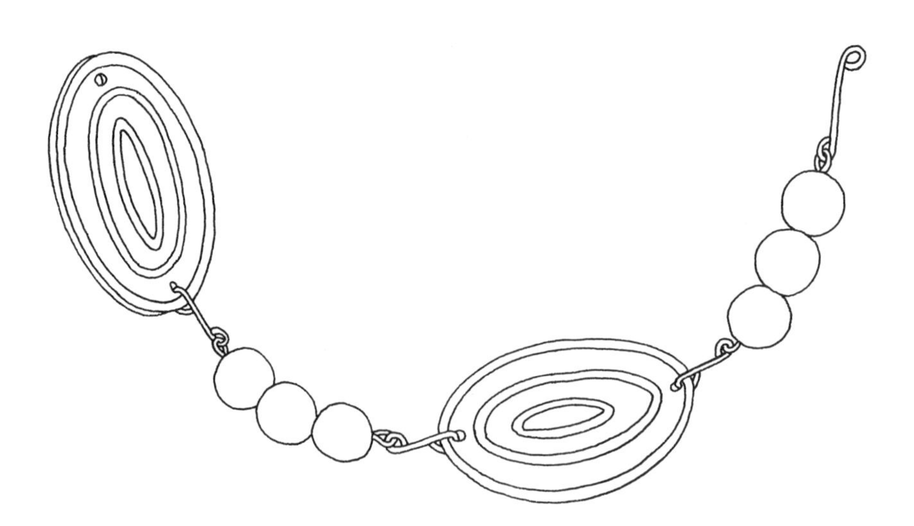

2. Matching enameled circles can be set into a backed bezel, and a cuff-link back soldered on.
3. For a necklace, enamel large ovals 1 by 2 inches in narrow stripes that follow the outline of the ovals, becoming smaller and smaller as they get toward the center. Use green, red, and white alternating. *Before* enameling, drill a hole at each end for the jump ring.

String three beads of a matching color on a stiff piece of wire with a loop at each end. Connect these with a plain wire, looped at each end, to the enameled ovals.

The number of ovals, the number of bead sections, and the length of the connecting wires is left to your discretion and taste.

AN ENAMELED MELON-SLICE NECKLACE

This design is based on the melon-slice necklace in Chapter 6 (pages 173-177). This version is made from a flat piece of copper *without* a center cutout. Instead, the curved center decoration is colored enamel, opaque or transparent, depending on your preference.

Opaque enamel is best used on silver as silver will not develop fire scale on the part not covered with enamel. If you use opaque enamel on copper, you must protect the uncovered areas with Scalex or its equivalent; otherwise you run the risk of fire scale developing on the exposed copper.

If you use transparent enamels, the whole copper surface must be covered with clear flux before the color decoration

in the center is added. And this can be lovely, as copper sometimes turns "gold" under clear flux.

Materials

A flat piece of 16- or 18-gauge copper 3¾ inches square; gold-filled chain 15 inches long; a short section of brass wire for the back hook, or a commercial spring catch, plus three jump rings; flux, and transparent enamels in your choice of color or colors.

Steps

1. Follow the directions for the melon-slice necklace, steps 2 and 3, page 174.
2. Follow directions for the melon-slice necklace, step 4, but do not drill or cut the center section of metal. Drill holes at top of the teardrop and at each end of the melon shapes, large enough for the width of the jump rings.
3. Wipe copper with powdered kitchen cleanser. Rub with vinegar and salt after washing off cleanser. Holding metal by the sides, and not touching the top, wash off under running water. When you remove the copper, a thin film of water should remain on the surface. If not, repeat the cleaning process. Let metal dry in air.
4. Wash the transparent flux in several changes of water until it is clear. Do the same for the colored transparent enamel.
5. Cover the entire surface of copper with the clear flux. (Silver needs only the center design areas covered with flux.) Dry, fire, and cool; stone the covering following the directions on page 235.
6. Enamel the center sections of all three pieces with transparent color. Apply a thin coat of wet enamel, filling in the areas between the center outlines. If any grains go over the scribed line, push them back with a small wet paint brush. Remove excess water with pieces of paper towel.
7. Dry all three pieces, and place in a preheated kiln. When the enamel changes from powder to black granular to liquid with a skin over it—it is almost done. Suddenly it

is a smooth shining liquid. Turn off the heat! Let everything cool off in the kiln, as any sudden change in temperature may crack the enamel. When you do take the pieces out, they may be slightly convex. This is all to the good, as it tends to make the pieces look heavier.

8. Now grind down the surface with the carborundum file until no shiny area remains. Wash well and scrub with a nail brush. This thinning out of the enamel will make it more transparent.
9. Add a second coat of color to all three pieces, following the procedure for the first layer. Fire, cool, and grind down the enameled center sections, leaving the clear flux untouched.
10. If the color is intense enough, put the pieces back into the kiln for their final gloss firing. Otherwise add a third layer of color.

    Copper can stand up under a number of firings, but silver has a limited life under repeated heatings—one of flux and two of color is about the limit.
11. You are now ready to put all the pieces together, following steps 7, 8 and 9 for the melon-slice necklace. The only difference is the substitution of two pieces of chain for the neck wire. The attachment of the chain is permanent; this means there is less chance of chipping the enamel. Attach it to the top points of the melon shapes with oval jump rings. Add a spring ring and jump ring at the back. Clean the backs of the pieces with steel wool and crocus cloth; apply clear nail polish to the backs to prevent tarnishing.

Variations

An additional thought for a wild necklace! Make the melon shapes into watermelon slices, choosing enamels of green, white, and pink. Starting at the bottom edge, make a strip of green, then a wider strip of opaque white, and finish with a broad area of bright transparent pink. The hanging center pendant becomes a larger-than-life seed of transparent brown. Or it can be a whole watermelon shape, striped in two shades of green enamel.

See drawings for suggestions for other enamel designs.

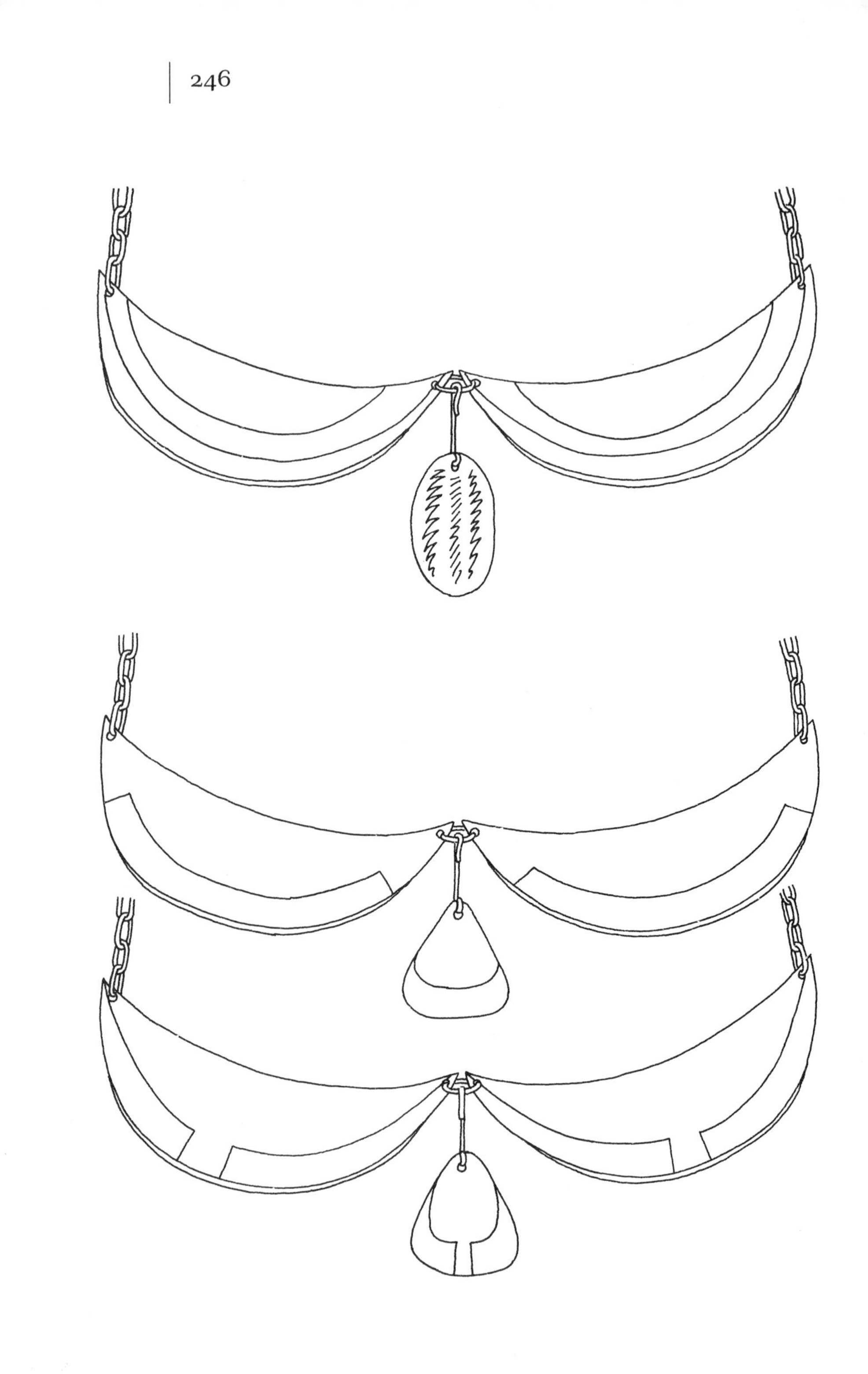

AN AFRICAN PENDANT

This design is taken from the wall decoration of an African house.

Materials

A piece of 16- or 18-gauge copper, $3^3/_8$ by $2^1/_8$ inches; transparent flux, and transparent enamel colors in red, yellow, orange, and green; a $^1/_2$-inch solid circle of copper; copper wire for hanging pendant and circle.

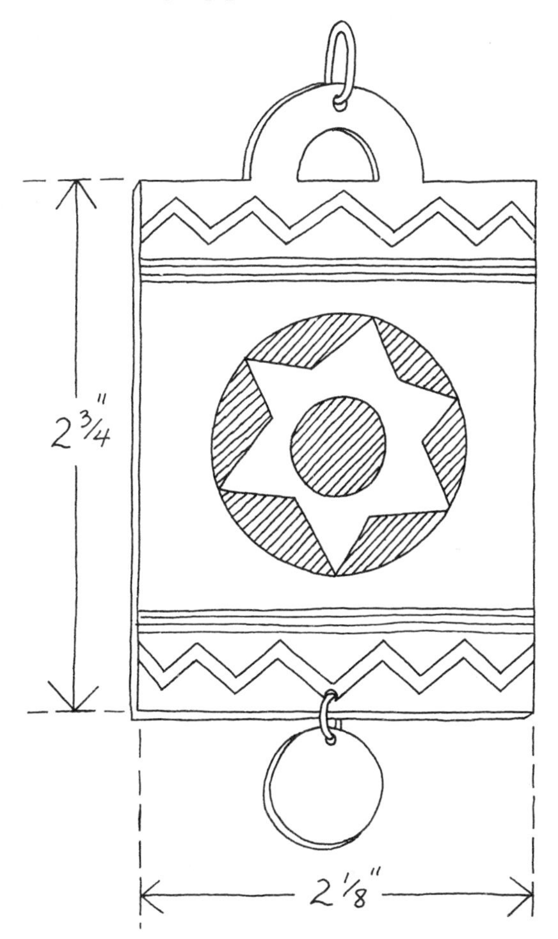

Steps

1. Make a paper pattern of the pendant. The rectangle should be 2 1/8 by 2 3/4 inches. The half-circle loop at the top is 7/8 inch wide and 1/2 inch high, and is cut as part of the rectangle. Add the surface design to the outline of the pendant pattern.
2. Now transfer outline and design to the copper, using carbon paper. If your supply sheet of copper is larger than the rectangle, then use one corner, which means you will have only two sides to saw out. After transferring, carefully follow design with the scriber. You will want to use a ruler for the straight lines.
3. Saw around the outline of the rectangle and the loop. Drill a hole just inside the inner line of the loop, insert the blade, and saw out the interior metal.

   File all edges smooth, and bevel them. Drill a hole at the center bottom large enough to take the width of the wire you are using. Make the same size hole at the top of the wide metal loop.
4. Next, using the round end of your hammer, and bracing the copper circle on the sandbag, hammer the circle so that it is slightly concave.
5. Thoroughly clean both pieces of metal and cover the backs with Scalex.
6. Wash the transparent flux, and apply to both the rectangle and the circle.
7. Follow directions at the beginning of this chapter for firing and cooling the enamel and stoning down the surface. Then add a second coat of transparent flux, and repeat the processes.
8. Now add the design of colored enamels. Since your last coat of clear flux will be frosted from stoning, you will have to moisten the area with a brush dipped in clean water in order to see through to the markings in the metal. Keep your pattern right beside the copper rectangle as you work, so that it will be easy to locate the areas of your design. If there are irregularities as you work along, that is all to the good, as handcrafted designs should never look like perfect machine-made products.

Starting at the top, make the zigzag of transparent green enamel, putting on only a thin coat and cleaning up the edges.

Next, add the line of yellow enamel, which can either be clear or opaque.

The center star is left clear, but the triangle shapes that make up the surrounding oval are covered with orange enamel. The center circle is yellow enamel. Or, if you would like to add another color, it can be red. The lower line is yellow, and the zigzag green.

Dry, then fire the enamel, and let cool in the kiln. Some colors may melt before the others, but keep the heat on until all the colors are shiny. Stone down the colored enamels on the *top* to a smooth surface to give the second coat something to cling to. Do not stone the clear flux, as this has already been done.

Add a second coat of the decorative colored enamels, and repeat the firing, cooling, and stoning down.

At this point decide whether or not your colors are intense enough for the effect you want, and either add another layer of enamel or put the pendant back in the kiln for the final gloss firing.

When it comes to using color, there are no hard and fast rules, as we all have our own preferences with regard to color, intensity, and final effect. These important decisions are, finally, up to you.

9. Clean the back of the pendant and circle with emery cloth. Polish with crocus cloth. Edges will have to be filed to remove fire scale. Cover back of the pendant and circle with clear nail polish to prevent tarnishing, and let dry.
10. Make two wire hangers. Attach one to the pendant top, and attach to the chain. Attach the second loop to the bottom of the pendant and the top of the circle.

A NECKLACE OF SHIELDS

This is a repeated pattern of an exotic design from the Far East.

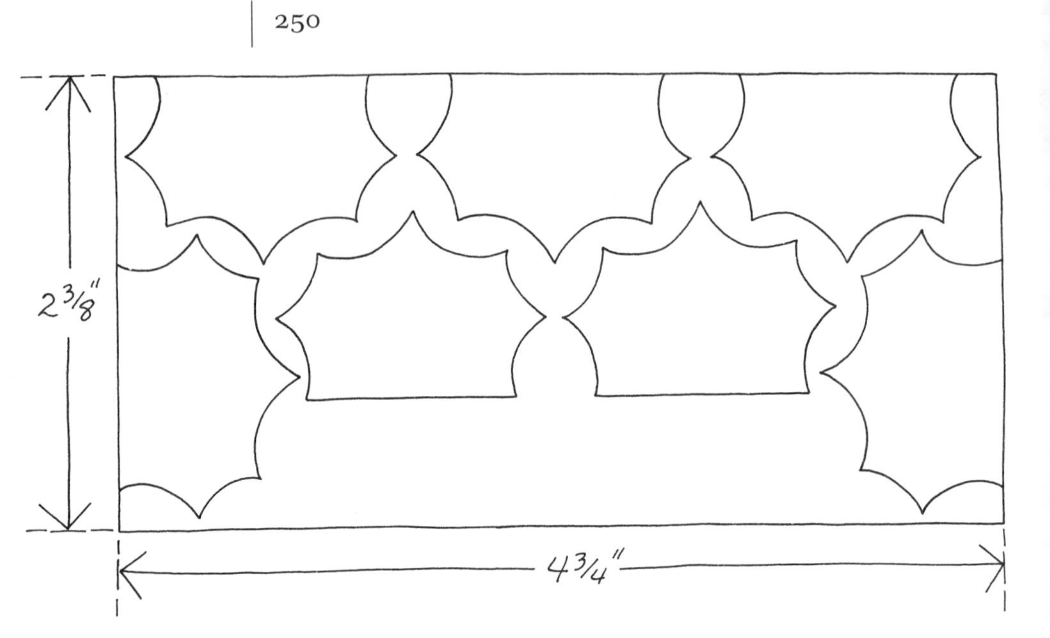

Materials

A piece of 18-gauge copper 2³/₈ by 4³/₄ inches; wire for oval jump rings, or eight commercial jump rings; a jump ring and a spring ring, or hook, for back closing; a length of chain 13 inches at the most; transparent flux and transparent enamels in a soft green and yellow, plus opaque white. You may want to choose other colors.

Steps

1. Copy the layout pattern for all seven shields on tracing paper. Transfer the diagram to your metal using carbon paper. Follow the outline and the interior design with the scriber. Use a ruler where necessary to achieve a straight line.
2. Cut out the shields with the jeweler's saw. File edges smooth, and polish the surface. Finally, drill holes at the top points of each shield for the wire links.
3. Clean your metal of all grease, then cover the backs with Scalex.
4. Wash transparent flux, and apply a thin coat to the shields. Put the copper into the kiln, fire until glossy, and cool.

5. Stone the surfaces, wash off, and apply a second coat of transparent flux. Repeat the melting process, and stone until smooth.
6. Now wash the clear enamels well. Only moisten the opaque white, as this does not need to be freed of dust.
7. You will now start with the top of each shield, adding the colors as you work downward. Do one color at a time, applying it to each shield in turn. Or, if it is easier for you, finish each shield before going on to the next

one. This is a matter of personal preference and working style. Put a white line at top edge, then a broad stripe of soft green, and another line of white. The colors should be separated by the narrowest line of the clear flux showing through. The zigzag is yellow, as are the spots.

As each design is finished, put the metal on the wire-mesh holder so it can dry in place and all the pieces can be put into the kiln at the same time without further disturbance.
8. When the shields have been fired and cooled, stone the top surface very lightly, just flattening the curved top of the lines a bit, leaving most of the enamel shiny. This will keep your design raised from the background of transparent flux.

9. The second coat of color is now added, following the same procedure as in step 7. Fire and cool, but do not stone, as you will want the design to have a slightly irregular surface.
10. All the shields should be cleaned of fire scale and the edges filed to remove any black spots. Cover the exposed metal backs with clear nail polish to prevent tarnish.
11. You are now ready to put all the pieces together. Link the shields with the oval wire jump rings. Cut the chain in half, and link each half to the jump ring on each end shield. The next step is to hold the necklace against your neck to check the length, and to cut off any excess chain if necessary. Add the spring ring and matching jump ring—the necklace is finished and ready to wear.

A THREE-CHOPPER NECKLACE

Three very modern hanging silver pendants are shaped like old-fashioned choppers.

Materials

A piece of 18-gauge sterling silver 3 by 3⅝ inches; a 17-inch length of chain or wire for a neck hoop; spring ring, or hook, and jump ring; clear flux and a transparent enamel in a color of your choice. The light shades are particularly lovely on silver, and are brighter than on copper—turquoise-blue, yellow, light green, azure blue are suggestions.

Steps

1. First trace the pattern for the three pendants using a thin paper, and then transfer by carbon paper to your piece of silver. Mark the outlines with the scriber, and then clean off the carbon lines.
2. Next, saw out the designs. Be careful to keep the excess silver in large, uncut pieces. These are useful for other designs. In fact, the pendant design shown on page 183 is made from the scrap silver of this cutout.
3. Curve the top of the shanks over to form hooks. Measure down ⅜ inch from the top, and make a mark with

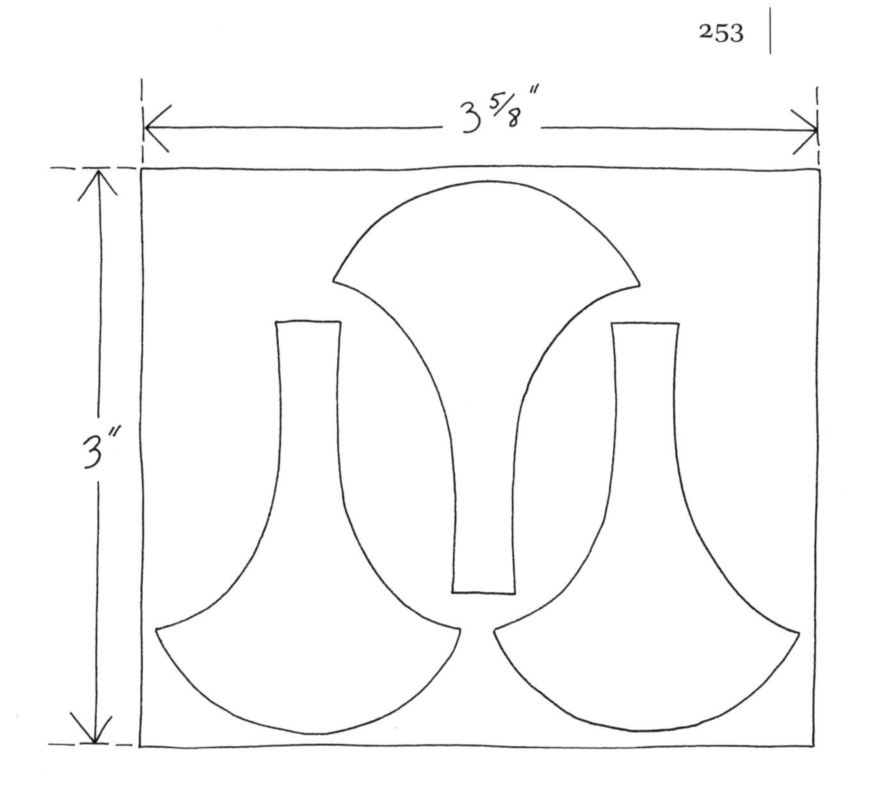

the scriber. Curve the metal forward at this point to form a U. Do not bring the metal too close to the main body of the pendant, as it will have to clear the enamel on the face of the metal.

To cut the slot at the bottom of the chopper, first measure the width of the shank at the bending point. The opening should be slightly longer than this, and a little wider than the thickness of the metal. It will be centered at the bottom of *two* of the pendants, 1/8 inch from the bottom edge.

Drill a hole inside the edge of the slot, insert the saw blade, and saw out the inner metal. File edges clean. Check the fit of the hook. The bottom pendant does not have a slot.

4. Prepare the silver for enameling, cleaning it of all grease.
5. Wash the clear flux for silver. Also wash the transparent enamel (for procedures, see the beginning of this chapter).

6. Apply the flux to the silver with a spatula. Dry, and put into the heated kiln. When surface shines, turn off the heat and let cool in the kiln. Smooth down with the carborundum file.
7. Repeat the process with the colored enamel, for both the first and second coats. Then put back into kiln for final gloss firing. You are safe with these four firings, but any more may affect the silver, and cause the enamel to crack and break off.
8. As silver does not get fire scale, the backs of the pen-

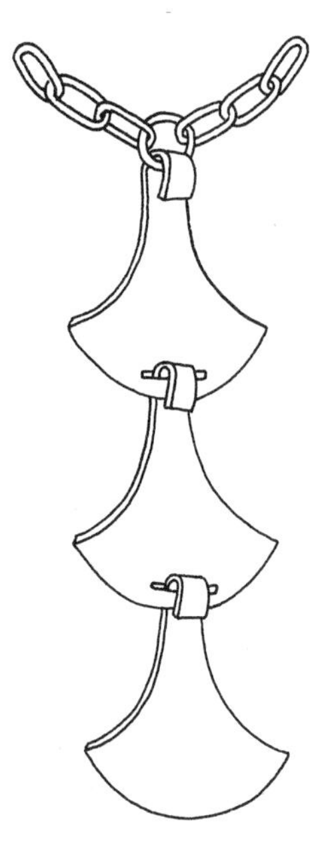

dants only need a light polishing. Then cover with clear nail polish, and let dry for several hours.
9. Slip the hooks into the slots. With the pliers, carefully bring the bottom of the top U closer to the rest of the pendant. The chain or neck wire will thread through this opening.
10. If you are using a silver chain, slip the pendant over it, and measure against your neck for the right length. Cut chain shorter if necessary. Add the spring ring, or hook, and matching jump ring. If you decide on a neck wire follow directions on pages 156-157).

AN ENAMELED ROOSTER BUCKLE

Materials

A piece of 16-gauge copper, $3\frac{1}{2}$ by $2\frac{1}{8}$ inches; transparent flux and enamels.

Steps

1. Follow directions for pewter belt buckle, page 184.
2. After final polishing and cleaning, cover the front of the buckle with transparent enamel flux and melt. Grind down, and add transparent colors to the rooster design in the center using red, blue, pink, and yellow. Fill in the background with a lively green.

   Add a second coat of flux to the two ends.
3. Melt the enamel in the kiln. When cool, rub with carborundum stick. Add a second coat of enamel all around, including the clear flux at the two ends.
4. Put buckle in the kiln and fire again, until the enamel is glossy. Do not grind down the second coat, as design should have an irregular surface.

A SUMMER-LEAF PENDANT

The enamel in this pendant does not have a metal background, but clings between the metal cutouts like window glass. It is called *plique-à-jour*, and is a classic form of enameling. It is a most impressive technique, a tour de force—but (shhh. . .) it's actually very easy.

Hang the leaf design by its stem from a hanger, which in turn is suspended from a neck wire.

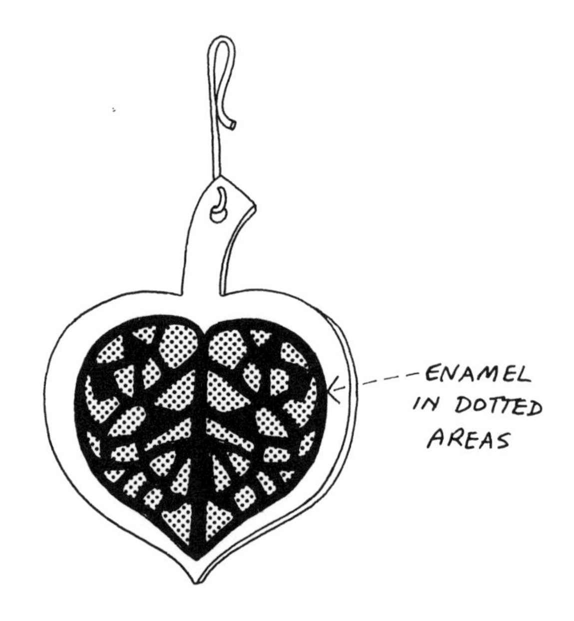

Steps

1. Trace and transfer the pattern, and mark it into the metal with the scriber. Remove the black lines with rubbing alcohol.
2. Now begins the careful sawing. You will want to take your time with this step. None of the openings to be filled with enamel should be wider than 1/4 inch in any direction. The leaf may seem to have an inordinate number of openings, but these small spaces are the reason the enamel stays in place.
3. Once the leaf is cut out, polish the surface, and drill a hole in the stem.
4. Put the metal on a piece of mica, and fill each opening with transparent enamel, making sure no grains spill over onto the surface of your design. Melt in the kiln, and let cool slowly.

5. Without removing the metal from the mica, fill the openings with additional enamel level with the metal surface, as the first coat will have sunk a bit. Fire again; this time metal and enamel should be even. Remove from mica. That is all there is to it.

Make the hanger for the leaf. Insert the round end in the pendant, hang the hook on a neck wire—and wear, boastfully!

9.

ONE of the most exciting parts of making jewelry is converting objects you find into new pieces of jewelry. This may involve reworking something that was already decorative, or it may mean taking something that no one thought of using as decoration and building a new piece of jewelry around it. The results are usually truly unique pieces of jewelry, pleasing to look at and satisfying to wear. After all, you will have "discovered" something that no one else has.

The only problem in this sort of work is that you may not always be able to do the "conversion" yourself. If you do not have the equipment or skills, you may not be able to work on precious metals. You may not want to take the chance of working on enameled pieces, or ones with stones in them. Or you may not know exactly of what metal your found piece is made.

It's best to start by taking the piece to a jeweler to get advice on the proper technique to use in your work. Unless you have the equipment, you will also want the jeweler to plate-work a different metal tone or to cover tarnish. If you do have a professional do the job for you, don't feel that the piece is any less important as a personal creation. After all, the "eye" is the most important thing, and if yours was expert enough to detect the possibilities of the found object, you've become a real jewelry designer.

It would be impossible, of course, in a book like this to give you examples of all the found objects that can be made into jewelry. Tomorrow you might go out and discover something that no one else ever realized had potential as a piece of jewelry. We can only suggest some things that have possibilities, in general, for such conversions.

TOOLS

You'll use the same basic equipment you have used in your other jewelry—at a minimum your pliers, solder and soldering gun, and hand drill.

MATERIALS

The major material for your work with found objects will be precisely that—found objects. These may be odd buttons you locate at a rummage sale, in a thrift shop, in an antique shop, or even in your local button store. Buckles, old coins, old necklaces, shells, cuff links, and lockets are some of the other objects for which you can be on the lookout.

These can be used alone, or you may create layers of found objects—a small button of one design on top of a larger button of another shape or design, and so on.

In addition, you'll need the usual supply of findings—jump rings, pin backs, earring backs, pendant hooks, chains, wire, and so on. Other materials will depend on the designs you create yourself.

Let's see what you can do with some of these, remembering always to check the metal content of the piece before and to decide if your skills are up to the work.

EARRINGS

Earrings are relatively easy to make and can often be put together from inexpensive findings. Among the possibilities:

1. Metal buttons from which the shanks have been re-

Silver-colored buttons, shanks removed, become earrings with the use of contact cement and earring backs. These were made to match the buttons on a dress.

A pair of old buttons becomes a pair of earrings, again with shanks removed and the use of contact cement and earring backs.

moved. Depending on the buttons, they are glued or soldered onto the earring back to make the classic button-type earring.

2. Cuff links from which the shanks have been removed. They are then glued or soldered onto the earring back.
3. Small shells through which holes are drilled. They are attached to the earring back with jump rings.
4. Odd beads and parts of chains from broken necklaces or bracelets that can be attached using the techniques of Chapters 2 and 3.
5. Two found objects joined to make a pair of earrings with more than one design element. For instance, a pair of cut-steel buttons attached to earring backs make pretty button-type earrings. But it might be even prettier to attach the button to an earring base with an attachment ring from which you hang another found object. You might try a small cut-steel buckle to which a tiny jump ring has been soldered. Or you can hang a stone or a bead or a silver-colored or enameled object (perhaps one you've made by following the directions in the previous chapters).

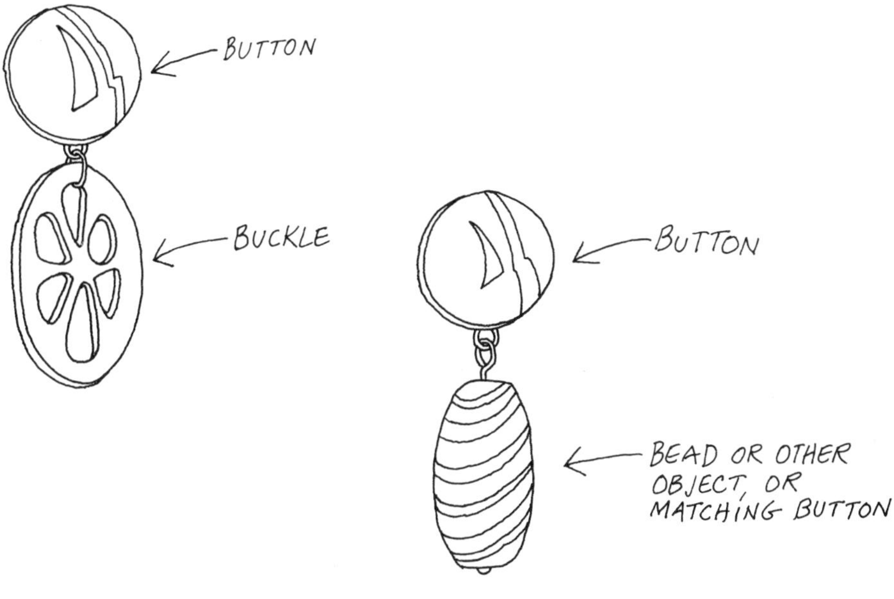

Left: multicolored beads are strung on a wire in a circle shape and the circle is wired onto an earring back, as shown. The center pearl is also wired on. Right: a pair of old buttons from which the shanks have been removed dangle from purchased decorative earring bases. A matching bead joins the button and base to add an extra designer touch.

A collection of earrings and cuff links, made from found objects. Top left: small gold-colored cuff links, backs removed, are soldered to the tops of larger cuff links, also with backs removed; the "new" units are mounted on earring bases. Top right: earring bases with pearls glued on have dangling bits of odd-shaped agates. These match the bracelet and necklace shown on page 273. Center left: a pair of odd bangles from an old pin hang from earring bases made from old cuff links. Center right: old buttons of enamel with a floral design ringed with cut-steel make modern earrings. Bottom: six mother-of-pearl and silver-colored buttons are used to make a pair of cuff links and matching earrings.

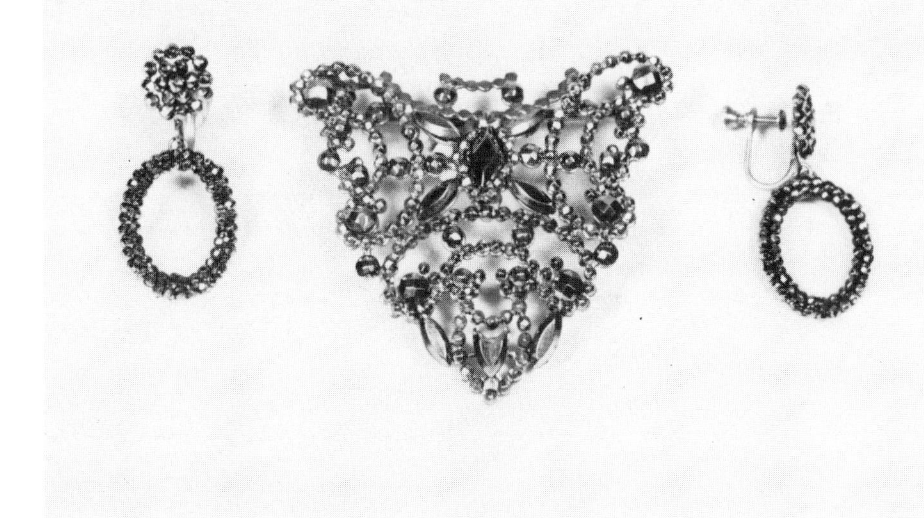

Small round cut-steel buttons are the base for a pair of earrings. They are glued onto screw-back earring bases with drop rings, from which small cut-steel buckles (salvaged from a pair of old gloves found in a rummage shop) are hung. The cut-steel buckle in the center is also old—it's not an exact match, but makes an interesting pin or pendant to create the effect of a set.

PINS

Many found objects lend themselves to conversion to pins of all sizes and types. If the backs of the objects are absolutely smooth and clean, pin backs may simply be glued to them with contact cement. This is not nearly as safe as soldering the pin backs on, however, and should be done only if you suspect that solder will not take or that the heat will spoil the metal, stones, or enamel of the piece. If you have any doubts at all and you care about the piece, work out your design and let a professional jeweler execute it.

Here are a few suggestions:

1. Odd belt buckles make attractive pins.
2. Old shank-type buttons in various shapes strung on 14-gauge wire make nice pins (see pages 46-50).
3. Large pendants with flat backs can be converted into pins.
4. Two or more design elements can be joined to form a pin;

for example, solder a jump ring to the bottom of a small pin back and then add another object.

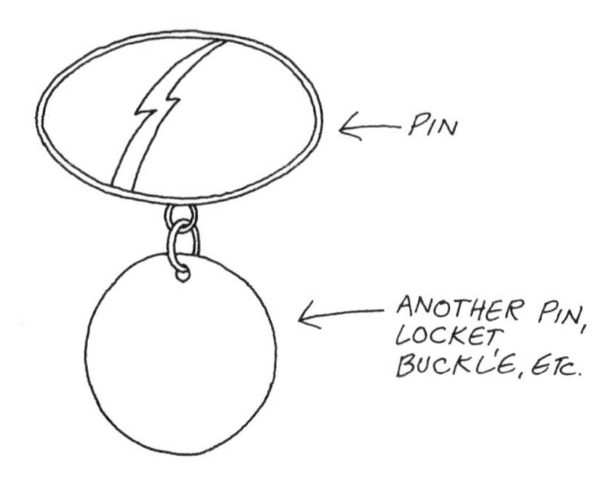

PENDANTS

Almost all of the objects converted to pins can also be made into pendants. Just solder a ring to the back, making sure it is large enough for a chain to go through. In addition, you may use old coins, as described in Chapter 3, or other odd pieces of metal or wood to which you have added beads, other pieces of metal or wood, shells, and so on, to make interesting hanging pieces.

You can make a very unusual pendant or pin by soldering a ring onto an irregularly shaped piece of metal. Or use buttons or cuff links from which the shanks have been removed—as well as anything else you think will make an interesting-looking piece of jewelry.

It is like wearing a charm bracelet in pin or pendant form. If you use a piece of metal, you can simply drill a hole at its top and insert a jump ring through which the chain passes. If you want to use it also as a pin, solder the ring onto the back above the pin back.

You can also use this treatment for pieces of wood that you have painted, stained, or lacquered. In this case, the objects are glued on with clear contact cement.

Some buckles and other found objects can take lots of ad-

Top: an old gold pin is joined to another old pin made of carnelian to create an unusual mixture. Bottom: a brass and plastic buckle is joined to a purchased wire chain to create an interesting pendant.

The chain encircles two pairs of old enameled belt buckles that have been made into pins. If you look closely, you can see that when the pairs are put together, one half fits under the designed edge of the matching half. Thus, each buckle makes two quite individual pins. Enamel is easily spoiled by heat, so the soldering was done professionally. The black pendant is one half of a celluloid belt buckle that dates from the early years of this century. It is inlaid with brass. A hole was drilled in its top, and a jump ring inserted so that it could be worn as a pendant. The other half of the buckle became a pin.

A 4-inch silver locket is dressed up with cuff links, tiny lockets, fraternity pins, tie pins, and a variety of other found objects that are soldered onto it to make a "hanging charm bracelet."

An old sterling silver chatelaine hook and half of an old silver belt buckle are the bases for new jewelry. In each case, the fobs (also old) were added. Pin backs and loops for chains were soldered onto the backs so that they could be worn either as pins or as pendants. The lower piece was plated gold, and is shown hanging as a pendant.

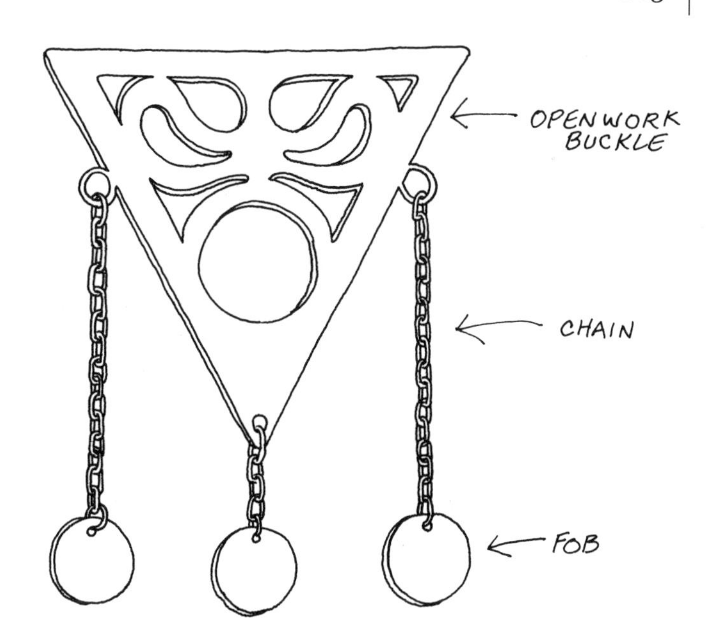

ditions. For example, the buckle shown here has been converted into a combination pin-pendant. Chains were attached (soldered on for extra security), and small fobs added to the ends of the chains. The pin back was soldered on and so was the ring for the chain. Then, because the elements were various shades of silver (some bright and shiny, others dull), the entire new piece was gold-plated to make an expensive-looking and unique object.

RINGS

Not too many found objects can be made into rings, but once in a while you may come across something that lends itself to this purpose. One of the nice things about making rings is that you don't have to look for pairs of found objects – one button or cuff link does very well for this purpose.

You might try:

1. A good odd button from which the shank can be removed. It can then be soldered onto a purchased ring shank.

2. An interesting large cuff link, to which you can do the same.
3. A small pin from which the back can be removed so that it can be soldered onto a ring shank.
4. A small locket, perhaps one that is dented on one side, that can be soldered onto a ring shank.

Sometimes one element can be soldered on top of another one to make an unusual effect—for instance, a small flat button or cuff link on top of a locket or another button or cuff link.

BUTTON CUFF LINKS

Cuff links are easily made from buttons. Ideally, the buttons should have shank backs.

Steps

1. Join two buttons with 1/2 inch of small link chain. If the buttons have flush shanks, attach the ends of the chains to jump rings that have been passed through the shank holes.

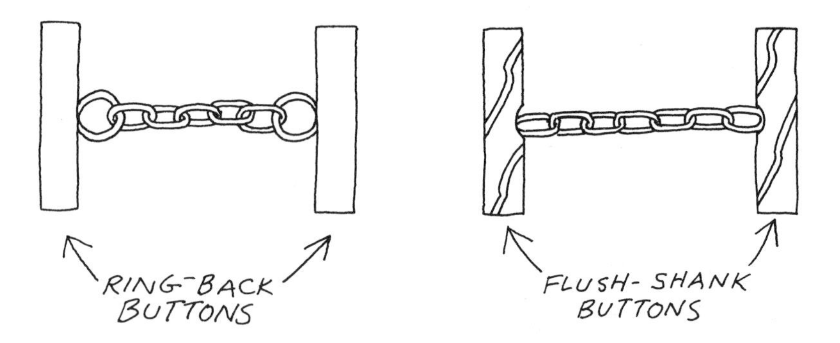

If the button has a ring back, the jump ring can be eliminated and the chain can be attached directly to the button backs. There should be approximately 1/2 inch between the buttons to make a cuff link that fits properly.

2. Repeat for the second cuff link.

You can use twisted wire in place of the chain to accomplish the same thing. Or you can use elastic cord knotted between the buttons. It does not show when the link is on the cuff.

Old coins (or new ones) can also be used for cuff links. Simply convert them to shank-type buttons by adding a small ring to the center of their backs, and then proceed as you did with the ring-back buttons.

BEAD CUFF LINKS

If you've found four really pretty beads that you'd like to make into cuff links, use 18-gauge wire to make them. Here's how:

Steps

1. Work with a 6-inch piece of wire. String two of the beads on it, and separate them by about 3/4 inch.
2. Knot the ends of the wire so that the beads are still 3/4 inch apart. Then twist the ends over the other side of the wire to draw the wire together. The beads should now be 1/2 inch apart, and ready to use as a cuff link—after you've made the other half of the pair.

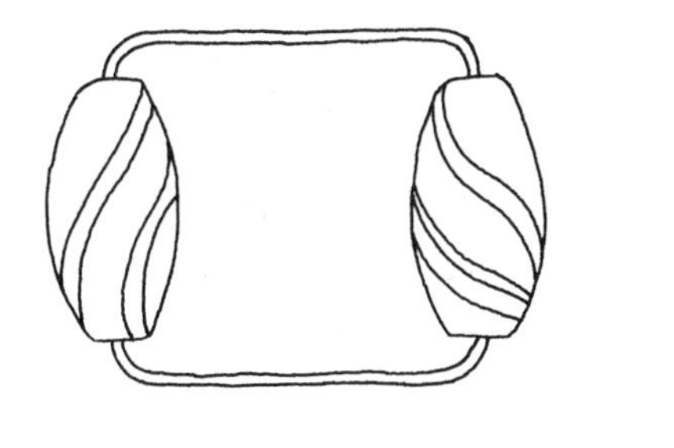

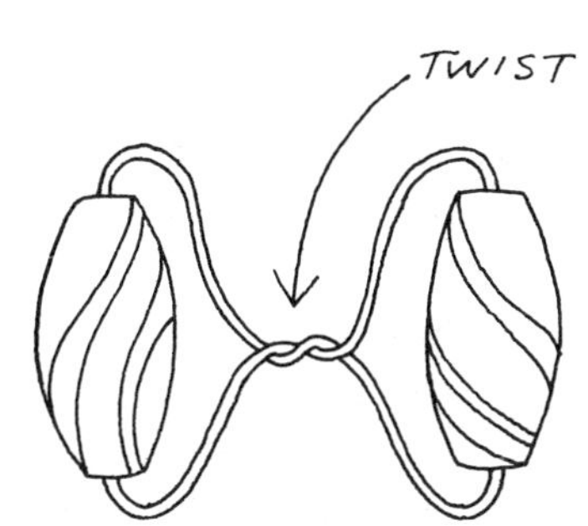

Necklaces and Bracelets

All of the techniques described in this book can also be used to make necklaces and bracelets from old buttons, beads, chains, and other found objects. It is simply a matter of seeing the potential of something you've come across, and designing a new piece around it. You may even find yourself starting with a good-looking clasp and using it as a base for a necklace or bracelet.

Belts

Almost anything you can do with found objects (or beads) for necklaces or bracelets will also work for a belt. This may be something like old coins linked together with wire (with or without beads in between), or beads, sequins, buttons, and so on sewn onto a fabric belt or a piece of ribbon. Or reverse the process—take a pin of the proper size and use it on the front of a belt, buckling the belt in the back.

The more expert you become in the technical aspects of jewelry making, the more conscious you will be of the possibilities of various materials with which to create your pieces. If you shop not just in notions departments and craft and hobby stores but try to see potential everywhere you go, you'll have greatly expanded the fun of your jewelry hobby! And just to encourage you, here are some samples of jewelry created from found objects.

A pair of Georgian (about 1825) agate and gold bracelet clasps were converted into this matching bracelet and necklace by stringing pearls onto the holes that already existed in the clasp sides. Originally they had been worn on wide black velvet bands, one on each wrist. The earrings in the photograph on page 262 were made to match this set.

Top: a gold chain is doubled over to make a bracelet base for the gold backs of small old watches. They are simply soldered onto the chain at intervals, and a spring ring and jump ring are used for the closing. Bottom: a heavy old silver bracelet (that could have been worn alone) was used as the base for this charm collection. The hanging pieces are neck pendants of the 1920s, formerly worn individually on silver chains. The stones are various types of quartz.

Top center: a silver decanter label was professionally transformed from "Rye" by having the old letters erased and the author's initials engraved on it. A pin back was added. The other three pieces are old brass drawer pulls (each cost under a dollar) that have had pin backs added.

Again, pins and pendants from buckles. The piece at bottom left was a two-piece buckle that was soldered together to create a single design.

Belt buckles transformed into pins and/or pendants. Top: two halves of a Georgian silver and cameo buckle soldered together with a pin back added. Left: an old buckle with a hand-painted miniature transformed into a pin. Right: a steel engraved buckle made into a pin. Bottom: a heavy silver buckle made into a pin with a pendant loop. The other half of the buckle was similarly treated and then gilded. Thus the original buckle was transformed into one gold and one silver pin-pendant.

Sources for Supplies

FOR retail store sources in your area look in the yellow pages of the telephone directory under the headings Arts and Crafts; Beads; Hobby and Model Construction Supplies; Jeweler's Supplies and Findings; Precious, Semiprecious, and Synthetic Stones; Rocks for Collectors. Hardware stores and variety stores carry many of the supplies.

Here is a listing of those companies that sell by mail order. Most supply a catalog, free unless otherwise indicated.

NORTHEAST AND ATLANTIC COAST

ABBEY MATERIALS CORP.
(Metal jewelry supplies)
116 W. 29th St.
New York, N.Y. 10001

AKG COMPANY
(Metal jewelry and clay supplies)
1442 Christians Rd.
Newark, Del. 19711
Catalog 35¢

ALBERT FINDINGS, INC.
(Jewelry supplies)
66 W. 47th St.
New York, N.Y. 10036

ALLCRAFT
(Metal and enamel jewelry supplies)
215 Park Ave.
Hicksville, N.Y. 11801

ANCHOR TOOL AND SUPPLY CO., INC.
(Metal and enamel jewelry supplies)
12 John St.
New York, N.Y. 10005

ARE CREATIONS, INC.
(Metal jewelry supplies)
Box 155 E
Plainfield, Vt. 05667

ADAMAS LAPIDARY & GEM SHOP
(Minerals and crystals)
8391 Market St.
Youngstown, Ohio 44501

ASTRO MINERALS LTD.
(Minerals and stones)
155 E. 34th St.
New York, N.Y. 10016
No catalog

BAYTON ELECTRONICS CORP.
(Kilns)
2709 N. Broad
Philadelphia, Pa. 19132

BERGEN ARTS AND CRAFTS
(All craft supplies)
P.O. Box 381
Marblehead, Mass. 01945
Catalog $1.00

JERRY BARKS
(Jewelry supplies)
29 W. 47th St.
Arcade Store #5
New York, N.Y. 10036

BASKIN & SONS, INC.
(Stones, metals, supplies)
732 Union Ave.
Middlesex, N.J. 08846

CEDAR HEIGHTS CLAY CO.
(Clay)
50 Portsmouth Rd.
Oak Hill, Ohio 45656

CERAMIC EXTRUSION
(Wheels, chemicals, clay)
369 Mill Rd.
East Astoria, N.Y. 14052

COLE CERAMICS LAB.
(Clay, tools, glazes)
Gay St.
Sharon, Conn. 06069

DAVIS CRAFTS
(Jewelry tools and supplies)
86 W. Old Wilson Bridge Rd.
Columbus, Ohio 43085
No catalog

WILLIAM DIXON CO.
(Metal, tools, enamels)
750 Washington Ave.
Carlstadt, N.J. 07072
Catalog $2.00

GAMZON BROS, INC.
(Findings, tools, equipment)
21 W. 46th St.
New York, N.Y. 10036
Catalog $1.50

GEM-O-RAMA
(Stones, findings)
64 Poole Circle
Holbrook, Mass. 02343
No catalog

GEMROCK UNLIMITED
(Stones)
9848 Bird Rd.
Miami, Fla. 33165
No Catalog

GILMANS
(Stones, metal, findings, tools)
Hellertown, Pa. 18055

GOULD MERSEREAU
(Wood rings)
35 W. 44th St.
New York, N.Y. 10036
No catalog

H. HARRIS JEWELRY, INC.
(All jewelry supplies)
209 Canal St.
New York, N.Y. 10013
Catalog $1.50

INDIA JEWELRY, INC.
(Stones)
18 W. 45th St.
New York, N.Y. 10036
No catalog

B. JADOW AND SONS, INC.
(Jewelry tools and supplies)
53 W. 23rd St.
New York, N.Y. 10010

KILNS SUPPLY & SERVICE CO.
(Clay and enamel supplies)
225 Mamaroneck Ave.
Mamaroneck, N.Y. 10543

KRAFT KORNER
(Enamel, jewelry supplies)
5864 Mayfield Rd.
Cleveland, Ohio 44124
Catalog $2.00

LAPIDABRADE, INC.
(All jewelry supplies)
8 E. Eagle Rd.
Havertown, Pa. 19083

LITTLE SLABROLLER
(Clay supplies)
288 S. 7th St.
Indiana, Pa. 15701

M & J TRIMMING CO.
(Beads)
1008 Ave. of the Americas
New York, N.Y. 10018
No catalog

PROBST'S WATERMELON WORKS POTTERY
(Pottery supplies)
Box 29
Penland, N.C. 28765

ROMANOFF RUBBER CO., INC.
(Metal tools)
153 W. 27th St.
New York, N.Y. 10001

SCULPTURE HOUSE
(Della Robbia Clay)
38 E. 30th St.
New York, N.Y. 10016
(Write for names of local distributors)

SHERU BEADS
(Beads and findings)
49 W. 38th St.
New York, N.Y. 10018

SMOKEY MOUNTAIN ROCK SHOP
(Stones, metal, jewelry supplies)
San Carlos Blvd.
Ft. Myers, Fla. 33902

C. W. SOMERS AND CO.
(Jewelry tools and equipment)
387 Washington St.
Boston, Mass. 02108

STEWART CLAY CO.
(Ceraclay)
133 Mulberry St.
New York, N.Y. 10013
(Write for names of local distributors)

TECHNICRAFT LAPIDARIES CORP.
(Rocks, stones, findings)
2248 Broadway
New York, N.Y. 10024

MYRON TOBACK INC.
(Metal, tubing, findings)
23 W. 47th St.
New York, N.Y. 10036
Catalog $1.00

G. WEIDINGER
(All jewelry supplies)
4404 Del Prado Pkwy.
(P.O. Box 5)
Cape Coral, Fla. 33904

X-ACTO, INC.
(Jewelry and craft tools)
48-41 Van Dam St.
Long Island City, N.Y. 11101

CENTRAL STATES

AMERICAN ART CLAY CO.
(All clay and enamel supplies)
4717 W. 16th St.
Indianapolis, Ind. 46222

AMERICAN HANDICRAFTS CO. (TANDY CORP.)
(All craft supplies)
1001 Foch St.
Fort Worth, Tex. 76107
(Write for names of local stores)

AMERICAN METALCRAFT, INC.
(Jewelry tools and supplies, enamel)
4100 W. Belmont Ave.
Chicago, Ill. 60641

CERAMIC COATING CO.
(Enamels)
P.O. Box 370
Newport, Ky. 41071

GEMCRAFT OF WICHITA
(Findings)
300 N. Main
Wichita, Kan. 67202

Geode
(Stones, metal, supplies)
106 W. Main St.
New London, Iowa 52645

The Globe
(Jewelry and metal supplies)
220 Albert St.
East Lansing, Mich. 48823

C. R. Hill Co.
(Metals and enamels, tools)
2734 W. 11 Mile Rd.
Berkeley, Mich. 48072

House of Ceramics, Inc.
(Clay, glazes, wheels)
1011 N. Hollywood St.
Memphis, Tenn. 38108
Catalog $1.00

Minnesota Clay Co.
(Clay supplies)
2410 E. 38th St.
Minneapolis, Minn. 55406
Catalog $1.00

Paoli Clay Co.
(All clay equipment)
Route 1
Belleville, Wis. 53508

Peoria Arts and Crafts Supplies
(Enamel supplies)
1207 W. Main St.
Peoria, Ill. 61606
Catalog 50¢

Southwest Smelting and Refining Co.
(Jewelry supplies and findings)
P.O. Box 2010
1712 Jackson
Dallas, Tex. 75221
Also
118 Broadway
San Antonio, Tex. 78295
Catalogs #172, F.72, both $1.00

Tandy Corp.—*see* American Handicrafts Co.

Thomas C. Thompson
(All enamel supplies)
1539 Old Deerfield Rd.
Highland Park, Ill. 60035

WESTERN STATES

Artcrafts
(Beads, seashells, novelties)
Box 1386
Santa Barbara, Calif. 93102
Catalog 25¢

Bead Game
(Beads, jewels, chains, metals)
505 N. Fairfax Ave.
Los Angeles, Calif. 90036

Bead's Nest
(Handmade beads)
P.O. Box 1257
Cupertino, Calif. 95014
Catalog 15¢

Bluebird Manufacturing Co.
(Clay, equipment)
100 Gregory Rd.
Ft. Collins, Colo. 80521

California Crafts Supply
(Metal, jewelry tools)
Box 3277
Anaheim, Calif. 92882

The Craftool Company, Inc.
(Metal, jewelry tools, clay)
1421 W. 240th St.
Harbor City, Calif. 90710
Catalog $1.00

Crown Manufacturing Co.
(Metal, jewelry supplies)
1188 Industrial Ave.
Escondido, Calif. 92025

Discount Agate House
(Stones)
3401 N. Dodge
Tucson, Ariz. 85716
No catalog

Gemex
(Cabochons, jewelry supplies)
P.O. Box 427
San Marcos, Calif. 92069

Gems Galore
(Metal, jewelry tools, findings)
1328 El Camino Real
Mountain View, Calif. 94040
Catalog 50¢

LDEN STATE GEMS
(Stones)
22475 Maple Ct.
Haywood, Calif. 94541
No catalog

IEGER'S
(All jewelry and stone supplies)
900 S. Arroyo Pkwy.
Pasadena, Calif. 91109

DE WORLD
(Jade)
7960 Uva Dr.
Redwood Valley, Calif. 95470

PIDARY CENTER
(Jewelry tools and supplies)
4114 Judah Street
San Francisco, Calif. 94122

NTANA ASSAY OFFICE
(Metal)
610 S.W. Second Ave.
Portland, Ore. 97204

BRIEN LAPIDARY
(Stone, metals, tools)
1116 N. Wilcox
Hollywood, Calif. 90038
Catalog $1.00

TTER'S GARDEN
(Beads)
208 Juniper
Fallbrook, Calif. 92028
Samples 50¢

CRAMENTO CERAMICS & POTTER'S SUPPLIES
(Clay supplies)
2552-C Albatross Way
Sacramento, Calif. 95815
Catalog $1.00

SHIPLEY'S MINERAL HOUSE
(Tools and Gems)
Gem Village
Bayfield, Colo. 81122

THE SWENSONS
(Jewelry tools and supplies)
9641 E. Apache Trail
Mesa, Ariz. 85207

TREASURE CRAFT
(Beads and pearls)
Box 42
Corona, Calif. 91720
Catalog 50¢

TSI
(Jewelry tools, supplies, and imported enamels)
487 Elliot Ave. W.
Seattle, Wash. 98119
Catalog $1.00

VAN HOWE CERAMIC SUPPLIES
(Clay supplies)
11975 E. 40th Ave.
Denver, Colo. 80239
Catalog $1.00

URANIUM CORNER, INC.
(Jewelry tools and supplies)
2153 Broadway at Champa
Denver, Colo. 80201

U.S. LAPIDARY SUPPLY CO.
(Jewelry tools, findings, stones, enamels)
1605 W. San Carlos St.
San Jose, Calif. 95128

WAY-CRAFT
(Enamels)
394 Delaware St.
Imperial Beach, Calif. 92032

Index